HELL'S ANGELS OF THE DEEP

By

WILLIAM GUY CARR

Author of "By Guess and By God"

With 8 Illustrations

Reprint edition, 2016
Dauphin Publications

HELL'S ANGEL OF THE DEEP

WILLIAM GUY CARR

THE "E - 11" IN DOCK

In this submarine Nasmith bobbed up suddendly
in the harbour of Constantinople - the first enemy
to make an appearance there in five hundred years.
On left: Lieutenant Brown, its navigator.
On right: Lieutenant D'Oyly Hughes who blew up
the Berlin-to-Baghdad tracks.

INTRODUCTION

It was necessary to offer some explanation as to how the title of my first book was arrived at. *By Guess and By God* described in the fewest words possible the manner of navigating a submarine. Most of the time while out on patrol in enemy waters you were forced to guess where you were and what to do for the best. Often you prayed that you had guessed right. My second book deals with men, ships, and places. All types of men, various kinds of ships, and my personal impressions of a wide variety of places.

I want my readers to realize that I was only a boy when I first went to sea; I was not then sixteen years of age. Naturally my first chapters record my youthful impressions and ideas. I was still in my teens when the war broke out, but I had grown old in experience and learned a lot about the ways of the world.

Having been educated in the secluded atmosphere of St. Joseph's College, Dumfries, up to the time of running away to sea I had been taught by the good brothers their conception of what was right and what was wrong, what was manly and what was mean. I want to acknowledge that I value highly the training I received at their hands. But when I found myself thrown suddenly into the sea of life where the storms of passion swayed men's souls and the struggle for life continued relentlessly regardless of the weaker ones who fell by the wayside, I began to wonder just exactly how the Supreme Being would regard the different kinds of men and women I came in contact with daily.

Take for example Captain B. V. Smith. Notwithstanding the fact that I wrote some hard things about him and called him some pretty harsh names, still in the final analysis I looked upon him as the most outstanding mariner it has ever been my privilege to meet. Old Ben, as he was known throughout the China Seas, was my impression of one of Hell's Angels of the Deep. In his rugged frame was the strength of the Vikings; he had the contempt for the weakling his type of men cannot help but feel. If he drank, his iron will never permitted his drinking to interfere with his duties as a master mariner, otherwise how could he have commanded ships for more than half a century and never been involved in a serious accident? If some would not agree with his morals let me say that they were superior to those of many men I have met ashore since leaving the sea, men who have not the slightest excuse for their dissipations. If B. V. Smith had a wife in every port I certainly did not meet any of them. Contrary to popular opinion I found the majority of officers I sailed with anything but the libertines some people would like to believe them to be.

In my wide and varied experience I have still to meet men ashore who so extravagantly admire virtue in woman as a sailor does. It is my experience than when a sailor married he set his wife on a pedestal so high above the particular type he is supposed to associate with, that he literally worshipped her, and during the long periods of absence would subject himself to the practice of self-control which was almost inconceivable in its severity.

What class of men in the whole wide world give as high a percentage of their salaries to their wives and children as do the majority of sailors? They may sow their wild oats during the years of their youth, but it is their extraordinary craving for experience and adventure rather than a depraved mind which urges them on during their youthful years. It is my firm belief that by far the largest majority of married seamen are as loyal to their wives and families as they are to the ships they serve. It was once my privilege to assist a dying seaman pen his last letter home. His dying thoughts were of his wife and family. He knew he was dying and he did not seem to mind having to "slip his cable" in the least. His worry was for his wife and the years of loneliness which were ahead of her. After dictating his message to me he grew rapidly weaker. Sheer will-power had enabled him to speak as long as he had. I had seen him hesitate once or twice during his dictation. He seemed about to say something and then changed his mind.

INTRODUCTION

I bent over the dying man and said: "Is there not something else you wish to say?"

The candle of life was flickering very low. In fact it had started to splutter and was about to flicker out. I had to put my ear to his trembling lips to catch his dying words, and what pearls they were.

"Tell her I'm as true to her to-day as the day we were married." He had been ashamed to confess his virtue, but the knowledge the pleasure such a message would give to his wife finally outweighed his reticence. If this man wasn't one of Hell's Angels of the Deep, what was he? He was tough as oak, and unyielding as a piece of granite. He could curse and swear when driving men or when roused to anger, but if he used his strength of body and power of mind to subject those under him to his will he also was strong enough to subject his own passions and his own desires.

Sailors are strange creatures. Take the A.B. or the ordinary stoker. Careless, happy-go-lucky, come-day-go-day, God-send-Sunday, kind of creatures. I have seen them come aboard a ship sodden with drink, and a few days later, after the sweet ozone of the sea had cleared the liquor out of their systems, the same men have performed heroic deeds of self-sacrifice. Surely these men had descended into the very depths of hell in their iniquity, but they had also risen to the very highest pinnacle of Christian charity when they had voluntarily offered to lay down their lives not for friends, but for mere strangers in need of assistance. Surely if the blood of martyrs washes away the stains of their sins, these men I write of wipe out the penalty of their human frailties by bringing to the surface, when occasion arises, those sterling qualities of mind and heart with which most of them seemed to be endowed.

This type of men are those I call "Hell's Angels of the Deep." Judging them from their talk and their rough exteriors they are as tough as the devil himself; but probe down underneath the surface, peel off the hardened coarse skin, and you will find, in the majority of cases, hearts of gold and souls as white as the pulp of the mangosteen which is hidden under a dark and repulsive exterior.

There is the other type one meets in every plane of life

and that is the out-and-out rotter. You find him in the best schools, in the church as well as out of it, you find some of this type at sea. They are rotten to the core and never change under any circumstances. They are cowards at heart and never conquer their craven fear.

I have met some of this type also, but they are hardly worth mentioning. I remember one man in particular. He was well educated, good-looking, conceited, and boasted that he was an atheist. This man believed in no hereafter. According to him, when we were dead we were finished. On this belief he claimed it was the right of every man and woman to enjoy themselves to the limit of their fancy during life because there was nothing to follow after. He denied himself nothing, even the seduction of his friend's wife, yet I saw him tremble and his face turn a yellowish green with fear in the face of death. Why ? If there is nothing in the hereafter, why did he fear death ? There are as many degrees of wrong as there are points of the compass. It is my contention that the greatest sinner is not the man who is rough and abrupt, who may at times succumb to his weaknesses, and do it in an unashamed way, caring little or nought for who see or hear him. The worst one can say of him is that he is a sinner, and we are told that Heaven is full of sinners who have repented. The type of men who are detested by men and unforgiven by God are those who are devoid of morals altogether, who claim there is no such thing, that we are the victims of repression, and that all is fair in love and war. It is not strange to my way of thinking that this type of moral coward has in my experience always proved an abject physical coward as well when brought face to face with death, and hesitated to take the step which may close the door of life and open up the roadway which leads upwards to the Judgment Seat.

I have often pictured to myself, as I walked the bridge from midnight to four o'clock in the morning, just what the meeting between Old Sailors and the God of Heaven would be like. I have pictured the sailor standing, at last, cap in hand, hands clasped behind his back, head bowed, calmly waiting for the Judge of Judges to speak.

I have tried to picture what thoughts would be passing through the mind of the King of Kings as He looked at the man who during life had been such a strange combination of vices and virtue. I could see Him glance at the Recording Angel's ledger. The debit side had a hundred entries to one on the credit side. Then I saw the Judge push the ledger aside. He looked keenly at the old Shell-back in front of Him and said :

"You have sinned often and variedly, but you never sinned for the direct purpose of insulting Me or offending Me, neither did you sin because you questioned My supreme authority over mankind ; you sinned rather from habit and due to the peculiar circumstances which surrounded your lives. You never thought. You never sat down deliberately and said, ' There is no God, and if there is I am going to show Him that I defy His authority by deliberately breaking His laws.' You sinned, not in order to offend Me, but for the sake of the adventure and the temporary pleasure the sin gave you. Against this long list of foolish indiscretions I notice that several times while on earth you risked your life to aid your comrades in distress. I notice you unselfishly gave up many things so that others might derive greater pleasure out of their lives. I notice also that you are one of those who, through the dangerous years of the Great War, signed on regularly and sailed ships back and forth through the submarine-infested waters so that the citizens of your country might have food and not be brought to defeat by starvation. I see you were torpedoed three times, but that you signed further articles as soon as you reached shore. You did these things because by doing them you thought you were doing what was right. You did these things because you considered it was your duty to do them."

I saw the Old Sailor look up gratefully at hearing the kindly words. He recognized that the Judge was a Being of great understanding. The Sailor recollected that he never had done the bad things just for the sake of offending God. He looked up more hopefully, and the Supreme Being spoke again.

"I see that you died far away from home in a hospital. That nobody seemed to care about you at the last. Your last thoughts were rather worried ones. You glanced back over your life and thought it had been rather badly spent. You had never given much thought towards the Hereafter, but just before you died you said a mental prayer. I heard it and it went like this, 'I have not lived exactly like I ought to have done. What I did I did because I was a darned fool and somehow couldn't seem to help it. I've sense enough to know that as we must have a compass to steer a ship by, so there must be " somebody " at the helm steering the destinies of the world. I never seem to have had much time to think about these things, and I don't think I've much time left to think about them now. I reckon that if You've got me entered up in the Heavenly Log Book as often as the various Skippers I sailed with have me entered up in theirs . . . well, I don't have much of a chance when I meet St. Peter at the Pearly Gates. It's not much use starting to cry over the past now, it's gone and done with, but, Lord, if You can let bygones be bygones I promise to take in the slack of my pants and steer a better and straighter course after I've passed through the Great Divide.'

" I heard that whispered prayer. I believe you are loyal at heart and willing now to obey My Divine Commands. You may enter into the Kingdom of God."

When I rewrote the pages of this book I was under the impression that Captain B. V. Smith had sailed for the " Port of missing ships " long years ago. To my intense surprise and pleasure I received a letter from Messrs. J. Chambers and Co. only the other day saying Captain Smith was still alive and living retired in Liverpool. It was my original intention to dedicate this book to the memory of my mother and Captain B. V. Smith, the two people in all the world I feel I owe most by the sterling example they gave me during the impressionable years of my life. Having heard that Captain B. V. Smith is still alive I have changed my plans and dedicate the book to my mother's memory and to him personally.

LIST OF ILLUSTRATIONS

WILLIAM GUY CARR	*Frontispiece*
	FACING PAGE
PORT SAID	24
THE BUND AT SHANGHAI	40
THE WRECK OF THE *DACRE CASTLE* AT KELUNG HARBOUR	96
MY GUN CREW AT THE OUTBREAK OF HOSTILITIES	152
H.M.S. *HAMPSHIRE* SUNK WITH LORD KITCHENER ON BOARD	176
LIEUT.-COMMANDER BOYLE, V.C.	216
SUBMARINE R 12 COMING UP AFTER HER FIRST DIVE IN THE TRIAL BASIN	256

HELL'S ANGELS OF THE DEEP

CHAPTER I

December 25th, 1910.

It is no use. I simply cannot stick it any longer. I never slept a wink last night. I remained awake listening to the howling of the wind and the roar of the waves along the sea-shore. Something inside of me actually ached, so intense was my longing to be out there on the ocean battling the elements. I craved to be aloft on the yards of a sailing ship, working with other men. I could see them in my mind's eye struggling to take in sail. The wind was tearing at their clothes; the rain beating in their faces; the mast swaying; the yards creaking as they jerked back and forth, and, as I gave full play to my imagination, I saw them plainer as the lightning flashed across the sky and sent vivid forks zigzagging through the dome of the stormy heavens. I could see the angry waves, lashed to fury by the gale, reaching up at them. I wanted to be with them more than I ever did before.

It is all very well for Father to tell me it is a dog's life. Probably his father told him the same thing, but I learned the other day that he ran away to sea himself and I'm going to do the same thing.

December 29th, 1910.

I have to make my plans. I am going to Liverpool to look the situation over. I want to get a sailing ship, if possible. I really don't know what I had better do. I would like to go straight to the Captain and ask him to sign me on as deck boy, or anything at all, to get a start, but if I do this, he might ask me some rather embarrassing questions and send me back home.

December 31st, 1910.

Things don't always work out as you want them to. I've had a ship and I lost it again. I went to Liverpool and wandered down to the Salthouse docks. I saw some sailing ships moored there. I went aboard each in turn. I am big for my age, standing five feet nine inches tall and look a good deal older than fifteen. I asked for the Mate, and said, as casually as possible, " Want any hands to-day, Mister ? "

" Know anything about ships," he queried.

" Been around them all my life," I told him.

He looked me over carefully. I evidently measured up to his standards, for he told me to report to the Bos'on and start work.

All this seemed very easy, but it was too good to last. Just as we were all ready to go up to the shipping office and sign articles, a policeman walked aboard. I was walked ashore and detained until my mother arrived from Preston to claim me.

January 4th, 1911.

Strange how things turned out. I was just about as low in spirits as the village " pub " after the Annual Fair ; I thought the outlook was hopeless, but it wasn't. My very dejection touched my mother's heart. She felt sorry for me ; we had had a long discussion and she promised to " talk to my father." Her talk to Father ended as such talks usually do. Instead of having to plan to run away again, Dad is taking me into Liverpool to see some shipowners. I feel like yelling " Hip-hip-hurray ! "

January 10th, 1911.

This is the last time I will write in this new diary until I am at sea. My sea-bag and chest are packed. Everything is ready. My indentures are signed. I am to serve with Messrs. J. Chambers and Company as apprentice for four years.

What funny things these articles of indenture are. I am bound for four years under bond of ten pounds. The firm undertake to teach me the duties of a seaman. They are to pay me two pounds the first year, four the second, six the third, and eight the fourth. I, on the other hand, have to be loyal to the Company and goodness knows what else besides to my masters and those over me. I have not to frequent alehouses, taverns, and a lot more places which are apparently frowned upon and placed out of bounds. There is only one fly in the ointment as far as I am concerned. The ship upon which I have to serve is not a sailing ship. She is the S.S. *Dacre Castle* trading between New York, Boston, China, and Japan. She never comes to England. She is under charter to the Barber Line of New York. The officers and apprentices are sent out from England to join her and are sent back home for a change every two years. Personally, I would have liked to go in a sailing ship, but they are few and far between nowadays. I must be satisfied. The long voyages will make the period of four years seem to go quickly.

Once Mother made up her mind to help me to go to sea, she has been kindness itself, and so has Dad. He, personally, supervised the buying of my outfit, saw that I got everything which was necessary and useful, and bought nothing which he termed " junk."

I am all excitement waiting to be off. My passage is booked aboard the White Star liner *Baltic* which sails to-morrow for New York.

January 12th, 1911. At Sea.

I am at sea at last. England has faded away in the distance. The future seems to lie before me like a book. I wish I could turn over the pages and glance at the things which are in store for me. I don't know if the next chapters of my life are to have a happy ending or not.

I feel quite important dressed in my new uniform. " Brass-bound " is what my father called it. I haven't felt the least bit sea-sick, although the ship did roll a little last night as we left the coast. I would have felt rather foolish if I had been sick while wearing a sailor's uniform. I felt quite " doggie " when passengers approached me and asked for information about the ship. They evidently thought I was one of the ship's officers.

January 21st, 1911. New York.

We docked this morning. What awful weather. Snow and sleet all the way up the Hudson River. I was met at the dock by an apprentice from the *Dacre Castle* named Robinson. He and I will be room-mates for the next year. His name is Dick, but everyone aboard calls him " Mickey." He is in the last year of his apprenticeship and seems very popular with the officers aboard the *Dacre Castle*.

But the ship herself.... What a shock I got when I saw her berthed at the foot of Forty-second Street, Brooklyn. She looks a perfect wreck. She is coated with rust, covered with refuse out of the holds, and the derricks seemed all over the place.

She has discharged her cargo and is waiting to go to her loading berth. She is a ship of 7500 tons, and is flush decked fore and aft. There is nothing beautiful about her. The idea which struck me when I first saw her was that she was built by the mile and cut off the length required. The ends look as if they had been sealed up. I mentioned my disappointment to Mickey, but he assured me that I was lucky to be appointed to such a fine ship. She is practically new and has a speed of twelve knots. He told me she would look much different when she was loaded and cleaned and painted. Still I don't like her.

I can't help but keep comparing her with a fine three-masted full-rigged ship called the *Queen Elizabeth* which is under charter for the Standard Oil Company and lying off Staten Island. There are quite a number of sailing ships here. I think I will visit some.

The Captain of the *Dacre Castle* is B. V. Smith. He is an extraordinary man in many ways. He is over six feet tall, must be well over sixty, and is reckoned a hard case. He is a huge man. His ruddy face is topped by a wealth of snow-white hair which looks like an untidy mop. He has a heavy, drooping moustache and bushy eyebrows. His voice is like a fog-horn. When he shouts you can hear him all over the ship. He is the commodore captain of the company and commanded their last sailing ship. He is said to be one of the finest navigators afloat. He has been in command over thirty years and has never figured in a serious accident.

When Mickey took me up on the lower bridge, I handed Captain Smith the letter of introduction as instructed by the owners when leaving Liverpool. He read the letter, looked me over like a butcher would a steer, then bellowed, "Another fool of the family sent to sea." A hot retort came to my lips. I was just about to reply, "Times have changed since you went, Sir," when I caught a look in his eyes which made me hold my tongue. Instead of the clever remark I meekly muttered, "No, Sir."

"Don't contradict me," he thundered.

I remained silent. My knees felt a little shaky.

"Who told you to wear that outfit ? " he demanded, pointing to my " brass-bound " uniform.

"The owners, Sir," I replied.

"Oh, did they ? Well, I'm Master aboard this ship. Buy some dungarees. Report to the Mate. Do as Robinson tells you. He's got sense," he barked at me.

"Very good, Sir," I answered, trying to be polite, but all I received in return was, "Don't very good me. Get to your quarters and change out of that damned uniform. We don't wear 'em aboard the ships I command."

"Aye . . . aye, Sir," I stammered, and was glad to get out of sight of the old despot.

Mickey took me into the half-deck, which is the official term for apprentices' quarters. He showed me my bunk. It was on the port side and the bottom boards were covered with old newspapers. When I lifted these, I disturbed thousands of cockroaches. My face must have changed colour, for Mickey laughed.

"You'll become accustomed to those roaches. They're clean," he said, and added, "It's the bugs I hate. I've taken every precaution to keep them out of the cabin since I joined this ship three years ago ; she was new then, but they've invaded the half-deck at last. We'll have to wait until we get to sea and into warmer weather ; then we'll strip the cabin right down to the bare iron work and fix them," he promised.

We lifted the bunk boards and examined them. The cracks and seams were alive with the horrible little brown pests. I cannot express how filled with revulsion I felt. Never in my life had I come in contact with this kind of thing. I must admit that my mind went back to the spotlessly clean, airy room I had occupied at home. I thought of the clean sheets and beds. The comparison was terrible.

As I stood looking at the place in which I was to sleep for the next two years, my face must have registered my thoughts, for Robinson said, " Come on, Carr, snap out of it. You'll have to put up with a lot worse than that if you intend to stay at sea. If you don't think you can stick it, you might as well quit right now."

There was something about the way Mickey spoke that made me like him right then and there. I think we will become good friends. He is a jolly, good-natured fellow; always ready to smile, but there is something about his appearance which makes me think he would give a mighty good account of himself if he ever got into a fight. He is about five feet eight inches tall, broad-shouldered, slightly bow-legged, and has the typical carriage and look of a sailor.

" Have you got a bed ? " Mickey asked me.

I told him I thought beds would be provided.

" I'll buy you a donkey's breakfast when we go ashore to-night. They are cheap and filled with straw. I dump mine at the end of every trip and buy another," he informed me.

We carried my sea-bag and chest into the half-deck and Mickey helped me stow them away. The cabin is about ten feet long by eight wide. It is situated amidships between the Third Officer's cabin and the lamp-room. Just inside the door is a wash-basin. Mickey informed me that he always washed on deck in a bucket and used the wash-basin and locker under it for storing " grub."

I thought we ate in the saloon at the second table, but I am wrong. Captain Smith does not agree with apprentices being treated as junior officers, but rather as ordinary seamen. The differences between ordinary seamen and apprentices aboard this ship, according to Robinson, are that we apprentices don't sleep in the fo'c'sle (forecastle) or mix with the crew except when actually working with them during our watch on deck, and ordinary seamen are paid for their services ; we are not.

I must admit that I feel terribly disappointed. In this ship I am to have plenty of dirt and hard work and none of the thrill life in sail would have given me as compensation for the hardships one is asked to suffer. From what my shipmate tells me, life aboard this ship is a continuous round of "watch and watch"; painting; cleaning brass work; chipping rust, and washing paint with suggie-muggie (whatever that is). I asked Mickey what "suggie-muggie" is and he laughed and told me that I would soon find out.

I have an idea. I think I will break my indentures before they are really started and go into sail as an ordinary seaman. Mickey told me that if he had to start his "time" over again, he would do that very thing.

He told me that the routine aboard these ships kept one filthy dirty the whole trip. You are kept busy chipping rust in the bunkers, cleaning cargo holds, overhauling gear and oiling decks, and after leaving Japan on the return voyage, you shovel coal off the decks into the bunkers for six solid weeks. Coal can be bought so much more cheaply in Muji, Japan; the ship's decks are piled high with "black diamonds," and the deck load is trimmed down below into the bunkers as soon as there is room for it. He says life aboard a sailing ship may be hard, but it is at least clean. If he had to choose between going in sail or steam he would take the sailing ship every time. He claims that in sail you at least learn to be a seaman, but in steam, the position you are best qualified for when you finish your time is that of a stoker.

He informed me that during the whole of the three years he had been at sea, he had never been on the bridge except to take his "trick" at the wheel, and to clean brass work. He has not been taught any navigation and very little seamanship.

We were sitting talking on the settee when the Mate came along.

"Tumble out there, you two, cover the hatches. It looks like more snow," he ordered. Then turning to me he added, "Stick around with Robinson and get the hang of things. Get out of those G—— D—— glad rags. You can put them away for the rest of the voyage. You won't wear them out on this ship unless the moths get ' at them.' "

Mickey told me that the Mate's name was Gough, and that "he wasn't a bad sort, but hard boiled." He is a tall man and gives one the impression of whip-cord with knots in it. He has a hard face and heavy jaw. Mickey said he left two seamen in hospital in Hong Kong last voyage. I disliked the *Dacre Castle* the moment I saw her, and my impression has not improved any since I came onboard and met the Captain and Mate.

"A MOTHER'S FAREWELL"

Dedicated to the memory of my Mother

My son, you're going to wander far
   O'er oceans wide and deep,
To Europe, Asia, Africa,
   And may God guide your feet.

Remember, son, where'er you go
   To always give and take;
Life's tides do ever ebb and flow,
   They're not made to stagnate.

Be brave, be truthful, never shirk
   Your duty as a man;
But buckle down to real hard work,
   And evil always ban.

Should dark temptations loom ahead,
   Just steer a steady course;
Remember, dear, the words I've said,
   To sin but brings remorse.

And when once more you're homeward bound,
   My heart will ready be
To overflow with love profound
   When you come back from sea.

WILLIAM GUY CARR.

Jan. 9th, 1916.

CHAPTER II

January 28th, 1911.

I don't think I will sail on the *Dacre Castle* after all. Mickey has turned out to be a real trump. He is an awfully fine fellow. Through him I met Mr. Woods of the Seamen's Mission. He is also a very fine man. I went around the harbour in the Mission launch last Sunday afternoon, picking up apprentices. We took them up to the Mission, had tea, and afterwards attended divine service. We enjoyed a social evening and were then taken back to our ships in the launch. In this manner I met most of the British apprentices in port. Mr. Woods is very popular and the boys all turn out for him when he comes around. He is, according to them, a man's man, and not a sloppy old "Bible Puncher" just in the game for a living.

I found out that the *Queen Elizabeth* is a good ship with a bad name. According to my information, the Captain is going to find difficulty shipping a crew. I was told if I went aboard just before sailing day and saw the Mate he would sign me on as ordinary seaman and be glad to have me. I thought the days were over when crews were "Shanghaied," but I am informed that the chances are they will have to shanghai a crew, or part of it, at least, before the *Queen Elizabeth* can put to sea. The apprentices say the Captain and Mate "haze" (bully) the crew so they will "skin out" before the end of the voyage. That saves paying them wages. The apprentices are not treated too badly. They don't have to pay them.

I'm going to take a chance. Mickey is going to help me ashore with my gear. I have taken a room at a boarding-house run by the man who is going to provide the crew. As I'm a willing member, he won't have to "dope" me, or knock me on the head with a black-jack.

I hate the *Dacre Castle* more and more every day. I have done little else but clean holds and bilges from seven in the morning until six at night since I joined the ship. The only variety in our work is when we are sent to clean the brass-work around the Captain's cabin and on the bridge. I never had a colder job in my life. We clean the brass with powdered bath brick, oil and vinegar. We rub the mixture on with a spun-yarn swab and wipe it off and polish with cotton waste.

The officers have arrived from England. They followed me out. Both the second and third Mates are elderly men. Look very much to me like " down-and-outers." Mickey says it is hard to obtain good officers to serve on ships that do two full years away from home.

I'm all ready for the night after next. I am informed that running away from a ship is called " skinning out." Severe penalties are provided for apprentices who " skin out " and thereby break their indentures, but Mickey says he does not think the owners will bother me because I have really not started mine yet.

The ship has been shifted to her loading berth. Gangs are working day and night. I have spent the last two days and part of the nights taking turn with the second and third Mates " watching cargo." If an officer or apprentice is not actually down the hold watching, the longshoremen broach the cargo and steal anything to which they take a fancy. We are loading a quantity of beers, liquors, and wines for the Army and Navy Club, Manila. The gangs did everything they could to distract my attention for a few minutes so they could open a case and then hide the bottles, to drink when opportunity offers.

I watched carefully, but when I relieved one of the Mates next shift, the longshoremen, in number two hold, were all feeling pretty merry. I don't know for certain, but I have an idea, that they were not the only ones who like a drink. Mickey told me not to be too over-enthusiastic or I'd get myself into a lot of trouble. I don't doubt it. The longshoremen around these docks are about the toughest bunch of individuals I ever saw. They are mostly " wops " (Italians) or Irishmen. They seem to take a delight in competing against each other. They are great workers, but the man who seems to work the hardest is the one who " rushes the Growler " (the pail in which they carry beer).

February 2nd, 1911.

A lot has happened since I wrote in these pages. I ran

HELL'S ANGELS OF THE DEEP 23

away. I got to the boarding-house all right. What a joint that was!

The night they shipped the crew aboard the *Queen Elizabeth* a big party was given by some "crimps" working for the "runner." These "crimps" brought plenty of booze and had women on hand. They horned liquor into the men and got them all very drunk. There were a dozen fights and brawls over the women, or supposed insults. It seems impossible that human beings could sink so low as to do the things I saw done that night.

There were two big blonde giants, Norwegians or Swedes, who broke up all serious trouble. They would knock a man out with as little compunction as swatting a fly. They had fists like hams, and I shuddered when I saw them swing their fists and heard the thud on the point of some drunken sailor's jaw. The sailors who frequent these ports must be tough or they couldn't stand the punishment they receive. I saw fights in which both bottles and knives were used, and I noticed one thing above all else. The man who escaped with the least damage was the one who was quickest and unscrupulous enough to inflict serious injury on the other man first.

I saw one weak-looking souse become quarrelsome. He talked big and made threats. He picked on one man in particular and accused him of having robbed him of some money. The man took no notice for a time, then he warned the other to desist. When the other ignored his warning, he laid him out with an empty bottle. The cut in that man's head would require at least half a dozen stitches to close. If the man's skull wasn't fractured, it is beyond me.

I wanted to leave the place and promised the "runner" I would return and go onboard the ship when he was ready. He wouldn't hear of my going. He offered me liquor and beer, and insisted that I stay around.

About one o'clock in the morning I was sitting in his office when he entered and told me they were ready. I threw my sea-bag over my shoulder and followed him down to the wharf. About a dozen men were in a fair-sized launch. They were all helplessly drunk or unconscious from one cause or another. An argument arose between the "runner" and the man handling the launch about taking the man with the deep cut in his head.

The "runner" argued to the effect that he was commissioned to obtain twelve men and that there was nothing in the contract which would allow the Captain to return damaged goods or simply accept them on approval.

We went down the river and over towards Staten Island. Soon I saw the tall masts of the sailing ship outlined against the starry sky. This was adventure. There were countless twinkling lights all along the water-front; the dark waters of the river swept onwards sluggishly towards the ocean. Strange cries and noises filled the darkness of the night; the tang of the frosty air helped me to realize that what was happening was real and not just another flight of my imagination.

The "runner" hailed the ship. He was answered by the swinging of a lantern.

The motor in the launch slowed down, spluttered, and finally stopped. We drifted alongside. The painter was made fast. A Jacob's-ladder clattered down over the side. The shanghaied men were passed aboard.

When the last man was aboard, the "runner" called the Captain. "Here's a likely youngster, Captain, a friend of mine, who wants to go to sea. Guess you'll make a sailor outta him. Here's his 'dunnage' coming aboard."

With this explanation he heaved my sea-bag over the bulwarks and told me to follow and slide aft with the men.

I climbed aboard, but before I could jump down on deck I nearly fell over backwards into the launch. Standing at the rail with the Captain of the *Queen Elizabeth* was Captain B. V. Smith of the *Dacre Castle*. The Master of the sailing ship was a friend of his. He saw me hesitate. If I had not done so, I doubt if he would have noticed me, but when I stopped climbing the ladder, the sailing-ship Captain bellowed, "Come aboard there. Get a move on. You'll move faster than that before I've had you aboard this ship very long." That drew Captain Smith's attention to me.

I gathered my wits together, then climbed quickly up the ladder. I was about to jump down on deck when I heard Captain Smith bellow, "Well, I'll be damned; if it isn't that new apprentice of mine. . . . Come here, you young rascal.

PORT SAID
Ships at the entrance to the Suez Canal.

What the hell's the meaning of this ? I'll teach you to try running away from a ship of mine. Get back into that boat there. Take your dunnage . . . dammit."

I did as I was told. There was nothing else I could do. I heard Captain Smith saying good-bye to his friend. He thanked him for the cordial entertainment he had received, wished him *bon voyage*, and then he joined me in the launch.

" Take me to the *Dacre Castle*. She's loading at Number Seven Bush Docks," he told the man in the launch.

" Aye, aye, Sir ! " he replied, respectfully enough. I realized then that Captain B. V. Smith was more than well known along the New York-Brooklyn water-front.

Captain Smith said very little until I was back onboard the *Dacre Castle*. Then he acted far differently to what I expected. He asked me for no explanation. He needed none. He could evidently understand the motives which were behind my conduct.

" Go to your cabin. Don't be a young fool. I know you'd like to go in sail, but you are lucky to miss that ship. You'd never stick it. You'd run away from her and start to drift. You'd continue to drift until you found yourself on the rocks with your life ruined as far as following the sea as a profession is concerned. This ship isn't perhaps just what you expected. Someone in Liverpool undoubtedly filled you full of ' bunk ' about how you would be treated. You'll get treated exactly the same as I always treat boys who sail with me. If you work hard and do as you're told, and give no trouble, you'll get along alright. If you don't, you'll be sorry. Get to your bunk. See you're on deck bright and early in the morning. No more nonsense now. You understand ? " he concluded.

" Yes, Sir," I answered, meekly enough, and I went below to tell Mickey what had happened. We ended up by having a good laugh. We both agreed that B. V. Smith is not such a bad old fellow after all. I expected much worse than I got . . . and probably deserved it.

February 8th, 1911.

We are at sea. I haven't been sick but I felt pretty groggy when the Mate put me to work down in the chain-locker and fore-peak cleaning it up and stowing the paint and oil barrels ship-shape for the voyage. We were bucking a fairly heavy sea and the reek of oil and smell of tar, added to the motion of the ship as she pitched up and down, made me feel as sick as a dog. The perspiration broke out all over my face and I felt like lying down and giving in. I don't remember feeling so miserable in all my life. I stuck it out, however, and soon felt better.

We are on watch and watch. Mickey is in one and I am in the other. We do four hours on duty and four off. During the time we are off duty we have to eat, wash our clothes, clean out our quarters, and sleep. Due to the dog-watches, the hours of duty change each day. One day we actually work fourteen hours and the next ten.

The ship has been washed down, the derricks secured, and cargo gear all stowed away. She looks entirely different to what she did in Brooklyn and is not at all a bad sea-boat.

We have a general cargo onboard, and our ports of call are Algiers, Port Said, Singapore, Hong Kong, Shanghai, Manila, Kobe, and Yokohama.

The food is nothing to write home about, but I am getting used to it. When one is really hungry you can eat almost anything. We go to the galley and receive our " grub " the same as the crew. We eat it off tin plates which we balance on our knees. We have no table in the half-deck.

We are allowed one small tin of condensed milk every three weeks. Mine only lasted one day, for I opened it with a can-opener and when I went to use it again it was full of cockroaches. Mickey, from experience, had only made two small holes in his tin. He forced the milk out, when required, by blowing into one hole with his mouth. After he has enough in his tea or coffee, he plugs the holes with matches. The cockroaches are an absolute nuisance because they eat holes in the bread if you leave it uncovered. They make it look just like a honeycomb. They annoy me by crawling all over me when I am trying to sleep. Mickey assures me that I will get used to these things after a while. I don't think I ever will.

I am learning to steer. It is not hard provided you keep your attention on the compass card and don't use too much helm. The " Old Man " is a crank on this matter and spends most of his time while at sea walking backwards and for-

HELL'S ANGELS OF THE DEEP 27

wards across the lower bridge watching the wake. He tongue-lashes the helmsman if he steers more than a couple of degrees either side of his given course.

I have not yet made up my mind in regard to Captain B. V. Smith. Sometimes I think he is a regular old tyrant and then at others that I actually like him. He fears neither man nor devil. We have some real hard cases aboard this ship amongst the crew. The Bos'on, a Frenchman, just recently got out of jail where he had served a term for stabbing a man in the neck. He is quite proud of his record, and his chief recommendation for the position of Bos'on seems to be that he is ten minutes more hard-boiled than the rest of the crew. But he is as an infant compared to Captain Smith. I don't know whether what happened the other morning was done intentionally or not, but it was a scream while it lasted.

The Bos'on handles the hose when the crew are washing down decks. The other day about six bells in the morning watch, the crew were washing down the upper bridge. Captain Smith was on the lower bridge taking an early morning "sight." We were just a week out from port and Captain Smith and Mr. Gough had been "Licking the crew into shape." Intentionally or not, the Bos'on put the hose over the top of the upper bridge and played it on the "Old Man" and his precious sextant. Captain Smith was on the upper bridge in a couple of bounds. He was dripping with moisture and frothing with rage. He must be somewhat of a lineologist, as well as a master mariner, for he told that Frenchman more about his ancestors than he could ever have dreamed possible. According to Captain Smith's version, they can't have been very nice people to know.

The Bos'on made some remark about the Captain's origin which was far from flattering and "Old Ben" let a roar out of him which made the compass dance around in the binnacle. He grabbed the Frenchman by the scruff of the neck and proceeded to wash the words down his neck with the nozzle of the hose. After he had about half-drowned the Bos'on he shook him like a terrier would a rat and threw the man from him as if he were discarding a piece of cotton-waste with which he had just finished wiping his hands. The "Old Man's" methods may be crude, but they are certainly effective. I don't think the rest of the crew will try any more " Monkey Business " this voyage.

The crew is composed almost entirely of foreigners. The cooks and stewards are Chinamen. The one compensation about this ship is Mickey. He is one of the best fellows I have ever met. He tells me what to do and what not to do. His advice prevents me getting into a peck of trouble.

Yesterday I was washing the deck-head in the port alleyway, using strong suggie-muggie (a washing solution made from caustic soda). I was whistling although I was really anything but happy, for the water was dripping down my sleeves and into my eyes. As I bent over my bucket, to wring out my swab, the Mate, Mr. Gough, happened along. I got a good stiff kick where it hurt most and fell forward on my face. Nothing was said and I was puzzled to know the reason for such treatment. Mickey, who was on his way from the galley with his breakfast, enlightened me. It is a serious offence to whistle at sea, at least it was in sailing ships. Mr. Gough, being a sailing-ship man until recently, brought his prejudices with him. I can hardly sit down, even yet.

February 23rd, 1911.

We passed through the Straits of Gibraltar and I saw the awe-inspiring sight which thrills all Britishers to the core. We called at Algiers and coaled ship. Captain Smith went ashore as soon as the ship was moored and didn't come back until it was time to sail.

The bum-boat men were soon alongside and sold the crew all the wine they wanted, and that was plenty. Almost everybody got drunk. They came into the half-deck and pestered the life out of we two apprentices trying to sell us post-cards of the filthiest pictures imaginable. I was a stranger to these things until a few weeks ago. I guess I know now, why my father didn't want me to go to sea.

Algiers is a beautiful spot. Looking at the city from the sea, the white domes and houses terrace upwards, from waters of the deepest blue. I thought paintings I had seen of the " Blue " Mediterranean Sea were exaggerated and unreal, but now I've changed my mind.

While I was drinking in this wonderful scene, a row started

on one of the coaling lighters. Two of the Arab coal-heavers entered into an argument. They talked with their hands as well as their mouths. All those near stopped work to watch the fun. At least I thought it was fun until one of the men stopped gesticulating long enough to pick up a coal shovel. He brought the sharp edge down on the other man's skull with all the power he could put behind the blow. The victim's head was opened from crown to chin. He died instantly.

Without any undue haste, the murderer gathered up his clothes and walked off the lighter. He climbed onto the wharf and went ashore. None of the other Arabs attempted to interfere. They simply dragged the dead man to one side and went on with their work, as if nothing had happened. When the police arrived, they came in a most leisurely way and made less fuss than if investigating an accident. "' What is written—is written and so it will happen—Why worry ! ' That is Arabian logic."

February 28th, 1911.

We are in the Red Sea and Suez is far behind. What a wonderful experience it was to come through the Canal. We had very little tying up to do and made the passage in fourteen hours. Captain Smith must think a lot of Robinson. He had him at the wheel most of the way through the Canal.

We did not get ashore in Port Said as we were there only a few hours, but the bum-boat men were just as pestiferous as they were in Algiers. They swarmed over the ship selling Turkish Delight, dates, figs, and mineral waters, but this part of their business is only a blind. They try to obtain entrance to your cabin and then produce their line of filth—immoral pictures, certain drugs, and all sorts of appliances used in immoral practices are offered for sale. These men are always on the alert and ready to steal anything that is left lying about, and they go out of their way to try and seduce young boys to their own depraved habits.

I was told to keep the anchor watch the night we were in Port Said. While making my rounds about four bells, in the middle watch, I caught an Arab in the very act of stealing one of the Manila mooring lines which was coiled up aft. When he saw me he pulled a dagger from his belt. I drew my old revolver. I had hidden it in my sea-chest and brought it to sea with me. I don't know what would have happened if I had fired it. Probably it would have been more dangerous to me than the Arab. It once belonged to my grandfather. The necessity for this experiment did not materialize, however, for as soon as the Arab saw the revolver, he took a flying dive over the rail and was picked up out of the water by two men in a boat who rowed him ashore. The men in the boat were undoubtedly accomplices waiting for him to pass the end of the mooring line down to them over the stern.

After leaving Suez, we steamed down the Gulf of Suez and saw Mount Sinai away on our port hand, and Ras Garhib on our starboard side. Mickey informed me that it was near the latter place where Moses parted the waters of the sea, leaving a dry passage over which the Israelites crossed and escaped from the bondage they had suffered in Egypt to the freedom of the Promised Land. Looking at it from the sea, the Promised Land doesn't look very much different from Egypt. All I could see were hills of burning sands and deserts stretching away as far as the eye could reach.

I saw my first mirage to-day. I was sent aft to read the log, and when I went up on the bridge to report the reading, I was dumbfounded to see the *Dacre Castle* was apparently in a land-locked harbour. Red sandstone cliffs, yellow sand-hills, stately palms, and green oasis stretched away around the whole horizon. It was as beautiful and magnificent a sight as was ever painted on canvas; then, as I stood and marvelled, I saw another ship coming straight towards us. She was steaming upside down over the top of the sand-hills and appeared to be suspended by the keel from the Heavens by invisible wires.

The Second Mate saw the look on my face and laughed. "It's only a mirage," he told me, indifferently. Even as he spoke, the whole picture, which looked like a scene out of Arabian Nights, dissolved, and I found myself transported instantly from a regular fairy land back to the decks of a drab old ocean tramp with a pail of oil and a wad of waste waiting for me on the rusty iron main-deck.

We are at present engaged chipping and oiling decks. First we chip all the rust off the iron decks with a chipping hammer, then we scrub the decks with steel brooms and rub oil on them with a wad of cotton-waste. Paint brushes are too expensive. We dip our hands into the tin and rub the oil well into the newly cleaned iron. The temperature, in the shade, was 99 degrees the last reading I took, but it is well over a hundred in the sun. The iron decks are hot enough to blister your knees, or "fry eggs on," as Mickey put it. You cannot bear to kneel on them without some burlap, or wood, between your knees and the deck.

I asked Mickey why we didn't get sunstroke. He laughed. "I dunno," he replied. "We work out in the sun without any sun-hats or other protection, and I never saw a sailor get sunstroke while at sea. I have seen men from below (the stokehold) go crazy with the heat and jump overboard, but it doesn't seem to affect the deck hands seriously. The sea-breeze or something must moderate the effect of the heat."

I don't know what he calls "seriously." My arms and shoulders are so sun-burned that they are peeling worse than they did when I had scarlet fever. Mickey informs me that I don't know what heat is like yet. He told me to reserve my opinions and comparisons about the Red Sea until I had experienced the heat at Port Swetman, in the Malay Peninsula, Manila, and one or two other places.

I think the heat is making everyone a bit grouchy. I hate the Chinese cooks and stewards. I always feel that they just gloat over the fact that they hold a position in this ship which gives them some authority over white men.

I complained to the Chief Cook about the stew he gave me for dinner yesterday. It was nothing but potatoes and some horrible greasy fat. I had not a bit of lean meat on my plate. "If you no likee . . . go to hellee," was his only comment. I would like to take that bunch of yellow-bellies (that is what all the crew call them) and throw them overboard. Mickey feels the same way. I suggested that we might give them a run for their money, but Mickey counselled patience.

He told me to wait until we near Singapore. The Chinks pay off there and we sign on another bunch. If we cause trouble now they will cut us short of grub and give us a dog's life. We must take what they care to give us for the present and give them a right royal send-off when we are about twenty-four hours out from Singapore. These Chinks are reputed bad actors. They would slit your throat just as soon as look at you if they thought they could get away with murder. The way they treat the mess-room steward is a crime.

There are five Chinese aboard. The Chief Steward, the second steward, two cooks, and a mess-room steward. The latter looks after the engineers. The other four have been giving the poor little mess-room steward a dog's life ever since we left New York. Mickey explained the situation.

They belong to different tribes or Tongs or whatever they call them in China. The cooks and stewards are Cantonese, while the mess-room steward comes from some province up-country. They love each other like a mongoose does a snake. I will be surprised if the cooks don't drive the mess-room steward out of his mind before we arrive in Singapore.

One of the Chinese took sick and was sent to hospital while we were in New York. This unfortunate we have onboard now was shipped in his place. I feel really sorry for him, but nobody seems to want to interfere.

Only the other day the Chief Cook placed the mess-tin, containing the engineers' dinners, in the oven until it was almost red-hot. Just as the mess-room steward was returning from serving the soup, the cook took it out and placed it on the galley table. As the mess-room steward entered, he spoke to him in Chinese, and told him to pick up the mess-tin and get it out of the way quickly. The mess-room steward obeyed, but the tin was so hot, he dropped the four dinners it contained on the deck and danced around with the skin literally burned from his finger-tips. The two cooks held their stomachs and howled with laughter. They thought it a great joke. After they had finished laughing, they abused the victim of their cruelty for his carelessness. They told him there was no more dinner for the engineers unless he wished to give them crew grub. He had no other option and, of course, got the full brunt of the engineers' wrath. This is only one incident of the cruel way they treated this poor devil.

Mickey was talking to the " Mess Boy " last night. He told Mickey he was convinced that the other Chinamen would kill him before the end of the trip. He said they were threatening his life continually.

CHAPTER III

March 3rd, 1911. In Hell.

We are actually in the nearest approach to hell on earth. We are in the harbour of Aden. The whole island of Perim is just a rock baked in the heat of a burning sun throughout the centuries. There is not a tree or a blade of grass to be seen. It radiates heat like the top of the galley stove, and yet British men, and even some women, hold this fort which is one of the most important links in the chain of the British Empire. It is the key to the Red Sea, like Gibraltar is to the Mediterranean. It is an important naval base as well as a coaling station.

March 15th. Leaving Singapore.

So many events have happened since last I wrote, I don't just know where to start. Perhaps I should mention that which happened last. The mess-room steward is dead . . . dead by his own hand, but just as surely murdered as ever a man was. It happened the night before we were due in Singapore.

The four stewards and cooks wore him down to a mere shadow. He failed until he was a most pitiful-looking sight. They worked on his nerves until he was afraid to shut his eyes. He dare not sleep. His celestial tormentors tortured him so persistently that the poor fellow grew to believe he was slated to die before he was " paid off." He undoubtedly killed himself to cheat the others of their revenge.

Mickey offered to let him sleep in the half-deck with us, but he would not accept the offer. We tried to tell him the stewards and cooks were only hazing him and dare not carry out their threats, but he wouldn't be convinced. Just as the palm trees, which cluster the islands situated at the entrance of Singapore harbour, came into view, the mess-room steward appeared on the main-deck. He looked towards the shore and then climbed the rail. He deliberately let himself slide down the side of the ship into the shark-infested waters of the Straits. He undoubtedly slid down the side in that manner to make sure that he would be chewed up by the propeller blades. Those of us on deck (it was about two bells in the first dog watch) gave the alarm and rushed aft to throw the man a lifebuoy. It was no use. All we saw was a blotch of red fast mingling with the dirty greenish-yellow waters of the wake. The propellers had done their work.

I was filled with anger against the other Chinamen. I felt they were morally responsible for his death. Mickey felt the same way about it. This tragedy happened while we were waiting at the galley for our suppers. The Chief Cook ladled us out a dish full of some vile-looking skilly. It was swimming in grease and hot as the dickens.

" What do you call this mess, you yellow-bellied son of a bitch ? " was the hard-boiled inquiry Mickey put to the cook. The cook picked up a wicked-looking knife, but before he could use it, Robinson brought the dish of boiling skilly down over his head and walloped him so hard on the jaw, he slid under the table and became all tangled up with his pots and pans.

The second cook grabbed the knife and attacked my shipmate. Mickey raced through the starboard alleyway and around the cross-bunker hatch through the port alleyway, the Chinaman after him. Round and round they went. The rest of the crew looked on, wondering what the end would be.

As Mickey passed me for about the third time, I stood ready with a short iron hatch batten about three feet long. It belonged to the cross-bunker hatch.

Mickey was well ahead of his pursuer at this particular time, and as he turned the corner into the starboard alleyway, he stopped, took the hatch batten from me, and as the Chink came racing round the corner, Mickey tapped him gently but firmly on the skull. He went down like a pole-axed steer.

Having disposed of one, Mickey went into the galley and shook his iron bar under the nose of the skilly-covered Chief Cook. (This was an action in itself which is almost unheard-of at sea.) It is indeed a daring individual who will step over the sacred dead line which shelters the exalted disher of hash from the rest of the common rabble aboard ship. The crime of breaking into the galley to steal food is comparable only to robbing the Bank of England.

" Anither word outta youse and I'll crown you like I did yer brother, yer good-fer-nothing son of a sea cook." Mickey was angry. His Irish temper aroused. He gave the trembling Chink a couple of flat-handed slaps across the face and then cleaned off the top of the stove with a sweep of the iron bar. The Chink dashed out of the galley to escape the steam and boiling water.

By this time the Chief Steward and the Mate were on the scene. Mickey explained what had happened and Mr. Gough walked back for'ard. I couldn't help but see the smile that hovered around the corners of his mouth. Mickey, in his estimation, has all the qualities which go towards making a good officer in the merchant service, at least in cargo vessels.

I might say that neither Mickey nor I ate any food which came from the galley until we arrived in port. I think those Chinks would like to have murdered us also.

I was ashore in Singapore. It was the first time I had set my foot on dry land since leaving New York. Mickey went with me. He knows these places like I know Liverpool. There are many things which puzzle me. I wonder why Englishmen ashore and holding good positions never seem to want to mingle or be friendly with ships' officers except the Captain.

If you go ashore in uniform you are about as welcome as the plague. If you go ashore in mufti it is not much different because every Englishman knows every other European in these Eastern ports. Go to the decent places and look for innocent amusement and you can't help but feel you are not wanted. You are not only not wanted but your presence is very much resented. They treat your advent into the better-class hotels and places of amusement as an impertinence.

I suppose it is for this reason that many officers off the ships gradually drift to those places where they are welcomed (for the money they have to spend). To me it seems hard that, after being cooped up aboard ship for a whole month, there is not some more cordial welcome awaiting ashore. In New York, it is different. Mr. Woods, who has charge of the Mission to Seamen, is a regular fellow. He seeks out the apprentices, junior officers, and engineers and makes it his business to see they become acquainted with respectable people. The Mission in New York is not just a place where they dish out religion, it is a place where Mr. Woods sees that the men who make use of it, come in contact with some of the nicest people it was ever my pleasure to meet. He introduced us to some of the most charming girls, and I know they were the daughters of very fine families. In New York we were treated as ordinary human beings, not as potential criminals and men of depraved habits and tastes. I know the boys and junior officers appreciate this kind of treatment because they treated the young ladies they met with a respect and consideration that was really admirable.

As soon as we set foot ashore in Singapore, the cab-drivers and rikisha men crowded around soliciting our patronage. They promised to find us " plenty nice girls," " plenty good drink," etc. etc. I can't realize I am only fifteen. I feel fully grown up. The curtain of life has certainly been raised for me with a vengeance. Two months ago I knew little or nothing ; to-day there is, or rather there seems to be, little left for me to learn. Mickey is a real good scout. He looks after me and advises me just like an older brother would do.

It is a strange, small world. During our many yarns, I found out that he knew many friends of mine. The maid in his home is none other than the maid my mother had when I was a baby.

Mickey and I were talking about the hospitality we meet with ashore. He claims there is just one country in the world where apprentices and officers are welcomed ashore and treated as ordinary human beings. This is Australia. All apprentices I have met speak of the wonderful times they have had in the Antipodes.

I heard a story which just about illustrates the conditions to which I refer. An apprentice finished his time and was home studying for his " Ticket." He sat at the table eating his dinner, and forgetting for the moment where he was, said, " Pass the butter ! "

His mother checked his rudeness by saying, " If you what, Jimmy ? " The apprentice, who had been away

HELL'S ANGELS OF THE DEEP

from the refining influences of home life roughing it at sea for four years, absent-mindedly remarked, "If you can damn well reach it."

It is little wonder that the veneer of respectability and decency soon becomes chipped and ultimately badly marred when boys are forced to mix constantly with men who are rough and obscene. You have to become hard-boiled in these ships or you would soon be nothing better than lackeys to the sailors. Only the other day they tried to make us clean out the heads[1] used by the crew. We refused, but if Mickey hadn't been able to lick the square-head who ordered us to do it, we would have had that job for the rest of the voyage.

We went around and saw the sights. Malay Street being one of the "sights," we went there also. It is a street of houses of prostitution. In these brothels are young girls of every type and nationality. English, German, French, Scandinavian, and Spanish predominate. These European girls are in the higher-priced houses. Chinese, Japanese, and Malay girls hold the fort in the cheaper dives. How do these girls arrive out here in the Orient? They all start life the same as any other woman. When are they first led astray? When are they first enlisted in the ranks of the professional prostitute? After they arrive at this level, what is the inducement held out to them to go to the Orient?

I was speaking to an officer from one of the P. & O. liners and mentioned these things to him. He gave a short, queer kind of laugh. "For every missionary, priest, and nun we bring out, at least four prostitutes travel on the same boat." This is the White Slave Traffic, and I am told some of the most wealthy and influential personages in Europe are mixed up in it. Where do these girls all end up? It is almost certain that few, if any, ever return to their native land. I noticed another thing. Natives rarely frequent these houses of ill-fame. The economic conditions are such that they marry young, and, from what I can gather, remain true to their marriage vows. If they tire of one wife, they marry another, but they don't renounce their responsibilities in regard to the first.

All this may meet with the severe disapproval of our

[1] Toilets.

Western minds, but it seems to me infinitely preferable to our hypocrisy, unfaithfulness, and indulgence in promiscuous love affairs.

The more I see of Mickey, the more I like him. Naturally he is a jolly, happy-go-lucky, cheerful fellow, but when he is angry or at outs with the crew, he is a wild cat and wolverine rolled into one.

Thank Heaven those Chinese cooks have gone. Nothing seems to have been done regarding the death of the mess-room steward. We have a new lot of cooks now. I hope they give us more to eat. I am always hungry.

At Sea.

We are headed for Hong Kong. We shipped some stores in Singapore, amongst them was a big ham. Every Thursday and Sunday is " Ham and Egg " day in the merchant service. That means we are supposed to be given ham and eggs for breakfast. We don't always get what we are entitled to, but it does not pay to " kick."

When the ham came aboard, Mickey eyed it like a cat does a canary. To-night it is my ten to twelve " trick " at the wheel. Mickey is on stand-by duty from twelve (midnight) until two bells. We are going to look into the question of that ham more fully.

Still at Sea.

We " won "[1] the ham. What a laugh ! Mickey certainly has brains. He got two man-helpers (long bamboo poles) and to the end of one of them he lashed a fork and to the end of the other a sharp-bladed sheath knife. The ham was hung from the deck-head in the store-room. Last voyage Captain Smith had all the doors and port-holes fitted with stout steel bars so the crew could not break in and steal the stores. The outer door of the store-room was open for ventilation purposes, but the steel bars were locked and in place.

After I had been relieved at the wheel, I joined my room-mate at the store-room door. Mickey gave me one man-helper and I jabbed the fork into the ham while he carved off a good-sized chunk with the knife he had lashed on the

[1] Stole.

end of the other. We worked away in this manner until we had the ham trimmed almost to the bone. When we had reduced its size sufficiently to allow it to come through the bars, I dug the fork solidly into the shank, while he cut the string. I pulled the bone through the bars so as to leave no evidence as to how the dirty deed had been performed. Mickey tells me it is an unwritten law at sea for apprentices to steal for their stomachs; the only crime is being caught.

When the steward served curry on Thursday morning instead of the traditional ham and eggs, " Old " Ben nearly threw a fit. When he heard the reason why ham and eggs had not been served, he raved like a madman. First he accused the steward of stealing the ham and selling it for booze. Then he demanded an investigation and told the Mate to search the ship from stem to stern. He vowed what terrible things he would do to the men who stole his ham.

When the initial search failed to reveal anything, Captain Smith sent for Mickey and me. We were cross-examined for fully an hour. We stuck out the third degree methods and came off with flying colours. All through the terrible ordeal I kept thinking how good the ham had tasted, and how good the next feed would taste if we didn't plead guilty and thus lose our spoil.

After threatening us, Captain Smith pleaded with us to tell him how we got the twenty-pound ham out of the store-room without removing the locks or bars. We tried to look innocent and remained silent. He raved and coaxed alternately but we stuck out bravely and he finally allowed us to go.

We ate all we could of the ham the night we stole it. The rest of it we wrapped in oiled paper and hid it in a biscuit tin in the starboard lifeboat. Nobody thought of looking for it there. To-night we are going to cook some more over a bucket of hot ashes. We will obtain them from the stokehold. It wouldn't be safe to use the galley just yet.

Hong Kong.

I don't see any reason in trying to write this diary from day to day. There is little or nothing happens at sea, so I will keep to places from now onwards and that will give me more space than filling up a whole lot of pages with entries like this :

Tuesday, April 1st.

Suggie-muggie in the morning. Chipping rust in the coal bunkers in the afternoon. Throat and lips so dry from rust and coal-dust that I tried chewing tobacco like the rest of the men do. Experiment not such a howling success.

An extraordinary event happened while we were anchored in the harbour of Hong Kong. Ships of all nations are there. Warships painted white, junks, passenger steamers, and even the odd sailing ship. Hong Kong itself nestled under the hill. Leave had been granted the crews of one of the American warships in harbour and also to the crew of the H.M.S. *Newcastle*. I went ashore with Mickey as soon as we had finished work. The Third and Fourth Engineers accompanied us.

I can only record the incidents of the early afternoon as they were related to me afterwards, but I was eyewitness to the events of that evening and night. According to the story as I heard it, some of the crew from the American warship became comfortably lubricated and while going along the water front looking for excitement, hauled down the British flag which was flying at the top of the flag-pole.

This incident was regarded as an insult by the crews of the British warships in harbour. A free fight ensued. The Britishers overpowered their American cousins and threw them into the waters of the harbour " to cool their ardour." Armed guards were sent ashore because the situation grew serious. Every time a party of British and American sailors met, there was a free fight. Casualties steadily mounted on both sides. Feeling grew intense. When we arrived ashore, we started what is known as a " pub crawl." I didn't take much to drink. I went along more for the fun of the thing, and out of sheer curiosity to see the sights.

The four of us were lined up before the bar of one hotel when Geordie Warren, the Third Engineer, got into an argument with some American sailors. " Geordie," as he is nicknamed because he comes from Sunderland, is a little short, thick-set man, and always ready for an argument. McNeil, the Fourth Engineer, is just the opposite. He is tall, well proportioned, and a fine athlete. He is never given to arguments if they can be avoided. Mickey is

THE BUND OF
SHANGHAI

Irish and, true to the characteristics of his race, is never happier than when in a fight.

I took all in and said little. The bar was a big one, stretching from one side of the room to the other. There was plenty of space for tables and chairs in front of the bar, and, at these, sailors of all nationalities were drinking. Geordie got into an argument about the incident to which I referred, and before anyone could interfere, a big lanky Yankee hauled off and knocked him down.

Mickey never spoke. He shot out his fist and down went the American. The fight was on. It was the first time in my life that I had ever been into anything like it. With Mickey, it was different. He picked up a chair, smashed it across the bar, broke off two legs, and handed me one.

" Take this and make for a wall. Get your back to the wall and fight your way towards a door. When you get there, beat it and wait until we join you outside. Keep your head," was the instruction and advice he hurriedly gave me.

As he spoke, a group of fighting seamen crowded over towards us. Mickey walloped another American sailor over the head and felled him as he would an ox. McNeil fought like a wildman. So did the Yanks. But it was anybody's fight. It was simply impossible to keep out of it.

Geordie got up and went down again almost as soon as he staggered to his feet. Tables and chairs were overturned, bottles were flung here, there, and everywhere. Some went high, or missed their mark, others swept the bar and the shelves behind the bar.

I took Mickey's advice. I got my back against a wall and worked my way towards the door. I felt wonderfully cool by this time. Not the least bit excited. If any one came near me who wasn't one of our own bunch, I brought down the chair leg where it would take most effect. For the first time in my life I felt the fire of battle alight within me. I experienced a kind of unholy joy when the heavy wooden club I held connected with somebody's head.

Just as I got near the door a sailor aimed a bottle at me. It missed my head by inches and broke with a crash against the wall just behind my ear.

Mickey seemed to be all over the place, but he was wonderfully cool. I saw Geordie Warren being trampled on,

McNeil was struggling with another man. I noticed blood was dripping from his coat sleeve. Mickey grabbed Warren and made a wild dash for the door. As he did so, he yelled for us to follow him. We had barely reached the door when the whole crowd rushed upon us, but somebody tore down the electric chandelier and put the place in darkness. A minute later we were panting up a lane outside. Mickey was still dragging Warren when McNeil pitched forward on his face as if shot. I bent over him. He was bleeding like a stuck pig. A hurried examination showed that he had been knifed in the arm. The blade had entered at the elbow joint and slashed downwards almost to the wrist. It was a terrible-looking gash and the blood spurted from the wound in horrible jets.

We made a tourniquet, stopped the bleeding, and took Mac to a drug store. A doctor arrived and proceeded to stitch up the ugly wound. It required twenty-two stitches to close it.

Geordie, who was really the cause of the whole affair, nursed a sore jaw and two black eyes for a couple of days, but, strange to relate, Mickey and I didn't have a single injury to show for our share in the battle.

As a result of these disorders, all leave was stopped and none of us was allowed ashore again.

Shanghai.

We met a Customs officer here who took us up to the club. We had a right royal time. He is only a young fellow and ran away from an English ship. He was lucky enough to land the position he now has.

He earns good money but he is dissatisfied with life on the coast. He drinks one absinthe after another. He insisted that we keep him company. He seemed just tickled to death to meet somebody to whom he could pour out his troubles.

Mickey is a wild actor. He is full of life and hellery. Last night he took me ashore and we met our friend of the Customs Service. We engaged three rikishas, and told the coolies to take us around and show us the sights. They certainly did as instructed. It is a crime the way whites treat Chinamen out here. This is their own country but every one seems to treat them as if they were about one degree lower in the scheme of creation than the animals in the fields. I saw a Sikh policeman publicly thrash a Chinese coolie with his cane for a trivial breach of traffic regulations.

We had not very much money. Mickey took charge of the expedition. As a matter of economy, we made a practice of ordering our rikishas to wait for us when we entered the various places of entertainment we called at, but we never left by the same door we had entered. In this way, we travelled a great deal without paying very much.

We went to the Savoy Hotel for supper. We were nicely dressed in white ducks and we waited until we met some English officers from another ship. We joined them and, as we planned it might happen, they paid for our meal. We vigorously insisted that we be allowed to pay for the meal, but the other officers were equally insistent that they should pay. They won the argument. I don't know what we would have done if they hadn't. We had about one Chinese dollar between the three of us at that time.

Mickey told them of the fun we had been having with the rikishas. We were all feeling pretty happy by the time the meal was over and they decided to join us.

We went all over Shanghai. We raised Cain with a vengeance. The real fun started about midnight when one of the rikisha men whom we had previously engaged but forgotten to pay, recognized us. He let out a whoop which would have turned a Red Indian green with envy. Others heard him. There was a back lash of Chinese gutturals and the chase was on.

Mickey seized his rikisha man by the pig-tail and made him run. To make him go faster he belaboured him with his walking-stick and balanced himself in the rikisha so that the Chinaman could not tip him. I followed his example and when my man became obstreperous, I drew my ancient revolver and pointed it at him. This action on my part had much the same effect on the Chinaman as the application of a match has to a rocket. He hunched his shoulders and simply flew over the ground. He turned a corner on one wheel and headed down the Bund towards the outskirts of the city. Mickey and the others soon followed and after a while they caught up with us. We had easily outdistanced our pursuers.

We were going along the Bund at a furious clip when, on

turning a corner, we ran smack bang into another group of sailors heading towards the city. As might be expected, the Europeans in both parties picked on the unfortunate Chinks and blamed them for the accident. After a brief struggle, we had them all prisoners. The question was what to do with them. One big sailor conceived a brain wave.

The burning question in China at this particular time is " to wear a pig-tail or not to wear a pig-tail ? " Those against wearing pig-tails seem in the majority, but some who are more conservative and old-fashioned in their ideas fear that if they discard their pig-tails their hopes of Heaven are pretty slim. They think that the pig-tail will give their friends a better chance of pulling them into Heaven if the decision of the judge is at all doubtful. Irrespective of what the reason may be, some Chinamen are still reluctant to cut them off, and those we held that night had theirs curled under their hats. When the hats were knocked off in the struggle, down came the pig-tails. The man I refer to thought it would be a splendid idea if we placed all the unfortunate Chinamen back to back and tied their pig-tails together. This was no sooner suggested than done, then half of us climbed in the rikishas while the other half got into the shafts. We left the Chinamen tied helplessly together. They were making more noise than a dozen hobbled geese.

Still in Shanghai.

You couldn't be dull long while Mickey is aboard. We, like most apprentices, have run short of money. Mickey devoted much thought and no little energy to the question of " raising the wind."

There happens to be a revolution going on. There always is. The only reason I consider this revolution worthy of mention is because it enabled us to obtain enough money to go ashore again.

While talking to our Customs officer friend, he mentioned the fact that one could almost obtain any price they wished to ask for revolvers and guns. He also informed us that the Government had issued an edict that any Chinaman caught dealing in firearms would be summarily beheaded. Lives in China just now are about as cheap as hen-eggs and yesterday we bought one hundred for one Chinese dollar

(50 c. or two shillings). The papers are full of stories of executions and executioners. This Chinese executioner is a regular fellow. He walks through the streets with a huge sword on his shoulder, guarded by half a dozen soldiers. If any unfortunate is caught committing any act against the edicts of the Government, he is simply made to kneel down, and, if he is in luck, and the executioner is in good form, his head rolls into the gutter at the first blow; if not, it sometimes takes more than one blow, but his head comes off all the same.

Being killed in China is rather a troublesome affair. There are many crimes calling for the death penalty. In some cases, the criminal's head is simply cut off. For looting and serious theft, his hands are first chopped off and then his head goes on the block. In the case of crimes which the authorities think really serious, the executioner spread-eagles the victim on a kind of heavy door and fastens him down; then he goes to work and chops him up piecemeal, starting at the ankles and wrists and working along joint by joint until he finally severs the head from the body last of all.

I have seen some extraordinary photographs of these public executions taken in Canton and Hankow. One photograph showed a mob rushing the executioner just as he had finished his gruesome task. I thought they were out for revenge, but I was informed that they were only trying to reach the body before the soul had taken to flight. There is something the Chinaman believes to the effect that the relatives must secure the body before life is properly extinct, or the soul of the deceased cannot find peace, and will haunt them for ever.

Whatever it is they believe, they certainly make enough fuss and noise when one of their relatives or friends decides to pass on. It is almost impossible to sleep at night because of the noise made by funeral processions on the river. I stayed up and watched one the other night. There were several sampans in the procession and they were crowded with the relatives and friends of the deceased. Professional mourners kept up the most hideous noise and wailings.

They lit flares and rattled tin cans and blew reed instruments incessantly. Every now and again, just to make sure that no devils had crept in through any crack in the barrage of sound, they fired off strings of Chinese fire-crackers. But this is all apart from how Mickey " raised the wind."

A Chinese pedlar came into our cabin and tried to sell us some tobacco, fruits, and candies. Mickey, while searching through a drawer pretending to look for money or something to exchange for his goods, allowed him to see the revolver. Some Chinamen are inveterate thieves. Mickey had not misjudged this one. His eyes nearly popped out of his head when he saw the gun.

Having bought what we wanted, we ordered him out of the half-deck, and after he had gone, Mickey told me his plans. We felt sure the Chinaman would return and try to steal the revolver. We secured the port-holes so he couldn't get into the half-deck from the outside, and then left the door unlocked and took up positions where we could see without being seen.

We hadn't watched very long when the Chinaman entered the alleyway. We came out of our hiding-place and saw him open the half-deck door. Mickey closed in on him from one end and I from the other. We followed him in and caught him in the act of hiding something inside his clothing.

We had taken the precaution to remove all ammunition from the revolver before we left the half-deck. As we entered the cabin, he whipped out the gun and pointed it at us. We jumped on him and pulled him down, knowing the gun was not loaded.

He was no match for the pair of us. We soon had him subdued and then the fun started. Mickey demanded to know what else he had stolen. He denied further guilt. Mickey insisted on searching him to make sure. I would never have believed it possible for a man to wear so many clothes or to hide so many articles about his person unless I had personally taken part in that search. We took off one layer of clothes after another. He had hidden all kinds of things, watches, knives, money, jewellery, etc. We decided to strip him to the bare skin and search him thoroughly.

After we had gone over him like a couple of Scotland Yard detectives search a suspect, we allowed him to dress again. Mickey asked me what I thought we should do with him. I suggested that we turn him over to the police. Mickey argued that if we did this, he would get his head chopped

off for trying to steal firearms. I told him that was none of
our funeral. We watched the Chinaman's face. They have
poker-faces, but this one registered considerable anxiety.
We knew he understood enough English to get the gist of
our conversation.

After a little more discussion, Mickey left the half-deck
presumably to call the police launch. He left the door con-
veniently open and I sat on the settee with none too firm
a grip on the Chinaman's arm. As I expected, he suddenly
jumped up and made a frantic dash for the door. I let him
go, and for all I know he has not stopped running yet. He
raced along the deck and jumped overboard and was picked
up by a passing sampan. I saw him land on the river bank
and head off into a swamp as if the devil and all his angels
were after him.

After he had gone, we returned to the half-deck and
counted our loot. It amounted in cash and valuables to
about $25.00.

"You don't think that was stealing?" asked Mickey,
evidently suffering some pangs of conscience.

I assured him I didn't, and pointed out that the man
had run away and left his things.

"I guess it served him right. He'd have cleaned us out
if he'd got the chance," Mickey remarked to soothe his still
troublesome inner self.

I agreed with him, and then we both rolled around the
half-deck howling with laughter at the thought of what had
happened during the last hour.

"MIDDLE WATCH REFLECTIONS"

> There's a time when all is restful,
>   And a tired world seeks repose,
> When the watch is called at midnight,
>   Till at dawn the old cock crows.
> You can pace the poop a-thinking,
>   Under skies of every clime,
> You can watch the moon a-sinking,
>   Just to while away the time,
> When the stars light up the heavens,
>   And the earthy ozone drifts

From the shores of dear old Devon,
  Or the land of the wild, wild Riffs.
That's the time your mind will wander,
  To the days that have gone by,
Or in dreams you'll madly squander
  Years to come before you die.

You can roam the whole world over,
As you browse in mental clover,
  You can chew the cud of memory sublime.
From Penang to white-cliffed Dover,
If you've been much of a rover,
  You'll find recollections you can put to rhyme.
When in southern seas you're sailing,
And the moonbeams leave a-trailing
  Paths, that dance and sparkle far behind,
Why, your thoughts can't help but turn,
And your heart for ever burn,
  With the joy of life and good things that you find.

Or if you're holding tight
To the weather shrouds some night
  When the stormy winds are raging o'er the Bay,
And you watch the mountainous seas
Lashed to fury by the breeze,
  You can still find food for thought in what they say.
For they tell a story plain,
Of your God (Who's no mere name),
  But a power that you must worship and adore;
For in every raging gale
You can think of those who fail
  And by wickedness are wrecked and cast ashore.

Though in storm you see God's anger,
  It's His mercy brings the calm,
And if you'll only trust Him,
  You can never come to harm.
You're as safe up in the rigging,
  Or upon the royal-yard,
When the vessel's madly swinging,
  Furling sail that's frozen hard,
As you are at home in summer,
  Walking down some quiet street.
For it makes but little difference
  Just where you end your beat.

CHAPTER IV

Nearing Japan.

The weather has been fine, and the run down to Manila was without incident except for strange craft and stranger sea creatures. I saw a gigantic sun-fish leap from the surface of the sea and spread itself in the air like a huge kite before it came down with a tremendous splash into the water.

In Manila I saw a submarine belonging to the American Navy. It was exercising in the harbour. I sometimes think I would like to join the Navy and serve in submarines.

Mickey has been up to his pranks again. I have not learned to swim properly as yet. I don't altogether fancy swimming where sharks are reported to be rather plentiful. Mickey said it was safe inside Manila Harbour. He is very anxious that I should learn to swim, so the other day, when I was on a swinging-stage painting over the bow, he cut the slings just at knocking-off time, and threw me and two of the crew into the water.

He yelled "Man overboard" and jumped in after me. I didn't know the rope sling had been cut. I thought it had parted accidentally, and I was more than grateful to Mickey for jumping in to my rescue until I learned from him later that he had simply done it for a joke. He is a wonderful swimmer. The natives here are marvels in the water, but I saw Mickey get the better of one in a sort of water wrestling match.

We have discharged most of our cargo and the ship stands high out of the water. Robinson accepted a bet and won it, so we went ashore here also. The Second Mate bet him $5.00 that he wouldn't dive off the top of the upper deck lifeboat davits. Mickey accepted the challenge. He climbed up to the boat deck, and scrambled out into the davit. He pulled himself up and stood poised on the goose-neck about seventy feet above the water. He made a magnificent dive —a swallow dive. He hardly entered the water before he was back on the surface again.

That same evening, nearly all the crew went in swimming. Suddenly the cry, "Shark! ... shark!" was heard. None of us thought it was serious; we thought one of the crew was trying to fool us and make us scramble out of the water. We went on swimming until one of the engineers came rushing to the rail and yelled excitedly for us to get out of the water.

"Get out of the water, you damn fools. There's a shark swimming around over by the next ship," he cried, and there was no mistaking the earnestness with which he spoke.

A Jacob's-ladder hung over the stern. Everyone made a dash for it. I was nearest because I had only learned to swim a few strokes, but I was second last to get on deck. All of the foreign crew raced past me. Some of them nearly drowned me in their frantic efforts to reach safety. All except Mickey. He remained behind in the water, kicking and splashing, and telling me not to feel nervous but to take my time.

I don't recall ever having experienced a sensation in my life exactly like I did as I swam for that ladder and began pulling myself out of the water. I felt numb all over. I expected to feel those cruel teeth close on my leg or ankle every second. It took every ounce of will power I possessed to keep from going into a panic.

After what seemed almost an eternity, I realized I was up about ten rungs of the ladder and safe. I turned to see Mickey just leaving the water and at the same time I saw the fins of a large shark cutting the surface of the water and heading straight for the ladder. I yelled a warning. My heart seemed to stop beating. Mickey made a frantic spurt and pulled himself up. His feet were just clear of the water when the shark turned belly up. Its huge jaws opened and closed. I shut my eyes. It struck at his feet and we were nearly thrown off the ladder as it jerked back and forth, but Robinson was safe. The shark had only grabbed the bottom rung of the ladder. After I got on deck, my legs seemed as though they were made of jelly. I had to hang on to the rail. I could not stand up.

The first thing Mickey did was to rush to the galley and beg the cook to give him some fat pork to bait a shark hook with. We were soon all at work. The shark hook was fastened

HELL'S ANGELS OF THE DEEP 51

to a length of chain and a heaving-line made fast to the end of the chain. We lowered the bait over the counter and floated it astern by means of a piece of cord or dunnage wood, but we had no luck. The shark was tearing around the harbour like some demented thing. It chased all over the place, here, there, and everywhere. It came so near to lighters that the natives prodded it with their long boat-hooks and pike-poles. I wonder if it was frantically trying to find a way out of the harbour through the breakwater?

The water here is lovely and warm, but I don't think I'll ever be tempted to swim inside Manila harbour again. I'd just as soon sleep with a rattlesnake as swim with a shark.

On the way from Manila towards Japan I saw an extraordinary sight. It must have been a meteor.

I had relieved the wheel at four bells in the middle watch. About five bells I saw a peculiar light sharp on the starboard bow. It was yellowish red and about the size of an orange when I first noticed it. The Second Mate looked in the same direction through the night glasses. He came over beside me, and asked me if I could see the light and what I made of it.

I could see the light, but didn't know what to make of it. Things happened quickly after that. The light moved towards us at a tremendous rate of speed. As it approached, it grew larger and brighter until we were completely blinded by its brilliance. My recollection is that it was white towards the centre, shading from yellowish red to a deep vivid purple on the outside.

I must admit I was terrified. I thought the end of the world was at hand. I shut my eyes and stood there trembling. Suddenly I heard a tremendous splash, followed immediately by a hissing, bubbling sound. I opened my eyes and the darkness was like the inside of a tunnel. I could plainly hear the water bubbling, then the ship rocked under the influence of the gigantic wave, and we were enveloped in a fog of steam. Gradually our eyes became accustomed to the darkness and things assumed their normal conditions. I could hardly believe my eyes. I know the Second Mate felt the same way, for he signalled a ship which passed us going towards Manila and asked her Second Mate if he had seen the strange phenomenon. He had.

If that meteor had dropped a little nearer it would have sunk a ship even the size of the *Dacre Castle*. If it had dropped ashore and fallen into a city, it would have destroyed the whole population.

Yokohama.

The last two weeks have been a period in fairyland for me. I find it hard to convince myself that I am not dreaming.

Japan is a beautiful place. The scenery is different to any I have previously seen. The mountains rise up from the sea with a peculiar symmetry of form which makes them look almost artificial, but in no way detracts from their beauty. Each mountain is capped with a white sugar-loaf of snow.

What a strange and wonderful nation this is. These are the little brown people who fought the mighty Russian Empire only a few years ago. I have been trying to find words to describe my first impression of Japan, and I think it reminds me more of a field of ant-hills except that it is infinitely more beautiful. Every island is cultivated, every town and village a hive of industry. The whole place seems over-populated, teeming with little people who hustle and bustle about, always energetically, never laggardly.

The streets are usually wide and clean. Everywhere is a riot of colour. The charming kimonos of the women, the picturesque dress of the men, the flowering trees and shrubs, the oriental architecture of the homes is only spoiled by the European style of buildings in the business section and along the water-front.

Amidst all this wonderful environment, I got into a peck of trouble. I had been "bawled out" by the Mate. I don't like the *Dacre Castle* any more to-day than I did when I first joined her. While Mickey and I were ashore, I met some of the crew of the Standard Oil barque *Calcutta*. She's a trim-looking packet and the "boys" give her a very good name. I'm sick of grovelling in filth all the time. We (that is Mickey and I) have hardly been out of the bilges since it was possible to get into them. Once the cargo was out of the holds, we were sent in to clean them up, and after we had the holds clean and the dunnage wood stowed away, we were put into the bilges to clean them out also;

after we had done that we had to scrape and paint them. Words have not been coined to describe the filth and stench one experiences in the bilges of a steamer. Japanese or Chinese coolies could be hired to do these obnoxious and filthy duties for about ten cents a day. But no—let the apprentices do them. It is teaching us to be seamen according to the terms of our indentures.

I kicked about doing this kind of work to the Mate. If I'd asked the King for a peerage, it could not have caused more excitement. His eyes popped out until they bulged into his cheeks. I could have knocked them off with a spoon. Strange to say, I didn't feel afraid. I thought he was going to strike me, but I stood my ground, and delivered the first speech I ever made in my life. I told him that I was willing to work and willing to learn, but that I didn't think we apprentices were expected by the owners to act as scavengers of the ship. I told him that if he had any respect for his British nationality, he would not humiliate us before foreigners by making us do tasks which only the lowest caste natives can be hired to do. I said all this and a lot more. The Mate listened until I had finished and then he let out a roar like the bursting of a typhoon. He cuffed my ears, introduced his shoemaker to my tailor, and told me more about myself and my ancestors in two minutes than I had ever dreamed possible. Boiled down, his ultimatum was to the effect that if I didn't like the way he was treating me, I could bloody well lump it. I'm going to "skin out." This time I mean it.

In Kobe.

What a time we had last night. The *Muncaster Castle* (Captain W——) arrived in harbour yesterday afternoon. She belongs to the same Company and Mickey knows some of the apprentices. We went aboard to visit them last night.

The Second Mate's name is Bonner—Charlie Bonner.[1] He's the greatest character I ever met. He had us howling with laughter from the moment we got onboard until we left. And say, talk about telling stories and yarns! W. W.

---

[1] This is Charlie Bonner who afterwards won the V.C. during the war while serving under Captain Gordon Campbell, V.C., in Q-boats or mystery ships, as they were called during the war.

Jacobs is in the infants' class compared to him. Bonner is a whole evening's entertainment in himself.

Captain W—— is a great student of wild animals and birds. He has made it a hobby, and every voyage he takes back to New York monkeys, bears, parrots, snakes, goldfish, Victoria pigeons, orang-outangs, and the Lord knows what else besides. Bonner calls it a lot of "Monkey Business."

Bonner told us the story of the last voyage to New York, and he had us nearly all dying from laughter.

Orang-outangs are hard to keep alive when first captured. Captain W—— learned that they could be prevented from fretting if they were fed as nearly as possible to the conditions under which they lived in their wild state. For the benefit of these huge apes, he carried dozens of eggs and a large cage of live pigeons. Whenever they got feeling blue or dumpy, he would make a nest and fill it with eggs, and allow the huge apes to rob the nest and suck the eggs. Other times, he would turn them into a cage with some live pigeons and let them satisfy their blood-lust by killing the pigeons.

I will try and tell the story as Bonner told it to us. We were all in the half-deck of the *Muncaster Castle* drinking Japanese beer—and very nice beer it is. I think there were at least ten people in that one small room. Some sat on the bunks, some on the settees, others on top of the lockers. Bonner sat on the only chair, and that was a canvas stool. He had a glass of beer in one hand and a big Manila cigar in the other.

"Captain W—— and I don't seem to get along very well together," he explained. "The trouble started when he came out of his cabin one afternoon and caught me trying to catch his precious goldfish with a bent pin and a piece of bread I'd rolled into dough. The fish were in a big tank on the lower bridge, and I found this fishing game a rather interesting way to pass the time while on watch when there wasn't anything doing. Captain W—— had previously suggested to the Mate that he might find us some sewing, to keep us occupied while on the bridge, but when the Mate asked me to make pneumonia jackets for some sick monkeys, I objected.

"That was the start of the trouble and it has been going on ever since. The day I said 'Grace' at the cabin table didn't improve conditions. We'd been having the same old hash meal after meal. There was never a change in the menu from day to day. We knew a week ahead exactly what we would receive for breakfast, dinner, and supper, on any given day. I hate a trouble-maker aboard ship, but something simply had to be done, so one day at dinner I bowed my head and said, 'Hebrews the thirteenth chapter and the eighth verse.'

"The 'Old Man' asked me what I was doing. I told him I was simply saying my Grace before meals. His curiosity got the better of him. He told the steward to bring his Bible. He opened it at the verse and read, 'Jesus Christ, the same to-day . . . yesterday . . . and forever.' I think it did the old beggar good, for we are getting a little better grub now." Bonner laughed, "More of a variety, anyway."

"Tell them about the orang-outang which shaved itself," suggested one of the other apprentices.

Bonner chuckled and settled himself down for the story. "Captain W—— had one brute aboard last voyage which was nearly as big as a man, but it was strangely tame and docile," he explained. "It wandered about all over the ship and made itself perfectly at home in anyone's cabin to which it took a fancy. Captain W—— prophesied great things for this monkey. He said he felt sure that with a little training it could be made to do almost anything. He wasn't far out, either.

"One night we were having a few drinks in my cabin when in walked the orang-outang. We welcomed it as we would *any* guest of the Skipper's and poured it out a drink of whiskey and soda. The huge ape watched us drink our whiskey and then it downed the drink at one swallow." Bonner laughed as he continued. "Talk about a lot of monkey business, say that fellow was a scream. It sat in front of a mirror and made grimaces and chattered to itself for nearly half an hour. When it got up on its feet, it staggered like a drunken man. Finally it laid down on his bunk and went to sleep.

"Next morning it woke me up and I honestly felt sorry. It was plain to see the ape was suffering the effects of a terrible hang-over. It waddled over and climbed on top of my washstand and placed its hot forehead against the cool mirror. When I opened the top of the washstand it dipped its head into the cold water and swilled its face.

"Do you know that monkey really got to such a state it liked to have a drink, but we never gave it enough to make it really tight after that. But to get on with the story of the shave.

"This monkey came to look upon my cabin as its own. Time after time, when I came off the bridge, I found it curled up on my bunk asleep. I had to turn it on the settee. One day it watched me shave.

"We were nearing New York and I knew the reporters would be aboard like a plague of locusts just as soon as we hit the dock.

"I like to see any man make money providing it is not at my expense," Bonner explained, as he continued his yarn. "I thought of a scheme by which I could help the Skipper clean up plenty of dough. After I had lathered my face, the orang-outang picked up my shaving-brush and began to imitate me. This gave me an idea. I shaved it and left it with a face as smooth as a baby's bottom.

"You never saw anything so comical looking in all your life. Everyone thought it a huge joke except the Captain. He got so mad he couldn't make up his mind whether he would shoot the monkey or me. I tried to tell him that he had something unique, a money-maker, but he wouldn't listen to me. I tried to point out to him that monkeys had been known to smoke, drink, and play cards, but never to shave themselves. I told him if he would only consent and allow me to be his Press agent when we arrived in New York, that I would make him plenty of money. He got so sore that he left the table and had his meals sent up to his cabin after that.

"I don't exactly blame him for getting sore because there are always some people who want to carry a joke too far."

Bonner winked at one of the *Muncaster Castle's* apprentices and there was a world of meaning in that wink.

"Captain W—— had not been in a very good humour for some days. He had been hazing the crew for bad steering, and finding fault with the officers. Nothing was just right. One day he raved for an hour about how much time we were losing due to bad and erratic steering. About two o'clock I noticed his monkeys were out of their cages. Somebody had released them by way of revenge.

"The Captain rushed on deck and soon organized all the ship's crew, both watches of officers and men, into a hunting party. Monkeys were everywhere. Up the masts, on the funnels guys, swinging from the awnings and the lifeboat davits. One bit the man at the wheel when he reached up and tried to grab it as it raced along on top of the awning spars.

"Every man was provided with a long bamboo pole with a wire noose lashed to the end. The monkeys were cornered and then, by a little judicious handling, the noose was slipped over the head and twisted tight. The captive was then grabbed firmly by the loose skin at the back of the neck and put back into its cage. This was no easy operation because the little beggars soon got wise to our plans.

"The work of recapturing the monkeys was progressing slowly but satisfactorily when one decided it would rather die than be captured again. It jumped overboard, and before you could say 'Jack Robinson' a dozen more had followed suit. Captain W—— was nearly frantic. His money, which he had turned into monkeys, was jumping overboard. He stopped the ship and ordered away the lifeboats.

"Many gallant rescues were performed that day. Some of us are still waiting for medals for rescuing life at sea. Captain W—— was sore about losing so many of his precious monkeys. When he read my entries in the log, his temper didn't improve any. I wrote:

"Noon to 1:00 P.M.—lost one minute due to bad steering. Captain logged helmsman one day's pay.

"2:00 to 4:00 o'clock—lost two hours attempting to rescue monkeys." Bonner concluded his story. We returned to our ship.

Still in Kobe.

I saw a different side to Captain Smith's character yesterday. We apprentices were, as usual, short of money.

Mickey asked the Mate for an advance and the Mate referred him to the Captain. We both went up onto the bridge to make our request. I, personally, didn't think we had a chance in the world of having it granted, but it is the unexpected which usually happens. To our intense surprise, he invited us into his cabin. He even told us to sit down, and asked us what we wanted. Mickey told him. He inquired how much. Mickey said five yen ($2.50 or ten shillings). "What are you going to do with it?"—" Buy curios, Sir," was Mickey's thoughtful reply.

Then Captain Smith gave us a talking to which made us almost dumbfounded. He spoke to us of the dangers we could encounter ashore. He warned us against bad women, and against the evils of drink. He told us how easy it was to ruin our lives and our health and how hard it was to repair the ravages of certain diseases. He then referred kindly to my desire to go in sail. He told me he was of the opinion that all potential officers should be trained in sail. He actually informed us both that we were " good boys " and that he was well satisfied with our work, but in the next breath referred to us as two " limbs of Satan " and again asked us how we succeeded in getting the ham out of the store-room without breaking the locks.

It was plain to see the loss of the ham was worrying the " Old Man " worse than he cared to admit. We maintained a discreet silence.

" I know you boys stole that ham. It's no crime for boys to steal for their bellies, but just let me catch you at it again and you'll know all about it," he threatened.

Both of us got up to go.

" Sit down ! " thundered Captain Smith.

We sat, or rather collapsed, onto the settee. Then we received the surprise of our young lives.

" I'm going to give you boys ten yen each. I'm making you a present of the money. It won't be charged up against your accounts," Captain Smith informed us as he peeled the bills off a roll he drew from his pocket. Then he added this last piece of advice :

" Go ashore, have a good time, but don't make damn fools of yourselves. Don't expose yourselves to danger or bring back a souvenir you'll find it hard to get rid of."

When we got back into the half-deck, Mickey looked at me and I looked at Mickey. Then we both looked at the money to make sure he wasn't playing a practical joke on us to repay us for the ham incident. The money was genuine. Finally Mickey burst out with, " Well I'll be doggoned, but who'd ever have thought ' Old Ben ' had that much generosity or sentiment in the whole of his two hundred and twenty pounds of hard-boiled cussedness."

That little homily he gave us did us a lot of good. We were both beginning to feel " fed up." Generosity and advice, coming from a man like him, made us both think.

We went ashore. We were hardly out of the sampan before we were approached by a " tout." He gave us a card each, bearing the name of a Japanese " tea-house." On the back of the card was a story. It read :

" In a certain fishing village lived two brothers named Brown. One lost his wife about the same time as the other lost his boat. The local minister, meeting the man who had lost his boat, sympathized with him, thinking he was the one who had lost his wife. To the clergyman's horror, the man replied :

" ' Oh, yer Reverence, keep your sympathy for someone who really needs it. She was no good, anyway. She was old and had outlived her usefulness. In fact, only the other day I had to turn her over and tar her bottom. But that last squall we had was too much for her. She simply couldn't stand the strain. She cracked up and busted. I had her well insured and I'm well rid of the old tub, anyway.' "

At the bottom of the card was a note informing us that pretty girls were available for our entertainment.

Mickey looked at me. I looked at him. We had both heard of this particular " tea-house " from others who had visited the place. We had allowed our curiosity to get the better of us and had actually intended to visit it and see the dance for which its girls were famous. Captain Smith's advice stood out in my mind in big letters. Evidently my cabin mate felt the same way. We pushed the " runner " aside and went hunting souvenirs of a kind we could send home to our relatives and friends.

The next evening we spent a very enjoyable time aboard

one of the " Blue Funnel Line " steamers and her apprentices agreed to take our presents home for us and save us freight charges.

Just before we sailed I received mail from home. I also received a letter from C——. She is a wonderful girl. Her friendship and example has often meant a lot to me when I stood on the threshold of making a darn fool of myself. I feel more than grateful to Captain Smith for a whole lot of reasons. In fact I honestly believe I'm beginning to like him. He may be two hundred and twenty pounds of hard-boiled cussedness but he is also 100 per cent real man, and I have a hunch that buried deep inside that great big hairy chest of his lies an honest-to-goodness heart. Being hard-boiled prevents most men who ship with seamen from attempting to take liberties. Should anyone be foolish enough to start trouble aboard this ship " Old Ben " snuffs it out like firemen do a blaze. No matter what others may think, his way of handling the crew saves a lot of trouble and the work is done.

CHAPTER V

Singapore.

We are finished loading and "Homeward Bound"! How I wish those two words were literally correct. The nearest this ship will ever be to home for the next few years will be when she passes through the Straits of Gibraltar. Mickey is not going to get home this voyage, either. We have made a quick passage and the chances are that he will be just short of completing his four years when we arrive back in Algiers next voyage. That means he will have to complete the round trip. Unlike convicts doing four years' hard labour, apprentices do not receive any time off for good conduct. The Board of Trade insists that they complete the four years at sea before they are eligible to sit for their Second Mate's Certificate. Mickey will be about one month short in his time, and he will have to serve an extra six months before he arrives back in Algiers. There is this compensation, he will be signed on the ship's articles as Able Seaman at the regular rate of pay—£4 10s. per month from the day he finishes his "time."

We have had a lot of trouble with the crew. They are an awful bunch of cut-throats and have been consistently drunk every time we were in port. There are a couple of Sea Lawyers amongst them and they have been instrumental in stirring up most of the trouble.

They persuaded the crew to "kick" about the food. There was the devil to pay for several days. Deputations carrying "Fannies" and other utensils paraded on the lower bridge demanding to see the Captain. The Captain told them the food was alright as far as he could see. They demanded that he taste it. He ordered them off the bridge. If it were possible to get away with a mutiny these days, there would be one aboard this ship.

Captain Smith did something which is very rarely done nowadays. He put the whole crew on their "wack." This means that every man had to parade before the Chief

Steward at the store-room each day and draw his own rations according to the rules and regulations as laid down by the Board of Trade in the Merchant Shipping Act.

I admit the food was terrible. The hard-tack was alive with weevils, the peas full of maggots, which floated on top of the soup; the coffee was thick with the remains of cockroaches which had gone through the coffee grinder with the coffee beans. The legs and wings formed a scum on the panikin. When some of the crew complained about the maggots in the soup, Captain Smith is alleged to have remarked, "Some men are never satisfied." Irrespective of the merits of the case, Captain Smith put the crew on their "wack."

Under this method every man received exactly what he is entitled to according to Board of Trade regulations, and not one ounce more. When it comes to weighing out the meat, the unfortunate who receives half a pound of gristle or bone is certainly out of luck. The amount allowed per man is half a pound of fresh meat, or a quarter of a pound of dried, salt, or preserved meat a day. The regulations do not say it must be lean or fat; so long as it is half a pound cut off a cow, a sheep, or a hog, it complies with the Act.

Thank Heaven the Captain's edict which put the crew on their "wack" did not apply to us apprentices. As a result, we have been having "cabin grub" since the trouble with the crew came to a head. What is more, since we started the homeward voyage, we have been allowed to "clean up" while in port. We wear decent clothes and are exempt from really dirty work. Our duties recently, while in port, have been watching or tallying cargo. Life is certainly a whole lot happier.

I think the reason for the change of treatment is because of the fight we had when leaving Muji, in Japan. The crew had been absolutely impossible. On the outward voyage, one man had answered Captain Smith back, when he was on the bridge, just as we were nearing Hong Kong. Captain Smith lost his temper and gave the man all he deserved. One of the Sea Lawyers referred to persuaded the man to lay an official complaint with the authorities in Hong Kong. The Merchant Shipping Act is now very severe on officers who manhandle members of their crew.

Strange though it may seem, my sympathies are all with Captain Smith. It would be impossible to describe just how utterly impossible, loathsome, and beyond the pale of common decency these men are. They are the riff-raff of the water fronts, the scourings of the world. Most of them have been driven out of their own countries to escape the law, or else they have deserted from the ships under their own flag; they are the dregs of New York. There isn't a Britisher or an American amongst the whole of our crew, and they are the first to take advantage of British legislation when it protects them from the consequences of their behaviour.

In the case I refer to, Captain Smith had reason to do what he did. A little upstart German was at the wheel. He had been steering all over the ocean, and had ignored with absolute contempt the Third Mate's repeated warnings to keep on his course. Captain Smith climbed on to the upper bridge. He addressed the helmsman.

"Look here, my man, you're going to steer properly or I'll stand behind you and con you with my hands," he informed him.

The man uttered an inaudible remark. Captain Smith went and stood behind him. Each time the helmsman went more than a quarter of a point either side of his course, the Skipper gave him a smart cuff on the ear delivered on the side corresponding with the error.

The man was obstinate. He refused to steer properly. The *Dacre Castle* is a good steering ship.

Captain Smith was just as obstinate as the German. Eight bells came and he refused to allow the new watch to relieve the wheel. He told the recusant seaman he would remain at the wheel until he decided to steer properly. The man became impertinent. Captain Smith grew angry. The climax came when Captain Smith gave him a rather severe cuff for going nearly a point to port of his given course. The man jumped away from the wheel and poured a string of foul language at the Captain. He called him a big bullying son of a bitch, a bastardly Liverpool Irishman, and everything else he could think of. Captain Smith nearly pummelled the life out of the mutinous seaman, and then, losing his temper completely, picked him up and literally dropped him over the top of the upper bridge rail on to the lower bridge deck.

Such situations are difficult to handle at sea nowadays. According to the law, the Master should have logged the man and fined him a day's pay for insolence and insubordination. I was working on the bridge during the whole incident and heard the man throw this fact in the Captain's teeth. " What the hell do I care for you, you big bully. You daren't lay your hands on me. It'll cost you your certificate. For two pins I'd take a swipe at you. It would be worth a day's pay," was the way he taunted the Captain.

Under the circumstances, I hardly blame Captain Smith. These foreigners, once they are aboard a British ship and under the protection of the British flag, become the most insolent and unbearable men imaginable.

Following the complaint to the authorities in Hong Kong, chaos reigned. The whole crew simply baited the officers. The officers, governing themselves strictly in accordance with the regulations, logged them for their various offences against discipline. Soon every man had been logged almost the amount of his earnings for the voyage. They didn't worry. They knew that when they arrived back in New York the Shipping Master would cancel most of the loggings. They were having plenty of fun for their money, but they reckoned without Captain Smith.

The little German was about as cocky as a game cock after its twentieth kill. He puffed out his chest and simply oozed insolence. One day I saw the Mate talking earnestly to the Captain. Shortly afterwards he sent for Mickey. When Mickey returned he informed me we had been taken off watch and watch and put on day duty. This was the best news I had heard since leaving home. It meant that we worked from seven in the morning until six at night, but we had our nights free both in port and while at sea.

When the change in routine was made, the deck hands were divided as follows : Three seamen were in each watch while one able seaman and we two apprentices worked " day work " with the Bos'on. The little German was put on day work with we two " boys."

The first task given us was to clean up the 'tween-decks in number two hold. Mickey had evidently received his instructions. He told me to watch him and take my cue from his actions.

The German was no sooner below than he found himself a comfortable seat and proceeded to light his pipe. "Get up there, you lazy scoundrel, and get a hustle on," Mickey ordered, and informed him that he had been put in charge down below.

The German told him to go to Hell and advised him to get busy with the work himself. Mickey got busy. He bent down and picking up all the dunnage-wood within reach, threw it into the corner where the German was sitting lighting his pipe. I followed suit and it literally rained wood on that poor fellow for about two minutes.

He rushed out, frothing with rage. What wasn't he going to do to us! We lit into him and cleaned up the hold with him. As he lay there with both eyes blackened, his nose bleeding like a tap, his lips swollen and some of his teeth missing, Mickey looked down at him and said, "Perhaps that will teach you to keep your place aboard a British ship and keep a civil tongue in your head. When we reach port, run with your story to the British Consul. A fat lot of good it will do you. I've no ticket they can suspend or cancel. Watch yourself for the rest of the voyage and tell your friends aft to do the same. You fellows have been looking for trouble all the voyage and you're going to get plenty of it if you don't behave." Having delivered himself of this speech, Mickey handed the sailor a broom and made him get busy cleaning up the hold.

Captain Smith and Mr. Gough were resting their elbows on the lower bridge rail when the three of us climbed on deck at eight bells to go to dinner. As the sailor started to walk aft, a smile spread over their faces. The smile gave place to spasms of hearty laughter when they saw the truly awful condition the man was in.

Our position as executioners-in-chief to the Captain was not allowed to pass undisputed. The crew all got riotously drunk in Muji. They knocked off work and refused to obey the Bos'on when he ordered them to turn to. As the ship was sailing next day, it was no use calling the police. That would only have delayed the ship.

It began to blow and looked like rain during the late

afternoon. Mr. Gough sent for Mickey. He told him to take me and turn the crew to, and batten down the hatches.

We went aft, but the crew told us to go to places and do things which were utterly impossible. They threatened to kill us if we set foot in the fo'c'sle (forecastle).

We went back and reported to the Mate. Mr. Gough flew into a rage.

"What's this you're telling me? Do you mean to say that you two fellows are afraid of a bunch of scum like we've got aft? Turn 'em to, and get those hatches battened down . . . or do it yourselves," he thundered.

Back we went again. Before going into the fo'c'sle, Mickey armed himself with an iron belaying-pin and I picked up a good-sized marlin-spike. "We've either got to clean them up or take a dog's life for the rest of the trip," Mickey said, as he led the way below.

"Out of this and up on deck or I'll crack the skull of every mother's one of ye," he ordered, reverting back to his native brogue.

A big blonde giant, a Dane, rushed at Mickey. He was the quietest man of the whole crew when sober, but when drunk he was terrible to see. If he'd ever got hold of either of us, he would have killed us. Mickey knew it. He stretched him out stiff and cold with a blow over the head. I thought the man was dead. He fell like a log and never moved. The air became alive with flying missiles. Knives, plates, boots, bottles, all arrived from the shadows at the far end of the crew's quarters. Back in those shadows we knew were five or six men. Five empty bottles stood on the filthy mess table. We grabbed these and threw them with all the force we could muster. I heard a splintering crash as one hit the ironwork, then a dull thud and a groan.

I was seeing red—fighting mad. I was not the least bit afraid. Before I realized it, I was into the middle of the sailors alongside of Mickey, hitting away with my iron club and experiencing the same unholy joy I had done during the rough house in Hong Kong.

We won that scrap, although both Mickey and I looked more like meat in a butcher's shop than human beings when we emerged into the light of day. But we drove four sailors up on deck ahead of us and we made them batten down the hatches. The other three men were completely knocked out and had to have medical and surgical attention. We left one of them behind in hospital.

I never realized until it was all over, but this victory (for we all consider it is one) was won on June 2nd—my sixteenth birthday. I can't realize I am only sixteen. I stand 5 feet 10 inches tall and weigh 163 pounds. I feel so well and so light and buoyant that I think I could lick my own weight in wild cats. This sounds as though I were growing egotistical, but I don't think I am, in the true sense of the word. I just feel proud as Lucifer that we put it over that bunch of foreigners. Everywhere we go there is talk of war with Germany. If it matures, I'm going to be in it, and no mistake about that.

My right arm is so sore I can hardly write. During the fight one of the sailors got his teeth into the muscle and chewed it until it looked like a piece of raw meat which had been through a food chopper.

Mickey had taught me a lot during the voyage and I followed his advice during that scrap. When any man tried to foul me, I put my thumbs in his eyes and gouged until they were out on his cheek bones. If you tried to follow Marquis of Queensberry rules in a scrap like the one we had in Muji, you would get so badly mauled your own mother wouldn't know you.

We had " Peace, perfect peace " after that fight, all the way to Singapore. There Captain Smith played his trump card and won the game. He took the whole European crew ashore and paid them off. What is more, the Shipping Master allowed most of the fines to stand against the men. They left the ship with hardly a nickel (shilling) and were returned to New York on another ship. We shipped a Lascar crew. They are under the control of a Serang and they give very little trouble. It has turned out better than ever for us two apprentices. The Mate couldn't very well put us to work with the native crew, so we are allowed to keep watch with the Chief Officer and Second Mate. At last we are beginning to learn the duties of an officer instead of just those of a seaman. I've given up the idea of running away from this ship now.

Boston.

Little of interest occurred the whole way home. I received plenty of mail from home. It is great to hear from your friends and relations.

I open these pages now to record a rather interesting incident which occurred here. I think everyone goes in for smuggling more or less, especially aboard these ships trading to the Orient. Mickey and I bought silk shirts, dress lengths, and Japanese tea-sets with some of the money Captain Smith gave us in Kobe. We can sell them in New York at about three or four times the price we paid for them in Japan. That will give us about twenty dollars each for pocket money —if the Customs don't find them first. One Japanese merchant actually trusted us enough to extend credit, saying we could pay him for the tea-sets next voyage. I consider this extraordinary.

Mickey knows the ropes. We hid the china-ware in the ashes under the donkey-engine fire box. If any Customs officer finds them there, he is welcome to them, for he will have to search in a temperature of nearly 150 degrees.

The silks we hid behind the wooden sheathing of the half-deck. We wrapped it all carefully in moisture-proof oiled paper, and after removing some of the sheathing, placed the silk on shelves between the angle-irons. We did this and replaced the sheathing before we painted our room on the homeward journey. Incidentally, we did as Mickey said we would, and went after the bugs and roaches. We stripped the room down to the bare iron and squirted a mixture of turps and carbolic acid into every nook and crevice we could find. After we had cleaned the cabin thoroughly, we scrubbed every piece of sheathing separately with the same mixture and let it dry in the burning sun. We went carefully over all our good clothes and uniforms and steamed all our bed-clothes and linen. The bugs sure got a " raw deal " as the Yankees say.

The Customs officers came aboard when we arrived in Boston. They examined our cabin carefully. They even noticed the putty in the cracks between the sheathing, but Mickey told them such a good yarn about the " bug hunt " that they laughed their heads off. I don't think we'll be bothered very much in New York. The Mate has a brother who commands a tug in the harbour and he'll land the stuff for us.

We went ashore last night. In my mail I received two pounds from Dad for spending money. He said not to mention it to Mother, and Mother sent me two pounds and said not to mention the fact to Dad. Just think! Twenty dollars all but a few cents. I felt like a millionaire when Mickey and I stepped ashore. But money doesn't go far in the U.S.A.

We went into a barber's shop. When our turn came, we asked for a hair cut and shave. We really needed the hair cuts—I'm not so sure about the shaves.

Every now and again the barber would say:

"I think your hair needs a shampoo," or "There are a few blackheads in your face which ought to be removed. A facial massage will just do the trick."

We spent about an hour in the chair. We thought these American barbers just wonderful . . . until they presented us with the bill—$6.70.

We asked them what they thought we were. We refused to pay it. They tendered us an itemized statement:

Hair cut	·50
Shave	·25
Shampoo	1·00
Massage	1·00
Singe	·25
Shoe shine	·10
Hair tonic	·25
Total	$3·35

My stomach felt queer and my "roll" seemed to be growing awfully small. I had invited Mickey in. It was up to me to pay the shot. Mickey wouldn't hear of it. He'd lick all the barbers in Boston before he'd let me pay nearly $7·00 for tonsorial treatment.

I put down $2·00 and we started for the door. The barbers blocked our way. One young fellow ran out of the shop. Mickey pushed the boss out of the way. The boss pushed Mickey. Mickey laid him out with a perfect hay maker to the jaw and the tonsorial expert crumpled up just as a policeman entered the store.

The policeman was as Irish as they make them. He inquired what the trouble was. We told him, so did the barbers. There was an argument as to whether we had ordered the treatment received. The barbers said we had. We said we hadn't. The policeman, with true Solomonly judgment, decided that there was a great deal of conflicting evidence and that the best way to settle the matter was to go fifty-fifty. He arbitrated the amount of the bill at $3.35 instead of $6.70. I paid this.

That ended that part of the trouble. The head barber wanted Mickey arrested for assault and battery. Mickey said he should receive compensation for his skinned knuckles. He pleaded guilty to hitting the man, but told the policeman he would never have done it if he'd known his head was made of wood. This tickled the Irishman's sense of humour, but he looked very severe and told us we would have to go with him. We went—but it was only around the corner. Once we were out of sight, he shook hands with us both. He asked Mickey what part of "Old Oirland" he came from, and told him he carried a wonderful wallop which was a credit to any Irishman.

Before parting, he gave us his address and asked us to come up Sunday afternoon and meet his wife and children. He was a really good sort, and Mickey has not forgiven himself for only hitting the barber once.

There is something about being abroad which makes you indifferent to public opinion. We would never dare do the things at home which we do here.

CHAPTER VI

Boston, March 2nd, 1912.

Another voyage is over and I have been more than a year at sea. I got out of the habit of writing my diary because nothing very much out of the ordinary happened until we were nearing port the other day.

Captain Smith may have his faults, but in my estimation he is the finest navigator afloat. He brought the *Dacre Castle* into Boston in a raging blizzard and he took her in without a pilot. I never saw such a gale or worse seas. They were mountains high and the cold was intense. Two of the Lascar crew died. The hail was so large it actually chipped the paint off the ventilator cowls.

When we finally arrived in harbour, we were coated from truck to water-line with ice about two feet thick. Half a dozen ships have been reported as lost, but we are safe in port. I couldn't help but think as I took my " trick " at the wheel what a splendid type of seaman Captain Smith really is. He stood behind me and coxed me with my steering and nursed that ship like a mother would a child. I was never so proud in my life as when he allowed me to stay at the wheel. He wouldn't trust the foreigners to steer in that kind of weather. The officers steered and he kept the bridge. He allowed me to steer while I was on watch, and that left the Mate free to work with the crew, securing tarpaulins and gear which broke adrift. I am senior apprentice now and keep watch with the Mate from four until eight in the morning and the same hours at night. (Mickey finished his " time " and went home from Algiers. I can't express in words exactly how much I miss him.)

I never imagined the weather could be so rough. The wind blew with hurricane force and the seas were such that one washed the foremast head-light away and swept the canvas from the bridge. It demolished the wheelhouse and wooden structures used as weather dodgers. We lost two ventilators and one lifeboat. The rails along the foredeck looked as if they had been damaged by shell fire. The deck-head over the cabins amidships was sprung fully three inches and all the cabins were "washed out."

It was a terrible experience, and yet I can honestly say that I was more thrilled than afraid. The vision of "Old Ben" Smith standing on the storm-swept bridge, calm and unworried, was an inspiration and an example it was impossible to ignore. He seemed unconquerable, almost a super-being as he stood, legs braced firmly to the pitch and roll of the ship, the salt water dripped from his oil-skins, and his unruly white hair tried to escape the bondage of his sou'wester. As I watched him, the comforting thought came to me: "The winds of the storm will wear themselves out, the waves will dash themselves to pieces with their very fury before Captain Smith begins to tire."

Hour after hour he remained unrelieved upon the bridge, his rugged frame refusing even to take advantage of the wind-break. He was out where he could see best. His eyes were narrowed to mere slits to protect the pupils from the driving sleet and hail, his face puckered and wrinkled, his skin looked like wet tanned leather. He never flinched from the cruellest sleet or from the angriest wave. He stood firm as a rock and guided his ship safely and fearlessly from the storm-swept ocean into the sheltered harbour of Boston.

No pilot boat was on station, coastal boats had run for shelter, passenger liners were hove-to, but the *Dacre Castle* kept on. From the vast expanse of the oceans to the narrows of the harbour entrance, she steamed as straight and true as ever an arrow was shot, and came-to all a-quiver as the engines went astern, and the cables roared through the hawse-pipes.

New York.

We have discharged our cargo and we are lying at Fortysecond Street, Brooklyn, waiting for a loading berth. We managed to smuggle ashore our tea-sets and silk. We have a young Customs officer doing night duty and he is "easy."

One of the stewards came along last night and asked me to take the Captain's laundry ashore. The Customs officer was present when he asked me. I agreed. I went along to his cabin and he gave me a sea-bag full of what I thought soiled linen. He gave me the address of a Chinese laundry to which I was to take it.

I made a note of the address and went into the half-deck where the Customs officer was having a drink with the new apprentice named Myers. I asked him for a pass and he gave me one. It was a miserable kind of a night, cold and wet, with the wind blowing hard from the north-east.

I found the address and walked into the laundry. I handed the Chink the bag and a note the steward had given me to give to him.

As he read the note, I actually saw him change colour, and when a Chinaman changes colour, there is something seriously affecting his emotions. I couldn't for the life of me fathom whether his emotions were those of anger or pleasure, or just plain excitement.

"You savey allee same this?" he asked me, pointing to the bag.

"Sure, allee same Captain's laundry," I replied in pidgin-English.

The Chinaman laughed. "You allee same come wrong place. You makee allee same follow me. Me show you light place."

He jambed an old hat down on his head. He struggled into an old coat, three sizes too large for him, and then using the sleeves of the coat like a muff, he led the way out onto the street.

"You allee same follow me. No walk with me? Savey?" he muttered. I understood what he wanted me to do, but I was at a complete loss to know why.

He boarded a street car. I followed. He got off and took the ferry across the the city. I did the same. We took the overhead and arrived at the Bowery. I was still carrying the bag of dirty clothes and wondering more and more over the strange behaviour of the Chinaman.

He left the overhead train and entered a street in the Bowery. I followed. He turned into a store where the proprietor sold Chinese fruits and vegetables as well as groceries. I hesitated a moment, and then entered also. I was shown into a back room where the bag was taken from me and placed on a table.

There was a consultation in Chinese between the man I had followed and the proprietor, and I felt I was the subject under discussion. They apparently decided I was " safe," for one of them said to me, " You allee same savey what you bling here ? " I was non-committal and simply nodded my head.

The Chinaman seemed satisfied. He picked up the bag and motioned me to follow him. He led the way through a passage, down some steps, and stopped outside a massive door at the end of the alleyway. The door was heavily barred on the inside. I knew we had entered on the street level and we were now at least ten feet underground.

He gave a peculiar knock on the door, which was undoubtedly a signal ; a grille opened from the inside and a pair of almond eyes squinted through.

A question was asked in Chinese and the answer given. The door swung open on a guard-chain and a further conversation took place. Again it was quite clear to me that I was the subject under discussion.

I have tried many a time since to account for my actions that night. It was a crazy, foolhardy thing to do, but my curiosity got the better of my caution. I had always wanted to see Chinatown. This was my opportunity and I followed on.

The first place we came to was a regular gambling den. A conglomeration of Chinese, whites, and even negroes gambled in this room playing fan-tan. They were terrible-looking creatures. A girl's honour, or a man's life would have been valued by most of them at less than a nickel (half-penny).

I had the feeling that the one thought in their minds, when they raised their eyes from the tables to look at us, was, " Are they worth murdering ? How much money have they got on them ? "

We only passed through that room. The next place we entered gave me a shock. It was a sort of Chinese theatre ; a play was being enacted on a low stage. The atmosphere was such that you could almost cut it with a knife. From what I gathered, as I passed through, the theme of the act was the abduction and seduction of a young Chinese girl. The applause all seemed to be for the villain of the piece.

We passed on into a den of prostitution. I seemed to be wandering on as in a dream, but my recollection is that the girls were exceedingly young and not limited to any one nationality. One girl rushed towards me when we entered and tried to throw her arms around my neck. She pretended to be amorous, but I am sure she was terrified to find herself in such a situation. I never got the chance to find out. A Chinaman grabbed her and threw her roughly away from me. He placed his finger to his head to indicate she was crazy. I fingered my revolver, but I knew I was helpless to do anything.

The next place was evidently our destination, for we stopped in a smaller room which was decently furnished, and we all sat down. The place reeked of incense, but this was a relief from the horrible atmosphere and stench of the other rooms.

One of my companions left and returned in a few minutes with another Chinaman. I was introduced to him in English. I was told he was a friend of the steward and that the bag I carried was for him. I handed him the bag and he placed it on the table and emptied it of its contents. Wrapped up in the dirty clothes were nearly one hundred small packages which can only have contained one thing—opium.

I was paid more money than I had ever seen, at one time, in my life before. The Chinaman who paid me this money told me to return straight onboard the *Dacre Castle* and hand the money over to the steward. He informed me that I would be followed all the way to the ship and that any attempt at treachery on my part would be summarily dealt with.

There was something about this Chinaman which made me feel he meant what he said. I had always been taught to avoid danger if possible, but to hug it close like a kicking horse if it were impossible to avoid. I realized I was in danger now, so I forced a laugh and told this Chinese gangster that, having brought the opium, I would like to see a real opium den. He spoke to another man in Chinese and then motioned me to follow him.

We passed through one room and into another. Chinamen and whites sat around with long-stem pipes in their hands. Some of them chatted to each other in a strange hushed whisper, others sat in stolid silence, a vacant stare in their eyes, their minds wandering in far-off places. The reek of poppy fumes filled the air and made me feel sick.

I was led into yet another room. It looked for all the world like the fo'c'sle of a ship. Crude bunks lined the walls three tiers high. They were filthy beyond description. The bedding consisted of rags. On these rags slept creatures of all descriptions. They had once been men. All were in various stages of insensibility.

I noticed one old man, perhaps he might not have been so very old, but he looked terrible. His body was nothing but a bag of bones. The skin of his face was dry and parchment-like. It was pulled so tightly over the cheek bones that he looked as though they would break through. His eyelids were closed and they hung like loose shutters over the eyes, which were sunk deep in their sockets. His face looked more horrible than any skull.

I can hardly describe the sensations I experienced as I walked out of the store and onto the street. I looked around to get my bearings and realized that I was almost a city block from where I had entered the grocery store.

On my way to the ship, my mind was occupied with many thoughts. How many of the girls who disappear in New York each year ended up in those dives? How many men who disappeared had their throats slit for the money they happened to have on them? I was hungry.

I went into a restaurant to get something to eat. The moment I left the street, two men were at my heels and I recognized them as two I had seen in Chinatown. My heart missed a couple of beats. They were tough-looking customers. I thought they knew I had that money on me and were planning to rob me. I got up, having in mind to seek protection from the police. Then I thought how foolish that idea was, and sat down again to think. One of the men crossed over and leaning over my table whispered, "Your orders were to go *straight* back to your ship. We're watching you. No monkey business, young fellow, or you'll be sorry for it." They were in the employ of the dope ring, not thieves or robbers. I must say that I felt relieved.

I ate a hurried meal and made my way back onboard. The

steward had turned in. I roused him out of his bunk. I told him what had happened and gave him the money. He counted it as he evidently knew how much there should be.

" You savey Chinatown, New York, plenty good now ? " he asked me, with a chuckle.

I told him I would like to see more of it, provided I could be sure that I wouldn't have my throat cut.

When I had turned in that night I thought things over. I had entered into the adventure innocently enough. I was clear in my conscience that I had no knowledge of what the bag contained until I arrived in Chinatown, but I couldn't help but think that if things had turned out differently I might have received a five-years' sentence in Sing-Sing. It would have taken a lot of arguing to convince any jury that I was the innocent victim of a gang of dope smugglers.

Still in New York.

Somehow, I can't forget the look in that girl's eyes when she flung her arms around me for that moment in Chinatown. She was only a child and she looked so horribly afraid. I shudder every time I think of her and those brutes of men I saw in the gambling den.

We sail the day after to-morrow. I think I will write anonymously to the police and tell them all I know without getting the ship into trouble. It is a strange law, but the ship and Captain would be held responsible if the authorities found out drugs had been landed from her.

I was talking to some people I met about their Chinatown and the Bowery and I remarked that it seemed almost incredible that such places could exist within a few blocks of central New York and in a civilized and Christian country. After hearing their explanation, I realize how futile it would be to try and do anything to improve conditions. In this particular world, the Devil himself rules. Graft is his Prime Minister ; the Almighty dollar, the Golden Calf before which all his subjects worship. His subjects are dope fiends, moral perverts, and criminals of every type. From this cesspool originated the insidious streams of graft which steep their way into the very heart of the nation.

I cannot understand why such conditions cannot be rooted out. If one nation insults another, or if one country kills or injures the citizens of another, or harms their interests, they go to war when diplomatic representations fail to solve the problem. On the other hand, I saw influences at work which are eating at the very heart of a nation and nothing is being done to clean up the mess because, from all accounts, gangdom rules New York and politicians are only the "front" behind which the criminals work.

I don't know why I write these things, but only the other day the Mate gave me the afternoon off. While ashore I happened to see a group of school children doing their patriotic exercises. When they grow up they will rush to arms if their country calls them. Why should truly patriotic citizens not declare war on grafting politicians and destroy the sink-holes of vice and crime which seem to be entrenched all over the city?

Coming back onboard late the other night, I accompanied the boys into a saloon. They wanted a "night cap" before they went onboard. Inside the saloon were a number of men all under the influence of liquor. They were amusing themselves pitching coins at the body of a naked woman who was laid out on the billiard table. To judge by their howls of laughter and ribald jests, they were thoroughly enjoying themselves. I hope I never grow so that type of thing would amuse instead of disgust me.

CHAPTER VII

A Chapter of Accidents.

The new apprentice who came in Mickey's place is a fine, good-looking chap, but I do not think we could ever become friendly. He is a German. What an extraordinary state of affairs which allows German boys to serve aboard British training ships and pass into the Merchant Service as apprentices! In twelve years this German may be in command of a British ship. What would happen then if the two countries went to war? He is German at heart, for he is never so happy as when he is speaking his mother tongue.

He has relatives and friends in New York, and although they could all speak perfect English when they spoke to me, they spoke German amongst themselves. Myers tells me he has no use for Germany. He says he is a Bavarian and claims it is the Prussians who are causing all the trouble. What he says may be alright, but in his case I am like the Scotsman, " I hae me doots." I caught him in the fo'c'sle the other evening talking German to one of the crew. I gave him a good dressing-down when he returned to the half-deck, and told him plainly that if he preferred the company of the sailors to living amidships, he must move his gear and live aft. I had enough of bugs and cockroaches the first voyage. We are clear of them now and I won't have Myers carrying such pests back in from the seamen's quarters.

There were several changes made amongst the officers just before we sailed. Captain Smith has gone home and Mr. Gough has been given command. To show how small the world really is, Mr. Lamb, the new Chief Officer, served in the same capacity under my father for eight years prior to the death of James Mark Wood. When the latter died all his ships were sold and his Captains and Mates all found themselves out of a job.[1]

[1] When James Mark Wood died he left handsome legacies to everyone who had been connected with his business ashore. His office manager received £50,000, his most junior office boy £50. James Mark Wood

Mr. Lamb gave me a good " bawling out " for staying ashore all night. He told me I would have to toe the line and behave myself or he would consider it his duty to inform my father. I don't feel hurt. It was perfectly alright for him to tear into me, but I don't care if he does write home because I stayed with a married cousin of mine that particular night. I would not like him to have seen me in those other dives.

Mr. Lamb is a very quiet man, but he is nobody's fool. He is a Welchman, and I have only seen him go ashore once since he joined the ship. To my mind he is thoroughly dissatisfied with the rotten deal fate has meted out to him, but it must be said to his credit that he does not vent his spite on others. He is not at all popular with the other officers. They say he is worse than a Scotsman and " too tight " to go ashore and spend a couple of dimes.

I don't think they judge him right. If I know anything at all, he keeps to himself because he doesn't want to be asked to go ashore. He has been out of employment so long that he can't afford to waste any of his pay. I met his wife when she travelled with my mother one voyage to meet the *Asama* when she was discharging in Antwerp. It was just holiday time and I went with my mother and had the trip around to Cardiff where the *Asama* took on a cargo of coal for Port Said. The *Asama* was my father's ship and Mr. Lamb was the Mate.

If he leads the life of a hermit, it is because he is a good husband and father, not because he is mean or close.

The new Second Mate is a man about fifty, with a very checkered career. He served in the Royal Navy and continued his career in the Merchant Service.

He once left the sea for ten years and was connected with some railway in India.

Mr. W—— is the name of the new Third Mate. He doesn't seem a bad sort. He'll be better after his head has resumed its normal proportions. He served his time in the fo'c'sle and is still suffering from a swelled head since he has passed for Second Mate. He is inclined to be a little too

started out in life selling newspapers. He died a millionaire. To a great extent he owed his success in life to the loyalty and efficiency of his seagoing employees, and yet as I write these entries, I know that most of his older Masters are serving as Mates and Second Mates in strange ships. Such is the ingratitude of the sea.

patronizing and officious, but he is generous with his money, so that about balances things up.

A new regime has been introduced which affects myself. We are to carry quarter-masters for steering and I am to be one of them. The others are paid better than A.B.'s wages and are rated as petty officers. I save the firm just that much money. Myers is to remain on day work under the orders of the Mate. I don't mind steering but I hate watch and watch.

April 15th, 1912.

We sailed from New York on the 12th. This ship isn't fitted with wireless. She ought to be.

I was at the wheel last night in the middle watch when we passed a steamer which signalled us. The Second Mate did not even bother to reply. The sea was calm and the ship was steering herself. I read the morse code signal. It informed us that the *Titanic* had struck an iceberg and sunk with the loss of nearly fifteen hundred lives. The signal said we would probably pass through the vicinity of the disaster about daylight and advised us to look out for ice and wreckage.

I called the Second Mate over and told him what the other ship had said. All he replied was this, " What a glorious death. Just imagine being able to order what you wanted from a bar like the *Titanic* would carry. You could get full to the neck. After you were that full, why worry if she sank or stayed afloat. If she sank, it would only be like taking one more extra long drink."

I can't explain why, but I have a feeling of pending disaster. When old women at home used to say they could feel things in the marrow of their bones, I used to laugh and wonder how such an expression originated. Now I know.

April 30th, 1912.

There is a lot I can't explain, even to my own satisfaction. I don't know why I am beginning to keep this diary again under the heading of dates. I don't know what made me send the first two parts of it home to my brother. I know something is going to happen, but I don't feel it is going to hurt me. I feel more as if I was on the verge of a big adventure.

We coaled at Algiers as usual. A new Second Officer was awaiting the arrival of the ship at Algiers in the place of the one who arrived in New York.

Myers went up 100 per cent in my estimation yesterday. We were coaling in Port Said and the ship was overrun with bum-boat men. Myers was off duty and I warned him against allowing any of the Arabs to enter the half-deck. Probably piqued because I had given him these instructions (Myers is older, but junior to me), he ignored them and allowed one of the pedlars into the cabin. The Arab made several repulsive suggestions to him and Myers, keeping his wits about him, told this moral degenerate to wait until he saw if the coast was clear. He called me and we informed the Chief Officer. It was little use calling the Arab police, so we took the law into our own hands and gave the man a good trouncing and kicked him off the boat.

I witnessed another murder while here. Life must be cheap or punishment very lax. The whole thing was very similar to the murder I saw committed in Algiers. Two Arabs quarrelled. A mob took one man's part against the other. They stampeded around the deck between the fiddle and the bridge. Suddenly one man picked up a huge piece of coal weighing many pounds. He brought it crashing down on the other man's skull, while he was bent over warding off the blows of his antagonists. The victim of the attack fell prostrate on the iron deck. Before anyone could give the alarm or interfere, every Arab near picked up a big lump of coal and brought it crashing down upon the unconscious man. He was literally pounded to pulp. Each man, as he threw his rock, walked on unconcernedly and continued his work.

The police came off in their launch. They took the mutilated body of the murdered man away, but I never heard what happened to the murderers. There must have been at least a dozen men-inflicted injuries, any of which could have proved fatal.

In strange contrast to these horrible crimes I have related is the other side of the picture. The Arab is abstemious except where excesses of the flesh are concerned. He does not drink intoxicating liquor and he lives up to his religion far more rigidly than we Christians do. His Koran is very similar to our Bible. Where the Christian and Mohammedan religions differ is that we believe Christ to be the son of God; the Arabs believe Mohammed to be the prophet of Allah. I always thought an Arab was a heathen until I had a long talk with an educated Arab gentleman the other day. They believe in one God. They believe the Koran to be the word of God as given to His prophet Mohammed by the Angel Gabriel. They believe that they would be justified in killing off opposition to make the world Mohammedan. We are supposed to believe in winning converts to the Christian faith by teaching and good example. They are openly avowed militarists; we are supposedly pacifists.

They heed the cry of their priest when he calls them to prayer. We don't, to a great extent, follow the advice of ours. The Mohammedan faces the east when he prays because he hopes that Mohammed will rise like the sun and enlighten the whole world. They wait for the second coming of Mohammed as we wait for the second coming of Christ. They believe he will sweep the world of spiritual darkness and leave it a paradise for true believers; we believe Christ will judge the living and the dead according to their lights and merits.

June 2nd, 1912.

To-day is my birthday. I am seventeen. It is over six weeks since I wrote in this diary and we are still at Suez. We have been wrecked, salvaged, repaired, and we are ready for sea again. My presentiments were not so very far out.

The Captain was tired after the journey through the Canal and the run down the Gulf of Suez. He laid down for a couple of hours' sleep and wrote instructions in the " night order book " for him to be called at two bells (1:00 o'clock in the morning), in order that he might alter course, so as to pass clear of Ras Garhib. I took over the wheel. I struck two bells. Half an hour went by.

It was a peculiar kind of a night. The dome of the heavens was light with the brilliance of the moon and stars. The calm sea shimmered under the rays of light. I was in the wheelhouse steering and my eyes were affected by looking constantly into the light of the binnacle. Suddenly I felt the ship tremble and shake. The compass needle jerked around. I knew instinctively we had hit something. I rushed over to the engine-room telegraph and put the indicator to full astern.

The Captain came racing on the bridge, as did the other two Mates. We were ashore on a coral reef twelve miles south of Ras Garhib. The Captain came over to the wheelhouse and looked in the binnacle. I was dead on my given course. He asked me if the course had been altered at two bells. I replied in the negative.

He asked the responsible officer why he had not been called at two bells. There seems to have been some mistake over this order.

Captain Gough ordered the Second Mate to go with the Third Mate and sound around the ship and instructed them to tell the carpenter to sound the holds and bilges.

There was nothing more I could do at the wheel. The ship was solidly ashore and the engines had been stopped.

We thanked Heaven that the sea was calm. The soundings around the ship showed her to be ashore with only seven feet of water for'ard and forty feet aft. She was embedded firmly in soft coral. Seven thousand tons had been driven ashore at a speed of twelve knots. It was little wonder she was tightly wedged in the bed she had made for herself.

There was no time to waste. All hands were put to work getting out the bower and kedge anchors. With a small crew, this was no easy task. The heavy bower anchors had to be carried out between two lifeboats and dropped well out, one on either beam. The kedge anchors were run out with less trouble, one on either quarter. The purpose of this was to steady the ship in case of a rising wind and sea, and to aid in helping to drag her off the reef.

While we engaged in this work, Bedouins appeared on the shore. They seemed to come from nowhere, like buzzards come to hover around the unfortunate who has fallen crippled or wounded by the wayside. With the advent of the Bedouins there also appeared the strange ghostly shapes of Arab dhows. The Captain thought it wise to call all boats back to the ship and to wait for daylight.

The European members of the crew, that is the officers and engineers, spent an anxious night. I had heard all kinds of tales of ships which stranded in the Red Sea being looted by Arabs. The Third Mate told me of a Shire line boat which had been looted and most of the crew captured and sold into slavery. He informed me that the story only became known because of the fact that the Second Mate put to sea in his lifeboat instead of attempting to land.

The Captain's action for the protection of the ship and her crew lent weight to the yarns told by the Third Mate. Lines of hose were connected up to the steam-pipes feeding the deck winches. This method, when you haven't got guns, is most effective in repelling boarders. Sentries were placed around the ship, especially at the bow and stern, and these were armed. I was aft with the Third Mate. I experienced the thrill of real adventure for the first time. This was living. This was life. I didn't think so after the next few days.

During the night we signalled a passing ship and told them of our plight. She happened to have wireless and reported it to Suez. Next day, about noon, the *Protector*, a Danish salvage ship, was standing by us and, as if to bear out the truth of the Third Mate's stories of plunder and murder, she carried two very useful 12-pounder naval guns and sufficient rifles, revolvers, and cutlasses to arm all her crew.

From this time onward, I hoped the Arabs would attack us, but my hopes didn't mature. After the first thrill was over, the adventure settled down to a job of real hard work. First we took the huge tow lines the salvage ship sent aboard and, instead of making them fast to the mooring bollards, we passed them right around the hatch combings of number four hold. We did this heavy work under the rays of a blistering sun and in a humidity which broiled the perspiration out of us like the moisture is rendered out of fried sausages.

Once the towing hawsers were made properly fast, the windlass took the weight on the bower anchors and the 4" wires, to which the kedge anchors were attached, were lead to the drums of the after winch. All ready, the *Protector* gave the signal and steam was turned on and the order given to " Heave away." The engines were put full speed astern with every ounce of power the boilers were capable of generating. The *Dacre Castle* never budged so much as an inch.

Tidal data was studied, but there is little, if any, rise and fall at this particular spot. The officers of the *Protector* came aboard and went into consultation with the Captain. A short while afterwards we received orders to uncover number one hatch and raise the derricks. For twenty-four hours we dumped cargo overboard. Steel rails for the railways in Manila, kegs of nails, huge steel safes were all hoisted on deck and dumped over the side. After the heaviest cargo had been lifted out of number one hold and dumped overboard, we put in another day trucking baled goods from number one and two holds and piled it high on the afterdecks.

The holds were like the inside of a Turkish bath. While working breaking out the bale goods, we came across cases of wines and beer destined for the Army and Navy Club, Manila, and the Service Clubs, Hong Kong. If the Club members were depending on those wines and beers, they certainly went dry. After we had lightened the ship in this manner, dozens of dhows arrived under charter and we loaded them and they took their cargoes to Tor, a port the other side of the Gulf.

An officer and one other man was sent over in each dhow to see that the crew did not steal the cargo. The British Navy is a wonderful institution, for it was only the threat of that great hidden power which made those Arabs hesitate to slit our throats and steal the cargoes which had been loaded into their dhows. Just imagine what a fortune 500 bales of American cloth would be to those Arabs! By the look of some of them, they would have murdered you for less than a nickel or shilling if they could have got away with it.

One vile-looking fellow showed plainly what he would have liked to do, had he dared. He kept drawing a wicked-looking curved knife from his belt, and after first pointing to the Third Mate and myself, he would draw it significantly across his throat for the amusement of his mates. I had brought along my old " rusty " revolver and I spent most of my time during the run over wondering if it would shoot or explode in case we were attacked by the villainous crew.

The Third Mate had a proper revolver strapped to his waist which had been loaned to him by the Mate of the salvage ship. I breathed easier when we arrived in Tor

Harbour. It nestles under the famous Mount Sinai which is nearly 10,000 feet high. As we sailed into the peaceful harbour surrounded by mountains of sand-coloured rock, I could see the road which wound its way up towards the monastery built high above the sea-level.

It struck me as being strange that right here in the midst of the Moslem world were the landmarks of Christianity with only a few monks and nuns holding the forts.

The voyage back to the ship was made late in the afternoon and it was dark before we arrived, but it passed without incident.

Next day a determined effort was made to refloat the ship but it was of no avail. For sixteen solid days we worked toiling in the sweltering heat before our efforts were rewarded.

On the sixteenth day it came on to blow. The diver from the salvage ship was sent down and he examined the bottom as best he could. Once when he came up to report, he said it was almost impossible to walk around the ship because of the number of empty bottles that littered the sea-bed. About eight bells in the afternoon watch we tried to get her off again. She moved for the first time, only to raise our hopes and then to disappoint us again.

Everyone was dead tired and the officers were anxious because of the threatening weather. About midnight we were all roused out of our bunks. The rising wind and sea did what our efforts earlier in the day had failed to do. After a series of bumps the *Dacre Castle* floated clear. The *Protector* immediately began to tow us stern first off-shore. We hadn't gone a quarter of a mile when she stranded again on another reef.

For two hours she bumped in a sickening manner while frantic efforts were made to tow her off. The carpenter reported she was making water in the after peak. All hands were kept busy dumping overboard the cargo off the main deck. At daylight, she floated clear once more, and, escorted by the salvage ship, we steamed slowly back to Suez for repairs.

As I write these entries we are ready for sea again. The Captain seems to have aged ten years.

CHAPTER VIII

August 12th, 1912.

I have neglected to write in these pages for some time. The reason which made me dig the diary out again was a strange dream I had last night. I can't put it from my mind. I dreamed that I was home and the scene I saw was the family gathering four years ago at Christmas—the only Christmas Father had ever been able to spend at home.

I saw everything as plain as could be. Each detail of what transpired that day passed through my mind and then just as dinner was over, my father's face changed from the happy, care-free expression we had all been accustomed to see, and he became serious, even sorrowful. In my dream I saw him get up and leave the table. All of us looked around wondering why he should have changed from the jovial to the serious so suddenly. He walked over and took up a favourite attitude with his back to the open fire. Then he spoke kindly but with a voice that was full of emotion. " I've been extremely happy to be with you all. I'm sorry I've got to leave you now. Good-bye." As he said these words, the vision faded and I awoke. I was trembling like a leaf. I still feel that something terrible has happened. I looked at my watch. It was just 3:00 A.M. The last I heard of Dad he was back at sea in the *City of Lincoln*. I do hope nothing has happened to him. He should be in Java according to my last letter from home.

While we were in Yokohama, the Emperor of Japan died. There was great to-do about it. Quite a number of people committed hara-kiri because they evidently felt there was no other way in which they could show just how much they thought of the old gentleman. I have a pretty patriotic fervour burning in my own heart, but I don't think it quite reaches that magnitude.

We were quite a long time in Yokohama because we had to go in dry dock to have the rudder post fixed and eleven new plates put in her bottom. I'm glad the job is done because when we ran into real heavy weather crossing the Bay of Bengal, some of us began to think the bottom was going to drop out of her. She leaked like a sieve, and to make matters worse, the cargo broke adrift. It had never been properly restowed after we had dumped part of it while we were ashore in the Gulf of Suez. We had a tough job for about twenty hours working down below securing cargo which had broken adrift due to the heavy rolling of the ship. One man had his leg broken. A barrel of oil went crashing across from one side of the hold to the other and, before he could get out of the way, it jambed his leg against an iron stanchion. With all the weight in the lower holds, the ship rolled like the pendulum of a clock, only not half as steadily.

I have heard some strange things about Japanese customs. There is certainly no false modesty in Japan. I was given to understand that the moral laws are the same for both sexes until they marry. They can follow their own inclinations and do as they like. Once they are married, adultery is considered a most serious offence and from what I hear it is almost unheard-of for a wife to break her marriage vows.

Chastity is not considered a virtue before marriage and I heard that it is considered no crime, or even a reflection on a girl's character, if she helps her family by selling her body. I can't vouch for the truth of this, but an experience I had leads me to believe there is something in it.

While in Yokohama, unloading the last of our cargo, one of the stevedores was struck by a sling of cargo, as he stood in one of the gangways, and was knocked overboard. I was near at hand when the accident happened. Being a good swimmer now, I jumped into the water and managed to hold him up until we were both rescued. There was nothing very heroic about the incident, as there were plenty of people on deck and a number of boats and lighters near the ship. The poor fellow didn't know how to thank me enough. His task was a difficult one because he couldn't speak English, but his gang foreman interpreted what he said.

He insisted that I go ashore and meet his family so they could thank me also. The foreman told me they would have some kind of a feast in thanksgiving for his rescue. Thinking it would be quite an experience, I agreed.

I was taken to a humble shack in the poorer quarter of the city. I was lavishly entertained by the man, his wife, and two daughters. They were young and extremely pretty girls.

They forced me to eat all kinds of things and got a great deal of fun watching me try to handle a pair of chop-sticks. I would have gone hungry if I had been left to my own devices, but I wasn't. The eldest of the two girls picked out titbits from the bowl of stew with her chop-sticks and placed them in my mouth. It was indeed a very happy gathering. The only trouble was that we couldn't talk to each other.

They kept offering me Sake and after the meal was over we had Oriental music played by all members of the family on Japanese instruments. The house was bare of furniture. We sat cross-legged on the rush floors until my joints ached. Imagine my surprise when about ten o'clock, the three other members of the family bade me " Good Night " and left me alone with the eldest daughter. She made gestures which I understood to mean I was to sleep there on the floor, for she brought in two funny-looking blocks of wood shaped out in the middle, which I understand are used as pillows. She also brought blankets and then put out the light.

This custom may be perfectly proper in Japan, but to an Englishman it savours too much of betraying the hospitality of one's host. I kissed my little companion "Good-bye" and made my way back to the ship. (I have often thought since that perhaps the girl was not his daughter at all.)

September 30th. Leaving Shanghai.

A very funny thing happened just before we arrived in Shanghai. China has been declared a Republic and our five Chinese cooks and stewards decided to dispense with their pig-tails to show their sympathy with the movement. One Sunday afternoon the five of them solemnly met on the main deck, and for a moment I thought I was going to witness another murder.

One Chinaman went into the galley and came out with a big meat-chopper. Another laid his head on a block of wood. The man with the chopper took hold of the other fellow's pig-tail and, stretching it out to full length, brought the chopper down smartly. He cut off the pig-tail—not the other man's head. The rest all followed suit and then they took turns trimming each other's hair according to the Western style.

We are making one or two calls and then we go across to Kelung in Formosa, to complete loading with tea for Boston. Owing to our stranding earlier during the voyage and being delayed in dry-dock in Japan, our mail seems to have gone astray. I've hardly had a letter from home all the voyage. They will catch us at one of the ports of call on the way home and we will be kept busy for a week, reading and answering the letters.

Hong Kong, October 30th.

It is no use trying to keep a diary; I might as well start and write a book. Since I last wrote in these pages, the whole outlook on my life has changed. The *Dacre Castle* is a total wreck, her bones bleach on the rocks of Formosa. My father is dead. He died the same day and the same hour I had that strange dream. He died in Samarang, Java. I am a distressed British seaman on my way home to England. Mr. Lamb is also dead. He was lost, together with three men, in the wreck of the ship. What a terrible difference a few days can make in men's lives!

I don't feel like writing, but like the actors say, "On with the show."

We were on our way from Shanghai to Kelung when we received the first warning. At noon, October 12th, we steamed into the harbour of Kelung. The ship was light, except for the water ballast, and ready to take aboard a cargo of tea for Boston, U.S.A.

During the previous late afternoon, and all through the night, an atmosphere foreboding evil seemed to have descended on the ship and her crew. The officers were short in their speech and irritable, the crew grouchy.

The sun, which appeared like a huge coppery ball, sank beneath the horizon out of a weird unnatural sky. The air was hot and stifling and still, with the horrible stillness of a death chamber. The space all around seemed close, stuffy, and confined. I wondered just what it meant and what it was all about.

I felt, as I did on certain occasions at boarding school, when I had been ordered to report at the headmaster's study and could think of nothing for which he could wish to congratulate me.

That night, when I reported to the bridge to take my " trick " at the wheel, the darkness was such that I felt as if I had been wrapped in a blanket—a damp, heavy, woollen one. The perspiration ran down my face. My clothes stuck to my limbs. The binnacle-glass was misty. Everything seemed distorted and unreal. I could hear the swish of the water under the bows as if the sound was being magnified through a loud-speaker. The steady pounding of the triple-expansion engines was the only thing which did seem real . . . and comforting ; everything else seemed dead or dying.

Before I left the bridge, I knew a storm was expected. The hourly reading of the barometer recorded in the log book looked like Judas's fall from grace.

Captain Gough kept the bridge all through the long hours of the night, talking in monotones to his officers as they relieved each other at the end of their periods of duty. There was no relief for him. He was like a general on the eve of battle. I often wonder if he anticipated what a tremendous battle he would be asked to fight against the elements of nature the following night.

When I read the log at 4:00 A.M., and reported the reading to the bridge, I learned the ship was doing thirteen knots. Her average speed was eleven, and I knew then that she was racing against time for the safety of the harbour. I was not so young and inexperienced that I didn't realize the dangerous position we would be in if we were caught at sea " light ship " by the pending typhoon.

Noon saw us safely berthed in the harbour of Kelung. Every kind and description of ship was crowded into the small, narrow harbour. Steamers of every class and nationality, sailing ships, men-of-war, junks, and sampans. We were the last in and drew the outer berth.

Because of the small size and narrowness of the harbour, all ships drop the port anchor, pay out cable, and then moor themselves bow and stern to huge mooring buoys.

We " hung " the starboard anchor and shackled the cable to the buoy ahead of us and secured the after part to the buoy astern, using every wire and rope available.

The whole atmosphere of the place was pregnant with

foreboding. All ships stopped working cargo. Lighters returned to shore. Hatches were secured and battened down. Most ships got up steam in case of emergency. I heard Captain Gough order the Chief Engineer to keep a full head of steam on our boilers.

A gorgeously uniformed, fussy, but very urbane Japanese official came dashing around the harbour about 4:00 P.M., making sure that all regulations had been complied with. He gave the final warning. He informed the ship masters that according to the latest reports received, the expected storm was the worst experienced in years. It had devastated the coasts of China and Japan. It was expected to hit the Island about 7:00 P.M. The centre would most likely pass right over the harbour.

A purple haze seemed to settle on the tops of the surrounding hills. The signal station, situated high above the town, flew the typhoon warning. In the town itself, people were hurriedly moving from the houses situated along the water front. To me, who had never experienced a tropical storm, the precautions seemed excessive.

As I stood with the Mate, Mr. Lamb, the carpenter, and the Bos'on, on the fo'c'sle head, I saw the sun sink again into a sea which looked like molten metal. The sky was like a sheet of hammered copper—the sun itself, a huge copper ball.

Looking out between the headlands, which guarded the entrance to the outer harbour, the world beyond looked like a gigantic stage. The wind was blowing fitfully with ever-increasing force.

Suddenly a dull ominous sound registered on our ears.

" It's coming . . . grab hold of something solid and hang on," the Mate warned.

A wall of dark clouds rolled up, shutting out the picture of oily sea and coppery sky from between the headlands. It was just like a curtain dropping after an act in a play.

The sound grew in magnitude until it reached the proportions of an angry roar. It was the roar of the approaching storm, and, outside the harbour, the seas topped with a cruel white curling foam, which looked like an angry grin. The dark curtain of clouds was torn now by vivid stabs of fork-lightning.

The storm hit and burst with the force of a high-explosive shell. Everything loose was hurled in the air and overboard.

Just as complete darkness descended, I saw the signal station blown off its foundations and hurled down the hillside. It was reduced to match-wood.

The full force of the storm struck the *Dacre Castle* as she stood high out of the water, presenting a huge surface to the wind. The after moorings parted as if they had been made of cotton thread.

The force of the wind made speech an impossibility.

The huge ship, moored only by the nose, swung back and forth at the length of her cable and crashed her stern into the side of the vessel moored next to her.

No ship could stand such punishment. It was only a question of minutes before she would break adrift or batter a hole in the side of the Blue Funnel liner. If she broke adrift, she would crash into others, breaking them adrift also. By morning, the harbour would have been littered with wreckage and clogged with sunken ships. It was then that Captain Gough made his decision. After viewing the damage aft, he struggled along the deck and climbed the bridge. He rang down "Stand-by" on the engine-room telegraph and ordered the Mate to slip the cable moored to the heavy buoy and heave in the port anchor. I went down to unshackle the cable from the buoy. What a task that was! We were soon headed out of the harbour—for sea. We felt our way groping into the inky darkness. Captain Gough was throwing away his own ship . . . and his crew, that the others might live.

Captain Gough always trained his apprentices to steer, and he insisted that they be at the wheel when the ship was entering and leaving harbour. He had little use for foreigners, and never trusted them at the wheel when the ship was in narrow waters, for fear they might misinterpret an order. For this reason, after we had unmoored the ship for'ard and secured the anchors, I was sent to the wheel. It was from this vantage-point I saw all that happened afterwards.

Once we were clear of the breakwater, the full force of the seas swept the decks like a mighty Niagara. The wind was of such force that it picked up the extra bunker coal, which was on deck, and hurled it through the bridge windows forty feet above. Within five minutes, the decks had been cleaned of nearly one thousand tons of bunker coal.

The darkness was like the inside of a tunnel. Men who had dressed themselves in oilskins had them ripped off their backs by the force of the wind. Mr. Lamb, the Mate, remained on the fo'c'sle head with the carpenter and Bo'son. Suddenly, out of the darkness ahead, borne on the wind, came the yell, " Ship right ahead, Sir ! "

A Japanese cruiser had run into the outer harbour for shelter and was anchored right in our way, blocking our exit. Blinding rain had hidden her from sight. Before we could get stern-way on the ship, we were on top of her. The sea lifted us up and then let us crash down again. We were so near the Japanese warship, that as we came down, we scraped her deck with our bow, tearing away the companion ladder and part of her rails.

We lifted high on another sea, but the engines were racing full speed astern and we descended clear of the other ship's side.

The wind shifted until it was right ahead. The engines were put ahead to stop our stern-way, but we were now completely at the mercy of the storm. We drifted steadily astern toward the towering cliffs and destruction.

It was impossible to shout orders from the bridge to the fo'c'sle head. The raging storm whipped the words out of the Captain's mouth. He took the wheel.

" Go tell the Mate let go the anchors," he yelled in my ear.

He thought with the anchors down and the engines going full speed ahead he might at least hold her from going on the rocks.

I struggled down the bridge ladder. The wind clawed at me like a hundred pairs of hands. Once on deck I had to lie down and crawl on my belly. It was impossible to stand upright. Seas swept the decks every second. When they did, I grabbed a ring-bolt or other fixture and held on for dear life.

Finally, I reached the fo'c'sle head and delivered my message. The starboard anchor roared through the hawse-pipe. The ship veered. Mr. Lamb let go the port anchor ; both failed to hold. The fury of the storm dragged the ship and her anchors as if they had been toys.

The brakes on the windlass wouldn't hold. Smoke and flame flew from the brake-bands and reddened the surrounding darkness. The ship lifted on a mighty sea. The windlass was torn clean out of the bows. Our fate was sealed.

Looking to port, we could see the cliffs only slightly darker than the surrounding blackness. At midnight we crashed. A mountainous sea lifted the *Dacre Castle* bodily and threw her onto a ledge of rock. She struck right amidships. Those of us on the fo'c'sle head were washed off. I picked myself up clinging to the rails back by the bridge.

We had struck right on the end of the reef. The ship was sagging in the middle. The Captain told the Third Mate to go and take soundings. I went with him. There was deep water under the bows and on the port and starboard side, forward and back aft as far as the bridge. We went aft. It was impossible to go along the decks. They were submerged and the seas swept over them in a white spurn. We crawled over the top of the engine-room, shinned along the lowered derricks, and gained the after-deck houses. We found deep water astern and on both quarters. The ship was resting on a ridge of rock which jutted straight out into the sea at right angles to the coast. We knew it could only be a few minutes before she would break her back.

We struggled into the crew's quarters, which were situated in the poop. Most of them were Lascars. We found them huddled and half-drowned down below. They were like a bunch of frightened sheep. To get them up on deck, we had to smash a couple of stools and use the legs as clubs and literally drive them on deck.

We instructed the Serang, who spoke English, to tell the men how to proceed along the derricks. We had to knock sense into him. Both he and his men were reduced to a state of utter helplessness through fear.

Every moment I was down in the infernal darkness of the crew's quarters, I could hear the creaking and groaning of the vessel's plates. I felt a horror of dying imprisoned down below. I wanted to be on deck.

We groped our way around and made sure the last Lascar was out. Then we struggled on deck ourselves.

THE WRECK OF *DACRE CASTLE*
AT KELUNG HARBOUR

As I crawled out of the companionway, the wind picked me up and hurled me against the after winch. I grabbed the first thing my fingers circled and held my breath while a sea swept the entire after-part of the ship.

Watching my opportunity, I made a dash for the derrick and swung myself above the swirling waters. One had to proceed like a worm. The wind gripped like a vice. It tore at me until my arms seemed to be dragging from their sockets. Every second, waves swept aboard. Sometimes I was on top of the derrick. At others, underneath, hanging on to the guy ropes upside down, like a monkey.

I reached the main mast and paused for breath. The superstructure amidships looked a mile away. It was in reality only sixty feet. I crossed the intervening space in safety and threw myself onto the boat-deck in the shelter of the galley skylight.

I heard the Third Mate shouting. He was only a few feet away, but his voice sounded like a whisper.

I pulled myself up level with the hatch. Just at that moment the searchlight from the Japanese warship lit up the scene of desolation. Silhouetted against the darkness, I saw the panic-stricken native crew trying to get into the starboard lifeboats. The Third Mate was driving them back with a club. I rushed over and gave him a hand. Gradually they fell back. To them, in their panic-stricken mood, a lifeboat was symbolic of safety. They were incapable of thinking for themselves.

I joined the Third Mate and we drove them back and herded them over the fiddle and on to the bridge. Hardly had we got them there when a gigantic sea swept the ship and lifted the starboard lifeboats high in the air. The hundred-mile wind got under them and tore the falls right out of the goosenecks. They sailed in the air like feathers and disappeared in a thousand fragments into the darkness.

As we reached the bridge, a wave larger than the rest lifted the entire ship bodily and crashed her down again on the ledge of rock. In the light from the searchlight we saw the funnel lift high in the air as the rocks pierced the ship's bottom. The *Dacre Castle* broke her back. A great jagged hole appeared in her decks just for'ard of the engine-room bulkhead.

The cold waters rushed into the boiler-room. The boilers exploded in a cloud of steam.

"The Second! . . . The Second! . . . He's still down below. He said he'd look after the dynamo when I told him to come up." It was Mr. Fairbairn, the Chief, who spoke.

Mr. Worral, the Third Mate, beckoned to me. Once more we made the journey aft. We had to jump over the jagged hole in her deck, clamber over the fiddle, and enter the engine-room through the port door.

We reached the top platform and found ourselves in a fog of steam. Worral grabbed a singlet which had been left to dry on a rail. He wrapped it around his head. I followed his example. He slid down the engine-room ladder. I followed. We found the Second Engineer in a state of collapse on the second platform. The Third Mate stooped and, taking a fireman's hold, lifted him onto his shoulders and carried him up on deck.

There is humour in every situation. As we arrived at the door of the engine-room, Worral turned to me and said, "You go into my cabin. Look in my locker. You'll find some whiskey there. Bring it along to the bridge. . . . We'll need a drink before this is over. There is also some crème de menthe; bring that, too."

Next day the wind dropped and the sea assumed its normal appearance. By noon it was hard to believe the happenings of the night before were anything but a hideous nightmare. The Japanese warship lowered her boats and came over to us. They congratulated the Captain on his wonderful seamanship. The ship was a total wreck.

The town was a shambles. Houses were thrown on their sides, roofs ripped off, Chinese junks were piled up on the main streets, but the other steamers which had been threatened with destruction when we broke our moorings were safe. All the crew were taken ashore and landed at Kelung.

The man acting as British Consul was a German. We were entitled to four shillings and sixpence a day as distressed British seamen. He saw a way to make a little money out of our misfortune. He provided accommodation for us in a third-class Japanese hotel, which was nothing but a house of ill-fame. The tariff was less than sixpence a day. We objected. That night we wrecked the place.

HELL'S ANGELS OF THE DEEP 99

I'll never forget that experience. Failing to correct the injustice by proper representations to the Consul, we started a rough house in the hotel. The proprietor objected, as was quite natural. We met his objections with wooden pillows.

Our sleeping accommodation in this third-rate hotel consisted of a space on the reed floor, a wooden pillow, and our salt-encrusted clothes for bedclothes. We didn't like it.

Our evening meal had consisted of rice and some concoction we wouldn't tackle, and we demanded ham and eggs. They were not forthcoming. When the meal did not arrive, we started the rough house.

The Third Mate jumped up in the air three times, and each time he landed the floor sagged. The fourth time it gave way altogether and deposited him in the middle of a party of Japs down below. We shifted into another room and prepared to repel boarders. Again we used the wooden pillows.

Somebody sent in a riot call and a detachment of police and troops arrived in charge of a lieutenant. The town was under martial law. We met them with a shower of well-aimed pillows. What were they to us—the yellow bellies?

The little Japanese lieutenant took no more notice of the shower of wooden pillows than if they had been bouquets of flowers. He strode calmly up the stairs. When he reached the top, he said in perfect English, "Gentlemen, there must be something very seriously wrong for you to cause a disturbance like this. . . . If you will kindly tell me what the trouble is, I will have it corrected . . . very quickly." He bowed until his head nearly touched the ground.

The sane, polite manner of this official made us feel ashamed. We told him our reasons for objecting to the place where we had been billeted.

"It is an outrage . . . a disgrace that gentlemen should be treated thus," he replied, after listening to our story. "It is unpardonable. . . . I will go at once and see the mayor."

The whole crew had been ripe for any mischief before the arrival of the little Japanese lieutenant, but after he had spoken to us and departed, we felt like a lot of punctured tyres.

Much to our surprise, he returned almost immediately and

informed us that we were to consider ourselves the guests of the town. He directed us to follow him, and we were escorted to the old post-office building which was of substantial construction. It had withstood the buffeting of the storm. A small army of coolies soon provided us with mattresses and blankets. They even rigged up mosquito curtains over each group of beds. We slept in peace.

Next morning we received an official visit from the mayor. Through an interpreter, he read us an address of welcome. It took an hour to read. The gist of it was that many years before, a Japanese ship had been wrecked under similar circumstances about the same place as the *Dacre Castle* met her doom. A British sloop, the *Lapwing*, sacrificed eighteen of her crew effecting the rescue of the other steamer's crew. The mayor told us that the citizens of Kelung had erected a monument in memory of the heroic men who had sacrificed their lives in the brave attempt at rescuing the Japanese crew. (We saw this monument afterwards.) The mayor informed us that though many years had gone by, the citizens of Kelung had never had the opportunity to show their appreciation in concrete form, therefore we were to consider ourselves the guests of the town, and as such we were to ask for anything we wanted, go into any store and take what we wanted, and the city would foot the bill.

The mayor provided a Jap, who had been a European chef, to cook for us. Gifts of food and beer were brought in such quantities that it was impossible to know what to do with them all. At night musicians came and played for us while all the unmarried girls in the town entertained us. We had dances and parties galore.

Our week's stay came to an end. We had to go by train across the island of Formosa and join a coastal boat at a little port called Tam-sui.

The first stage of the journey was across the island by train. The track was so uneven that the train took an alarming list to port or starboard every few yards and it proceeded at a snail's pace, but the journey had its compensations. We were honoured guests. Word had been sent ahead that we were on our way. At every station a delegation met us. They insisted that we get out of the train and have our photographs taken. Then they formally presented

HELL'S ANGELS OF THE DEEP

us with enough cases of beer to go around, one case to each man of the European crew. They informed us that they were at a loss to know just how to show their appreciation of our visit, but that they understood all Englishmen liked beer, which wasn't a bad guess.

When we arrived at Tam-sui, it took a special conveyance to carry the beer we had left over, aboard the ship which was to take us to Hong Kong.

High up in the mountain fastnesses, where they had been driven by the Japs, lurked the Dyaks. These fierce pirates had never accepted any authority. Driven from the seas, they had taken refuge in the mountain and it was impossible to dislodge them from their strongholds. Every now and again they would sweep down and attack some isolated post, murder the troops and the inhabitants; cut off their heads, and retreat, carrying with them the heads of their victims and the fire-arms of the slaughtered troops.

There is a stop on the railway called some Japanese name, which in the British means "The Veil of Tears." It derives its name from the fact that it rains there for some portion of each day in the year. Just near to this place the savages made a raid while we were in transit. We actually saw the looted houses as we passed. They were still smoking.

The news of the typhoon, the wreck of the *Dacre Castle*, and the raid of the head-hunters reached civilization all about the same time. It was too much for an enterprising reporter, representing one of the large American dailies. He wrote a wonderful story, weaving into it all three incidents. When we arrived at Hong Kong, we read that we had been wrecked during a typhoon on the coast of Formosa, captured by head-hunters, and brutally done to death.

. . . . . .

There are one or two things I neglected to write down which are rather necessary now in view of what has happened. When we arrived in Singapore on the outward voyage, Captain Gough secured a new Second Mate, Mr. Knight.

Mr. Lamb survived the actual wreck of the ship but sacrificed his life in a gallant attempt to rescue three coolies, a day or two after the storm.

We had loaded pigs of copper in Shanghai and after the

ship was wrecked, it was decided to salvage this valuable part of the cargo.

The European officers returned onboard the ship after the wreck, as did the apprentices, until final arrangements were made for the disposal of the ship and her cargo. During that time I was appointed cook and Myers as my assistant.

During the second night after the wreck, the wind and sea rose and the two ends of the ship parted company. The stern remained where it had first stuck, while the fore part floated several hundred feet down the coast and stranded again. My job of cook next day was rather difficult because the galley and most of the stores were in the other part of the vessel. Strange as it may seem, I hustled around and provided a meal which the officers claimed was the best they had ever tasted. Admittedly they were hungry and they were certainly ignorant of the true story behind that stew.

Hunting around I found some tins of oysters, a few onions, three dead chickens (they had been drowned during the typhoon), some tins of milk, flour, and seasonings. (Thank God for the seasonings.)

I skinned and drew the chickens and after making a fire in an empty ash-bucket, I cut them up and put them on in a pan to stew with the onions. I peeled some potatoes and added them, together with some unsweetened tinned milk. Just before the potatoes were done I added a generous supply of tinned oysters to the general concoction. When all was ready, I ordered Myers to sound the dinner-gong. I served the stew with great gusto. Even the Captain congratulated me on my effort and insisted that I sit at the table and have my dinner with them. There was no way out. I had to do as I was told. I had to take a dose of my own cooking.

The Captain was not so pleased when I served the dessert. While hunting around I located a case of champagne and a tin of Huntley and Palmer's Fancy Biscuits. I knew in my heart they were the Captain's own private stock, but being something of a socialist, I placed them on the table for all to enjoy. He looked rather sour but couldn't say very much.

I saw the Third Mate was enjoying the joke, so I topped off the meal by serving *his* crème de menthe as a liqueur. Not such a bad repast for a group of shipwrecked mariners on only half a ship.

That afternoon the representatives of a salvage company came off and next day we started to unload the cargo into lighters. We opened the after-peak, where some of the copper was stowed and three Japanese coolies went below to break cargo. We threw down some slings and lowered the fall. The Mate came along and, looking down the hold, noticed the men had collapsed and were gasping for breath. Without a moment's hesitation he descended the hold and, placing the sling around the stricken men, gave the order to hoist away on the fall.

The men were lifted on deck, but the exertion had been too much for the Mate. Chlorine gas had formed, due to the action of the salt water on the copper. He collapsed before he could climb out of the hold. I was sent aft to report to the Captain, and when I got back the Mate was on deck. Somebody had gone down into the death-chamber and slipped the cargo hook into his clothing and then climbed quickly up on deck again.

Medical men were immediately sent onboard from the Japanese warship, but although they worked over the Chief Officer for hours, he passed away, as did one of the men he had so gallantly attempted to rescue.

This deed, to my mind, deserves greater merit than any ordinary act of life-saving. The Good Book says, "Blessed is he who lays down his life for his friend." Anyone who knew Mr. Lamb knows that Orientals were no friends of his. He had no use for them at all, yet when duty called, he never hesitated, even at the cost of his own life.

"THE CYCLONE"

Skies leaden grey hang low o'er Bengal Bay,
   Long oily swells roll on as fades the day,
Down sinks the sun a dull and coppery sphere,
   Warning the sailor that the storm is near.

Quickly the mercury settles in the glass,
   And sea-gulls on the shoreward journey pass.
A small black cloud appears o'er the horizon's line,
   No bigger than a hand . . . Yet the most ominous sign.

Short gusts of wind spring up from here and there,
    A weird depression impregnates the air,
Oppressive silence reigns, as men secure the gear,
    For past experience warns and dangers real appear.

Men rush aloft and quickly furl all sail,
    For look ! Low o'er the horizon comes the threatening gale.
Driving on before it a wall of smothering spray,
    And a Stygian darkness takes the place of day.

Dark nimbus clouds roll up from out the west,
    And mighty billows raise their milk-white crests.
The voice of fiends scream in the tempest's roar,
    Which drives their barque towards the hostile shore.

Helpless as a feather borne upon the breeze,
    She falls away before it, battered by the seas.
It seems as though the very Gate of Hell had opened wide
    And loosed the pent-up furies of the damned upon the tide.

The Captain at his post does stand, and nurse her in her need,
    The boys there in the half-deck, go upon their knees and plead,
And offer up a silent prayer to Him who reigns above,
    For He alone can save them, to return to those they love.

Through the hours of darkness, before the storm they scud,
    The crew are sorely worried but they trust in Him above.
For God in His great mercy looks kindly on the brave,
    And often from the jaws of death will reach a hand and save.

Slowly the dawn dispels the omnivorous night,
    And reveals to view a truly awful sight,
Huge mountainous seas in perfect symmetry rear,
    Their mighty crests to heights that inspire fear.

Towering o'er their staunch but storm-racked barque,
    Battering her like cannon do their mark,
They rake her fore and aft, and tear and sweep,
    All moving objects to the deep.

Then comes the rain . . . A mighty deluge pour,
    With such effect that waves their heads do lower ;
But this slight pause does not denote the end,
    The worst is still to come, before they start to mend.

HELL'S ANGELS OF THE DEEP

It is but the pause as they the centre near,
    That dread position which all seamen fear;
The sinister lull . . . the rest . . . which breeds new power,
    Ere it bursts with a fresh frenzy, which make the bravest cower.

" O! God of Might, champion us our cause,
    Raise up Thy hand, and bid the furies pause,
Beat back the terrors which escape from Hell,
    Exert Thy power, before which Pharaohs fell."

With faith renewed they settled down to wait,
    Impotent now till God decides their fate;
The wind with hellish cunning from all four quarters blows,
    And even mightiest billows in mad confusion throws.

Waves break . . . and pound her port and starboard beams,
    Both fore and aft they rear;
They rack, and twist, and start her every seam,
    And still, O! gallant barque, she shakes them clear.

Masts, spars, and wreckage spread around,
    A more piteous object scarcely could be found.
Sensing their victory the fiends of Hell once more,
    Renew their deadly efforts and drive her towards the shore.

But God in Heaven sends forth a welcome sign,
    And wisps of blue amid the clouds define;
He opens wide Heaven's flood-gates . . . torrents downward pour,
    And beat the maddened wave-crests till they raise their heads no more.

Terrors quickly vanish, just like the nightmare flies,
    And as the daylight passes, stars peep from out the skies;
Tired weary men their prayers of thanks do send,
    Then clear away the wreckage and tattered sails rebend.

Quickly they work and get her under way,
    For loud booms the surf on the shores of Bengal's Bay,
But they succeed, and lay her course off shore,
    And bright breaks the dawn, and peace does reign once more.

                                                WILLIAM GUY CARR.

CHAPTER IX

December 25th, 1912.

Yes, it is Christmas night. I am at home. It has been a sad, quiet Christmas. We all missed Dad very much and my home-coming reopened the scars of sorrow so recently healed. I travelled home on the P. & O. liner *China*, and strange as it may seem, poor Dad's effects came home on the same ship. Everyone has gone to bed except myself. I don't feel like sleep. I thought I would bring this diary up to date.

It is just two years since I tried to run away from home. What a lot has happened since!

Mother has aged ten years and she is in very poor health. She was still in bed suffering from shock caused by the news of my father's death when she picked up the *Journal of Commerce* and read in big headlines:

"*Dacre Castle* wrecked in Typhoon—
Heavy loss of life feared."

This second shock caused her to suffer a serious relapse.

I met most of my old friends after I arrived home. They seemed to look upon me as something of a hero. The owners wrote and told Mother that according to the reports received from Captain Gough, I had acquitted myself very creditably during the last disastrous voyage. They said they hoped to be able to reward me for my conduct. I have to go to Liverpool to see them next week.

January 20th, 1913. *Algiers.*

I am starting a new diary and I have a lot to write about. I am onboard the S.S. *Wray Castle* under Captain Howe. She is a new ship. She is chartered by the Barber Line of New York.

To put things in a nutshell, Captain Gough must have highly recommended me. I am not aware of having done anything very special, but I have been promoted to fourth officer of this ship, and before I left Liverpool I was notified that I had been recommended for an appointment as Midshipman in the Royal Naval Reserve. What is even more, I have been placed on salary and I received a grant of £10-0-0 from the owners before I left Liverpool.

I like Captain Howe very much. He is a young man and smart as a new pin. The Chief Officer, Mr. F——, told me point-blank that he didn't agree with the practice of promoting apprentices before they had finished their time. This ship carries a Lascar crew. To show me his disapproval, he gave me some of the most menial and filthy jobs to do as soon as I arrived onboard.

December 1913.

I have nearly forgotten that I had ever kept a diary. Nearly a whole year has passed and I have never opened the pages. Life aboard the *Wray Castle* was not happy. Mr. F—— was determined from the very start to make it as uncomfortable for me as possible. He had to allow me to keep watch on the bridge with him, for that was the Captain's order, but when in port he put me to work painting over the ship's side on the same stage with the coolie crew.

On one occasion he sent for me just as we had come off watch at eight in the morning and said, " If the owners think I need a lackey to keep watch with me, you might as well be a real one. Go to the galley and bring that shaving-cup full of hot water and shave me."

I did as I was told, but not in the way he expected. When I arrived at the galley the Serang was mixing some strong suggie-muggie for washing paint-work. I dipped the shaving-cup in the pail and returned to the Mate's cabin. He was leaning back in his chair, legs outstretched, with a towel round his neck, waiting for the shave. I gave him the closest shave he ever had. I dipped the shaving-brush in the strong soda mixture and proceeded to lather his face. I had the lather well on before I noticed the suggie-muggie was so strong that it was dissolving the bristles of the brush. The Mate gave a howl and rushed over to the wash-stand and buried his face in the water.

When he looked up, his face was brown and white in

patches. I dare not record what he said to me during the next five minutes. I tried to look innocent. I was not afraid of him. I believe I could have licked him in a fight. I told him I had gone to the galley and done his bidding. I explained that I took a cup of hot water out of the pail I found standing inside the galley door. I explained that I was neither an experienced valet nor a barber, and expressed the hope that if he was tired of shaving himself, he might find someone else amongst the crew who would give him greater satisfaction.

The big joke of the whole thing was that the Captain and officers kidded the life out of him for being such a darn fool as to try and soften his whiskers with caustic. He could not very well tell them how it happened for he knew he had no right to order me to shave him in the first place. After that the battle was on. It waged all the year. Twice I had the satisfaction of knowing that Captain Howe reprimanded him for his conduct towards me. I never made a complaint officially.

Unfortunately, for me, Captain Howe was relieved by Captain Gough when we returned to Algiers. Mr. F—— told him that I was suffering from a swelled head due to my promotion, and announced his intention of curing the ailment. Captain Gough was ignorant of what had led up to the trouble, but he called me over the coals for my conduct reported by Mr. F——.

One day after we had been taken off the China run we were nearing Ghent. Mr. F—— told me he was going to report me to the Marine Superintendent when we arrived in port. He claimed he had enough on me to have my indentures cancelled. His concluding words were to this effect, " I'll show you what you've run up against. I'll *get* you if I have to *frame* you. I'll teach you, you can't fool with me, you young bastard."

He hardly had the last word out of his mouth before he was down on the deck. I literally drove the words down his throat. He got up, spitting out broken teeth, and I hit him again and again. I saw " red " for the first time in my life. I held him up with my left hand and pounded him with my right. I think I might have killed him if the Captain had not come rushing down from the bridge and ordered me

HELL'S ANGELS OF THE DEEP 109

to my cabin. F—— was still in bed when we docked in Ghent.

I was sent home. It looked as if my career at sea were ended. I was ordered to appear before the owners. Mr. Chambers gave me a fair hearing. My indentures were not cancelled. I was reduced from fourth officer and sent as apprentice to another ship, the *Hornby Castle*.

If ever there was an old crock sailed the ocean, she is one. The main steam pipe burst, while we were crossing the Atlantic, and two men were killed. It was very rough weather and the S.S. *Baltic* stood by us. She would have sent a doctor onboard had the weather moderated before the men died.

We got into further trouble going up the Sabine Canal to Port Arthur in Texas. We picked up a towing wire with our propeller and it wrapped itself round and round the propeller shaft.

Captain H—— was going to send to Galveston for a diver to clear the wire, but I went to Mr. Bennett, the Mate, and offered to try and clear it by diving without a suit. After working for eight hours from one of the ship's boats, we finally cleared it. It was no easy task for we had loaded grain in Galveston and the ship was deep in the water. The water was filthy and thick with mud, and the harbour was alive with alligator-gars—horrible-looking creatures which are half fish and half alligator. For three days afterwards I was sick at the stomach due to swallowing so much foul water.

On the voyage home, we ran into some terrible weather. The *Hornby Castle* was a well-decked ship. She had a cargo of grain in her holds and a deck-cargo of lumber as high as the bridge. When we ran into the bad weather, she wallowed in the seas like a sow heavy in litter.

Our steering gear broke down. We fell off in the trough of the sea and the ship tried to roll the funnel overboard. Investigation showed that the wire leading from the steering engine to the quadrant on the poop had parted under the deck-load.

Because I was thinner and more agile than most members of the crew, I was asked to crawl under the creaking deck-load and reeve off another wire. We first tried to pass a wire through the casing, but the end kept fouling on projections. I woke up with nightmares of that experience for weeks afterwards.

The deck-load consisted of heavy timbers. A casing had been built around the steering gear (which ran over blocks alongside the hatch combings), to prevent the timbers jambing it in case the deck-cargo shifted slightly during the voyage. The huge deck-load was lashed solid with wires and chains, but in weather such as we experienced that trip, it was a creaking, groaning mass, threatening to break adrift every second.

I know of nothing quite so nerve-racking as the experience of creeping under that tremendous load. There was only room to wriggle along on one's belly. Every inch I crawled I could feel the timbers working and threatening to cave in. Waves washed aboard and I was often nearly drowned like a rat trapped in a sewer before the water receded from the decks. I was nearly frantic from fear before I managed to reach the end of the wire which had been passed through from the after end but which had become foul about halfway through the passage under the deck-load.

Wriggling my way back was even worse than pulling myself ahead. I had to lie perfectly flat with arms outstretched ahead of me and push my way slowly backwards. There was not space enough to bend my knees. I kept going through sheer pig-headedness. I did not want Captain H—— to think that I was afraid. I had had trouble with him when the other apprentice and I had been washed out of the halfdeck. The other boy was a frail bit of a lad and it was his first voyage to sea. One of the officers remarked that he must have been sent to sea to save funeral expenses. It was a cruel, callous remark to make, but it was not altogether unjustified. The boy was ill when he came onboard. He was desperately sick during the passage home.

The half-deck is situated in the port alleyway, which opens off the after well deck. The apprentice was confined to his bunk. The deck-head was sprung and leaking. There was a foot of water washing about the deck inside the cabin, and waves washed aboard every minute. Our clothes and bedding were saturated. I knew that if my cabin-mate were left in conditions such as those, he would never survive the trip. I asked Captain H—— if I might make a bed for him on the chart-room settee or some place else where it was dry. Captain H—— looked upon my request as an impertinence. He ordered me off the bridge.

The Mate and Second Mate fixed us both up with a bed on their settees. In fact, the Mate gave the sick apprentice his own bunk. Both incurred the Captain's displeasure by doing so.

During my interview with the Captain he remarked, " You boys are too soft. You want too much coddling. You don't want hardship. You don't want to work. All you come to sea for is to save the expense of a Cooks Tour. Roughing it a bit will make men of you. If you can't stand it, you are better dead."

We had just nicely got the ship under control again when the carpenter reported her as making water in the fore peak. This was serious. We were loaded deep enough as it was. The scuppers were almost in the water, and if the fore peak filled it would put her down by the head and make her impossible to steer. Loaded as she was and with waves forty feet high battering her from all sides, it would only have been a matter of time until she became one of the missing ships.

Examination showed that some of the bow plates had been sprung due to the pernicious practice followed in Galveston of screwing three bales of cotton into spaces where only two could be stowed by hand. Expert longshoremen can, by using screw-jacks, load three bales where normally only two should go. I hear that the I.M.S.G. (Imperial Merchant Service Guild), of which organization my father, Captain F. H. Carr, was one of the first members, is trying to have a stop put to this dangerous practice. After the experience I had in this last voyage, I wish them every success.[1] I wish I had the courage to write to the papers and suggest that inspectors who are supposed to watch the loading of ships in foreign ports be supplied with spectacles, gratis.

Why a ship and her crew should be endangered for the sake of a few extra dollars which are earned by " screwing " the odd extra bale of cotton into her seems unreasonable,

[1] I understand this practice has been discontinued.

unless it is that the ship is worth more " dead " than " alive."
In that case the crew do not matter.

I think Samuel Plimsoll must turn over in his grave when some of these ships are sent to sea.

We had to heave-to and " break " the cotton out of the fore peak so we could build cement boxes around the leaks. It only takes a few words to write that down, but it took hours of the hardest work I ever put in to accomplish.

I mustn't grumble. I came to sea to seek adventure. I've had my share and I am finding out adventure spells " Hard Work." It is good experience, however, and teaches one what to do in emergency.

To cut a long story short, we arrived back in Antwerp safe and sound, but the other apprentice was sent home to die. Although none of us knew it at the time he had contracted enteric fever while in Port Arthur.

Antwerp, July 12th, 1914.

Another voyage is over and we had a lot of fun this last trip. We loaded a general cargo for the Gulf of Mexico ports. When we got there, the revolution was in full swing.

I don't know if anyone was aware of the fact when we loaded the cargo in Antwerp and Hamburg, but we had a quantity of arms and ammunition aboard billed as general freight. The reason I know this is because, while down the hold watching cargo, a sling broke and some cases marked " axe heads " fell from the level of the hatch combing to the floor of the hold. The cases burst open, and instead of axes they contained rifles of German make.

This fact aroused my curiosity. I informed the Mate, and we examined some other damaged cases. One was marked to contain condensed milk of a well-known Swiss brand. As a matter of fact, it contained ammunition for the rifles. This was none of our business, so we nailed up the cases again and sent them ashore. The Mexicans are always having a fight of some kind. I suppose they must have arms with which to fight or their favourite pastime would be stopped and they would have to content themselves fighting bulls. It is a case of everyone to their own liking, like the old woman said when she kissed her cow.

We unloaded cargo at Puerto Mexico and Vera Cruz.

While in Puerto Mexico, I went ashore with the Third Mate and two of the engineers. We took in what sights there were to see. A train arrived in town under armed guard. The guard rode in an open coal-car placed in the middle of the train, which was protected with sandbags. On our way back to the ships we were arrested. I don't know for what reason, but the experience was exciting while it lasted.

We were walking down the road towards the ship, when suddenly we were overtaken by some mounted police or troops; anyway, they were men on horseback. They surrounded us and motioned us to bunch together and go along with them. The Third Engineer thought he would break away. He dived past one of the horses and ran. The ship was only a few yards away when the incident happened. One of the Mexicans wheeled around and followed at a gallop. When he got near the sprinter, he just threw his lasso and turned, also at a gallop. The Third Engineer arrived back on the end of a rope, and he looked such a sorry mess we didn't try to follow his example.

We spent the night in jail, a filthy place full of insects and vermin. Twice guards approached us and asked how much money we had. We told them very little. They shrugged their shoulders and made significant gestures with their hands to their necks.

If we were to be hung, I wanted to know the reason why. I thought of those guns and ammunition we had landed from the ship. I asked the guard what we were charged with, and he answered one word, " Spies."

I was never able to find out just the why and wherefore of this strange happening, but we were released next day. The Captain was unreasonable enough to give us the dickens for being absent without leave, and told us he had a good mind to log everyone of us a day's pay. Can you beat that ?

We finished unloading at Vera Cruz. I rather like Mexican style, and I enjoyed a very pleasant evening up in the main square. There was a good band, and it was a colourful sight watching the uniformed officers walking around with their pretty señoritas. I noticed the mother or some elderly lady was always in tow. Unmarried girls have about as much privacy in Mexico as goldfish.

I went along to the Casino and was lucky enough to win nearly one hundred dollars playing roulette before I went back to the ship. I contented myself with backing the odds or evens and the red or black. My luck was in.

From Vera Cruz we went to Galveston to load for home. To our great surprise, these orders were cancelled, and we were chartered by the American Government to act as a transport and carry stores down to Vera Cruz for the American Expeditionary Force. Trouble had arisen over some real or supposed insult, and the Americans decided to occupy Vera Cruz.

I don't want to be unkind, but the citizens of Galveston made so much fuss over the departure of those troops one would have thought they were going to a real war. What tickled our fancy more than anything else was the consignment of several hundred coffins which we took onboard. These were taken along so the heroes who died fighting the foe might be brought back and buried in " God's Country." Personally, I feel that when I die, the place where they bury me will be my least worry. The Yanks certainly take their *wars* seriously.

We sailed and I witnessed the " battle " of Vera Cruz. Being a British ship under the British flag, we steamed into harbour and tied up right alongside the wharf.

I went ashore the night before the " battle." The city and everything in it looked perfectly normal. I heard the troops were to withdraw from the town before daylight to save the buildings from being damaged. The Americans planned to land and occupy the place until satisfaction was given them for the insult they had suffered. Incidentally, an American here is just about as popular as the toothache with the Mexicans.

Next morning bluejackets and marines attempted to land from the American cruisers which were anchored in the harbour. A number of cadets from the naval and military academy ashore decided they shouldn't. Before the Americans were half-way to the shore, these young gentlemen opened fire on them from the roof and windows of the academy. They also occupied the top of the lighthouse on the end of the pier. What is more, they certainly shot to some effect.

I don't know how many occupants they provided for the coffins we had onboard, but they certainly let them know they weren't going to land for any tea-party.

The boats pulled back to their ships. I do not wish to insinuate that they were forced to retire. They were not. The did this simply to save loss of life. The Mexican youths kept sniping at the ships, and they didn't seem particular which ships they shot at so long as they fired at something. The reason I mention this is because they wounded a fleet surgeon on one of the British warships, which happened to be in harbour at the time.

When the boats arrived back alongside the American ships, the real fun started. Slow and deliberate shooting from some of the American cruisers' smaller guns soon reduced the lighthouse to plain bricks and mortar. The Naval and Military Academy was treated in much the same way. I got a big thrill watching those young Mexican cadets bolt from one building to another and keep up firing. When their new position came under fire, they would bolt like rabbits to some other place of vantage and start shooting again.

The waterfront was soon cleared of the "enemy" and the Americans landed. During the night sniping broke out afresh. The Mexicans, shooting from the house-tops, picked off several members of American patrols. This wasn't a very pleasant experience for green troops, and, if my information is correct, it led to a serious tragedy.

Some of the less experienced troops got the "wind up" or "jumpy." This resulted in a marine officer being shot by one of his own sentries. During the night, two American patrols are reported to have engaged each other in a skirmish which resulted in serious casualties on both sides before they discovered their mistake.

Conditions ashore were not altogether what they should have been, because armed patrols visited our ship looking for deserters on numerous occasions. I asked one patrol sergeant why any of the troops would want to desert, and he replied, "Oh, some of these guys think that if they skip our outfit and join up with the Mexicans, they'll be promoted to generals in a couple of weeks. They are just crazy to get into a real scrap." Very well put.

We unloaded our stores and supplies and sailed for Tampico. Here there was more excitement. I don't know whether the rebels were inside the city or on the outside, but while we were there those on the outside decided to come in.

When we arrived in port, everything was quiet. On the way up the river, somebody was shelling the oil tanks, and the resultant fire was a sight well worth seeing. The blaze from the burning oil tank lit up the country for miles around.

After we had tied up, several of us decided to go ashore. We made our way to an open square where a kind of fair was in progress. We amused ourselves playing games of chance. The sounds of rifle fire could be heard every now and again just outside the city limits.

We were so engrossed in playing roulette and trying to win some money that we didn't notice the sound of firing drawing nearer until some soldiers rushed through the square shouting at the tops of their voices that the enemy were upon them.

The fellows in charge of the gaming tables didn't even wait to pick up the money. They just took to their heels. We didn't quite know what to do. The roulette wheel was still spinning; when it stopped the number I had played won. I picked up the money.

It is not every day one can witness a real battle, so we decided the best thing to do was to go into one of the houses which surrounded the square and watch the fun from the upper windows. We felt sure that if the troops came into the house, we could explain that we were English, and not Americans.

We had no trouble gaining admittance to the house. It turned out to be a house of ill-fame. Two of the girls were Americans. They were frantic with the thought of what would happen to them if they fell into the hands of the enemy. They begged us to take them with us and give them our protection. We told them to get into their street clothes and warned them to pretend to be Britishers should they be questioned. One thing was certain, we could not pull that gag and remain where we were. British tourists would not be likely to take their lady friends into a house of that kind. We bundled the girls into their clothes and ran for the central square in the middle of the city.

We had just cleared the house when the invading army arrived. We ducked and ran. Bullets spattered against the walls ahead and behind us, but none of us was hit. We dodged around the first corner and kept going in the general direction of the ship.

We made a turn to the left and were just about to enter the square when a real fight started. As far as I can gather, the troops which broke into the town outwitted the defenders. They attacked at a weak point and reached the heart of the city before anyone realized what had happened. Reinforcements were rushed from the other sections of the city and they all met the invaders in the central plaza. One unfortunate member of the invading force got as far as the bandstand before the other troops arrived. He was cut off when his companions retreated and hid under the bandstand. When the rest of the invaders had been driven back out of the city, the troops returned, and being informed that an enemy was hidden under the bandstand, they bolted him like a rabbit and shot him dead as he made a break for freedom.

I couldn't understand this method of procedure until, upon inquiry from a man who spoke English, I elicited the information that prisoners were a costly proposition and difficult to take care of. A dead man was no more bother than a cat or dog which had been killed by the traffic. The garbage collector looked after them all.

While we were standing around wondering what we would do with the two ladies of easy virtue who had forced themselves upon us, the problem solved itself. The British and German warships lying in the harbour landed a force of men and decided to evacuate all the American population in case the Mexicans took it into their head to avenge the shelling of Vera Cruz. We handed the "ladies" over to the kind attentions of the sailors. They may have already made the acquaintance of some of them. They certainly seemed happy.

From Tampico we went to Galveston and the Gulf ports to load for Antwerp. We arrived back this time with nothing more exciting than a fire in our bunkers. The poor old

Hornby Castle was becoming pretty decrepit. She has been sold to the Greeks. I wish the new owners, and the crews which sail in her, plenty of luck. They'll need it.

I have been transferred to the S.S. *Sizergh Castle*. We sail for Hamburg to load general cargo for Buenos Aires. War clouds are gathering thick and fast over Europe. I hope we sail from Hamburg before the storm bursts. There is just this fact to record. I have been promoted to fourth officer again and this seems to be a very happy ship.

"IN THE STOKEHOLD OF A 'TRAMP'"

Dedicated to the "Black-gang Squad"

BILL LOBB and Mike O'Dare,
   Used to laugh and curse and swear.
They were two of the hardy breed
   The stokeholds of steamers need.
They were pals from their very youth,
   And the scraps they'd fought ; s'truth !
It'd make your hair turn grey,
   Just to hear the things they'd say.

It was one dark night
   We were hove-to, right
In the teeth of a raging gale.
   We rolled and pitched to beat all hell,
And the screws raced clear as we rose and fell
   From crest to trough of the waves.
Down below Bill Lobb and Mike O'Dare
   Piled on coal as they'd curse and swear
At the water which washed about their feet.

They lifted a manhole, a kind of door,
   To drain the water from the stokehole floor.
They were taking a spell, for they'd cleaned their fires,
   When they heard a bang, like some bursting tyres.
'Twas the main steam-pipe had given out.
   Mike grabbed Bill Lobb and threw him down
The manhole they'd been stood around,
   And with his body he covered the hole.
'Twas the bravest deed that ever was told.

HELL'S ANGELS OF THE DEEP

We found him there nigh cooked right through,
   A sight to sicken the stoutest crew.
As he wasn't quite dead we'd have carried him out,
   But he said, " Bill first," did that game Old Scout.
" Guess I'm a goner, boys," he said.
   " I'm not much account, alive or dead.
Bill there . . . I threw him down below.
   He's got a wife and kids in tow."

His harsh old voice grew husky,
   The glaze on his eyes appeared;
His body was grimed and crusty,
   But his soul can't have much to fear.
He'd shielded his old pal Bill,
   With that body of his own,
From the scalding, blinding steam,
   For the sake of the kids at home.

" Bill . . . I'm feeling jiggered,
   I guess I'll have to go,
But I hopes that you pull through, Bill,
   You've got the wife in tow.
I'm feeling kind-a chilly,
   Though I'm par-boiled like a ham.
If you make the grade, Bill,
   Give m'love to little Sam.

" Mister, it's hell upon these coffins,
   Piling coal on down below;
You can hear cold death a-knockin',
   For their guts are on the go.
God ! . . . It's hell when bloody owners
   Send such rattle-traps to sea;
But they only think of dollars,
   Not the likes of you and me.
Just as long as the blamed insurance
   Will cover the risks they own,
And they carry their freight at a decent rate
   We can all take the short cut home."

WILLIAM GUY CARR.

CHAPTER X

August 3rd. Buenos Aires.

The whole atmosphere is charged with war. It is said we will join the French and help give the Germans hell. I hope we do. Life is growing monotonous since the Mexican show.

I received my appointment as Midshipman in the Royal Naval Reserve the last time I was home. It was dated April 1st. I hope nobody made a fool of me. If war does break out, I'll be called out by Royal Proclamation and sent home.

The *Cap Trafalgar* and several other German liners are here in port, and rumour is wild that they are all carrying guns below decks and are ready to be transformed into commerce raiders the moment war is declared.

I cannot help but feel excited. The little bit I saw of the Chinese turnout in 1911 and the excitement we had at Vera Cruz and Tampico has whetted my appetite for war, and life onboard this old tramp as fourth officer is anything but exciting. I am going ashore to-night with some of the officers.

August 4th, 1914.

We went ashore last night and we had plenty of excitement. We made a tour of the hotels to start with, dined well, if not too wisely, and then proceeded to take in a show.

The first part of the show was all right, but after midnight —Ye Gods ! The film showed a drama dealing with the kidnapping of girls by white slave traffickers, bogus ministers of religion who used their cloth to lure victims to their doom, and the forcible seduction of females in all the most lurid details.

I don't know if it was bad liquor, the stuffy atmosphere, or the picture, but I felt sick. All through the performance after midnight, girls wended their way amongst the audi-

HELL'S ANGELS OF THE DEEP

ence and tried to coax the men into the curtained cubicles which surrounded the main part of the theatre. It is a wonder an earthquake or a tidal wave doesn't put this modern Sodom and Gomorrah off the map.

The real excitement started when a German sailor went beyond the limits one is supposed to go, even with the class of girls who frequent these dives.

After mauling her about, the German took offence at something she said or did. He was a big burly brute, and he picked the girl up like a child, and placing her over his knees, turned back her dress, and, amidst shrieks of laughter from the rest of the party, proceeded to administer a sound thrashing. The girl's limbs were innocent of any underclothing whatever.

An English sailor could not be persuaded that it was no business of his. He jumped over three rows of seats and hit the fellow a smashing blow in the face.

The whole atmosphere was already pregnant with trouble. It only needed a spark to touch off the blaze. Several German sailors (they were off the *Cap Trafalgar*) attacked the Englishman. Several Britishers attacked them. The rough house started. Soon it was raging all over the theatre.

Bottles were used as clubs or missiles; girls screamed and fainted. Someone yelled " Fire ! . . . Police ! " Absolute pandemonium broke loose. We fought our way back to the stage and escaped via the rear emergency exit.

August 5th, 1914. Still in Port.

We went ashore again last night. The whole city was seething with excitement. Crowds were gathered in front of the German, British, and French Consulates, as well as the telegraph and cable offices. They were reading the various bulletins and trying to obtain information.

Towards midnight the excitement seemed to die down, and we decided to go onboard and get some sleep.

The excitement was not all over, however. As we turned a corner, the sounds of tumult reached our ears. We ran in the direction of the noise.

War had been declared. The official news had arrived by cable. A crowd immediately mobbed the German Consulate.

Everyone went crazy. Riots broke out in several places and Germans and their property were severely handled.

All Reservists were ordered to report at the office of the British Consul. I reported and afterwards I met a gentleman of the name of Mr. B——. He was a fine type of Irishman and he imparted some very interesting information to me.

According to his story, the *Cap Trafalgar* was equipped with 4·1-inch guns and gun-mountings. The guns were suspected of being hidden down one of the holds, probably in packing cases. Other German ships in harbour were suspected of being fitted out as supply ships for the "raider." Mr. B—— suggested that I go and, if possible, prove these suspicions to be true. He pointed out that if I could obtain evidence that such was the case, representations might be made to the proper authorities which would result in the ships being interned providing they remained in port longer than the twenty-four hours allowed armed ships under international law.

He warned me to exercise every care and to avoid capture. He pointed out that I would probably receive short shrift if I were caught by the Germans acting the part of spy. He also informed me that what I did would be on my own responsibility. If I were caught I could expect no support from the Consul. I understood the reason why.

My objective was the *Cap Trafalgar*. I was soon standing in the shadow of the freight shed looking the situation over.

I saw a quartermaster on duty on the main companionway, otherwise the decks seemed deserted. As I stood there figuring out the best way to get onboard, I heard sounds of hammering down one of the for'ard holds. That decided me. I had visions of winning a decoration before the war was really started. I circled the shed and stood on the dock under the towering bows of the big German passenger ship. Nobody was around. I reached up, grabbed hold of one of the mooring lines, and climbed aboard.

Arriving on deck I flattened myself in the shadow of the windlass while I recovered my breath. The first part of the adventure was over, but I couldn't prevent my heart from pounding a tattoo against my ribs. I realized that the most dangerous part of the task lay ahead.

As I crouched there, breathing heavily, I could distinctly hear the sound of work going on down below. As soon as I was rested, I crawled cautiously down onto the main deck and crept to a large ventilator. I knew the ventilator would lead down into the lower hold. I placed this ventilator between myself and the man who was on gangway duty and pulled myself up into the cowl.

Down below I could see a light. The ship was empty of cargo and every now and again I saw men pass back and forth below the ventilator shaft. Once or twice they stood immediately underneath, forty feet below. They sought the benefit of the cool breeze which entered the lower hold down the ventilator shaft.

At one bell (quarter to four) the sound of hammering stopped. I looked around the ventilator and saw seamen climbing on deck out of the hold. They came forward towards where I was hiding. There was nothing for me to do but lower myself down the ventilator shaft and hang on to the lip of the cowl by my finger tips.

The men passed within a foot of me, and I wondered what would happen if one of them noticed my fingers as they passed. My arms grew tired. I could still hear the men on deck. I moved my feet around to try and find a possible toe-hold on a plate joint. In doing this, I unintentionally kicked the plating and, to me, the noise sounded like the ring of a heavy bell. My discomfort for the moment was forgotten as I listened breathlessly and waited to see if the sound had been heard by the sailors standing on deck.

I heard a match struck; evidently they were smoking. Would they never go away? My arms seemed to be pulling out of their sockets. I had just reached the point where I had either to pull myself up or let myself fall, when I heard the voices receding. I gritted my teeth and held on another minute, then, with a great effort, I pulled myself up and seated myself inside the cowl again.

Now was my chance. The hold was apparently empty. There were two ways I could get below. One was to risk discovery and sneak to the ladder at the after end of the hatch. The other was to lower the end of a guy-rope down the ventilator shaft and shin down the rope. I had noticed plenty of guy-ropes coiled on deck, and I decided to get into the lower hold via the ventilator route.

Looking carefully around to see that all was clear, I climbed down on deck and picked up a rope end with plenty of length to it. I lowered the loose end down the ventilator until I felt it touch the floor of the lower hold. I then made the other end fast to a ring-bolt in the deck.

All appeared plain sailing. I climbed back into the ventilator cowl and lowered myself hand over hand down the rope.

As my feet touched the deck, I was grabbed from behind by two burly Teuton seamen. With all my caution and care, I had never thought of the possibility of a guard being left in the lower hold.

I saw the guns. They looked like 4-inch semi-automatic. They had just been taken out of large packing cases. I shot my legs out and tried to trip my captors, but I only started a fight in which I decidedly got the worst. Strange as it may seem, I thought of some of the cheap fiction I had read when a boy, the kind where the hero gets into all kinds of tight places and fights his way out against seemingly impossible odds.

While serving in the Merchant Service I had always been taught that one Britisher was equal to at least two or three foreigners, but the harder I fought, the worse of a beating I received. Boots and fists seemed to rain upon me. The three of us rolled over the deck for a moment or two. Then one of the big brutes put his knee fairly into the pit of my stomach. I wished I could have lost consciousness. It would have been less painful.

An officer descended and came over and questioned me. I kept my mouth shut. I had learned that habit before I had been very long at sea. " Least said soonest mended " is one of the truest proverbs ever made. The officer asked me who I was and what I was doing ? He questioned me in several languages—French, German, Spanish, and English. I kept absolute silence and simply shook my head from side to side, pretending not to understand.

I realized my only hope was to appear stupid and try to convince them that I was only a common thief intent on pilfering cargo or a young man trying to stowaway.

Much to my delight, the officer ordered my captors to take me on deck. He led the way, the others followed behind me.

I was feeling about as happy as a man awaiting the executioner. About the easiest thing for me to picture just then was a firing party and a deep-sea funeral after the ship sailed from port.

I would have dived overboard and swam for it if I had got half a chance, but one of the sailors walked each side of me, holding on to my arms.

As I was marched aft I noticed two policemen standing at the foot of the gangway amidships. I was never anxious to land in a jail until that moment. I realized that if I could only be arrested by the local police I would be comparatively safe.

To think was to act. I owed the big brute on my left a grudge for putting his knee into the pit of my stomach. I fixed my eye on the bottom of his chin and measured the distance carefully, then, when we were exactly opposite the gangway, I gave my right arm a complete circular twist, broke my captor's hold, and finished the swing in a perfect haymaker to the point of the other chap's jaw. I never experienced such a sensation of complete satisfaction in all my life as when my fist connected. If he didn't have a broken jaw, it was because his jaw was stronger than my knuckles. I smashed three of them.

Before the German seaman had recovered from the unexpectedness of my attack, I was bounding down the gangway, into the arms of the representatives of the law. I submitted to arrest without a struggle. The German officer followed me down the gangway. He emitted a flow of guttural curses. He demanded that the two policemen deliver me back into his custody. He became excited, insistent, and finally abusive. The policemen became annoyed at his aggressive attitude, and, if I understand Spanish at all, told him to go to Hell. They led me off to jail.

I am not at liberty to tell how I did manage to escape from the hands of the law, but I did, and it was not long before I was back in the Consul's office. I told him I had been aboard the German ship and that I had actually seen the guns. I signed a document to this effect and the Consul made a very complimentary speech and promised to report the incident to the proper authorities for recognition.[1]

It was decided that I had better go home on the R.M.S.P. *Aragon*. Nothing could have suited me better. It seemed as if every man of British nationality in Buenos Aires who had ever shouldered a gun, went home on the *Aragon*. It made one feel proud as Punch. To all those men England was "home." There were Naval Reservists, Army Reservists, Legion of Frontiersmen, ex-Naval and Army deserters; men who had left home years before for the good of their health, or because they valued their freedom, but when the clarion call went forth calling her sons to battle, when the old Lion roared, these exiles in South America responded to a man.

The banks had all closed their doors when the news that war was actually declared was made public. But passage money didn't bother these men. They were going home to fight, and they were ready to fight anyone or everyone who tried to stop them. The *Aragon* ceased to be a passenger ship—she became a troop ship.

Typical of the fine patriotic spirit these exiles showed is that of Leading Seaman Fisher of the Fleet Reserve. He sold his goods and chattels and sailed for home on the *Aragon* with his wife and four young children, and left a good position to do so.

Prince Louis Napoleon is also onboard. The French do not recognize his title, but that doesn't worry him a bit. He's going to join a crack Cossack regiment as Colonel.

He climbed in the rigging and made a speech just before we sailed. He worked everyone up until they were so crazy mad to fight that some men who had come down to the wharf to see us off climbed aboard and sailed with us. Two other chaps started a fight right there. I never found out what it was all about. Prince Louis can speak and he certainly hates the Germans.

Every cabin is full, and we have a thousand more pas-

[1] AUTHOR'S NOTE.—I never heard any more about this incident. As everyone knows, the *Cap Trafalgar* was allowed to go to sea. She mounted her guns and raided and sank our merchant ships until she herself was finally sunk in battle with the British armed liner *Carmania*, September 14th, 1914.

sengers to take aboard on the way up the coast. They'll have to sleep on deck or in the lifeboats.

I'd like to put down how I feel, but I can't explain it. I feel proud as a game-cock, light as a swallow, and as full of fight as a grizzly bear.

I'm determined I'll keep this diary up to date, but it's getting trying already. I'm alone in the writing-room. The ship's headed down the river. Dinner is over and the whole of the volunteers are in the first-class smoke-room drinking toasts to the Allies and damnation to the Germans.

While I'm writing this they have sung, "It's the Navy, the British Navy," "Rule Britannia," "God save the King," the Marseillaise, "The Girl I left Behind Me," and a dozen more good old songs.

There is a young Irishman onboard who is already accepted as a leader of good times. He is now standing on a table with his arm around Prince Louis' neck, acting as song leader. I'm afraid of only one thing—if he cuts loose with that Irish blarney of his amongst the fair sex, there'll be some broken hearts before we land in London. He is good-looking and full of hellery. His wit is as sharp as a lance and he has a silvery brogue which can't help but lull the fears and suspicions of the most timidly inclined. From what I have seen already, women fall for him like leaves before the autumn gales.

August 9th.

My good intentions have gone west already. I've missed two days and it would take me a week to write all about them. The whole ship's gone clean war crazy. It has been absolutely impossible to separate the different classes. Human beings going home to fight are as thick aboard this packet as a plague of locusts. They sleep in relays. The only division possible to make is that the regular third-class passengers, mostly Portuguese labourers, have been stowed away for'ard for sleeping quarters. These men and women are going back home after making a little money in South America. They are a queer lot.

I've been made Fifth Officer of this ship. Everywhere else except the officers' quarters is too crowded for comfort, and we won't get to London before September 1st.

There are quite a number of really fine-looking girls aboard, but there are too many men in the running for their favours for anyone to get a chance of five minutes alone with them.

There is no canoodling going on up on the boat decks this trip. The simple reason is that even the boat decks are too crowded. There is one girl I'm going to teach how to " shoot the sun " some afternoon. If that is a success, we might study astronomy in the evening. The only place that is not overcrowded is the navigating officer's quarters immediately under the bridge.

I've caught my Irish friend playing with the children of a certain very important personage. I doubt if it is the children he is interested in as much as their very charming and petite governess.

August 10th.

Rumours are rife: Number One—the British Navy cleaned up the German Navy and the war is all over but the shouting: Number Two—the *Kronprinz Wilhelm* is waiting to intercept us: Number Three—we have been ordered to proceed without lights at night from now on: Number Four—the Russians have nearly captured Berlin.

It is the general consensus of opinion that the war will be over in less than three months. The war fever is dying down. Nobody aboard seriously thinks that we will get a chance to personally take a wallop at the Germans.

As an officer of the ship, I do happen to know that the Captain feels anxious about the presence of German armed merchantmen. I heard him tell the Chief Officer that we intercepted a SOS from a Union Castle boat which had been captured. The signals stopped suddenly, so we don't know what really happened. If we are sunk with all this crowd aboard—three times as many as there is lifeboat accommodation for—we'd be like Barney's Bull.

We've got two fine 4·7-inch guns mounted on the poop. These may scare the enemy away. I did hope they wouldn't until I discovered we haven't a single round of ammunition for them. This seems unbelievable, but it is nevertheless true. We have two perfectly good guns, at least six first-class gun crews, and not a single round of ammunition. Poor old England—I guess we are a nation of shopkeepers after all. The German passenger boats are all armed to the teeth and the larger cargo-boats detailed to act as supply ships. The proof is they've started commerce raiding already.

I hope H.M.S. *Glasgow* sinks the *Cap Trafalgar* before she gets to sea.

August 12th.

I've been too busy to write the last few days. We left the South American coast and are now headed across the Atlantic for Lisbon to land the Portuguese passengers. Now I'm beginning to prevaricate. I've been busy, but not too busy—the trouble is I don't know how to write what I want to put down.

It certainly seems as if the glamour of war upsets the equilibrium of the fair sex as much as our own. Why do they worship and adore a warrior, even a would-be warrior? They do and always have done. It is the same to-day as before the Battle of Waterloo a hundred years ago. Dress up in uniform, label yourself for the boneyard via the smoke of battle and bursting shell route, and girls will take you in their arms and call you their hero and a lot more nice things besides, all of which seem silly now, but it is rather nice to listen to at the time.

My lady friend aboard this boat is a very charming French girl. She is desperately in love with her marvellous France. I wrote a lot about . . . my friend, but I have torn out the pages. I wrote the entries when the memory of them was still burning in my brain.

The things which happen when one is alone in the company of a charming companion, in the romantic atmosphere of soft lights, sweet perfume, and hushed music, which floats down into the cabin from above, while the water plays a gentle lullaby as the keen bows rise and fall to the motion of the waves, seem so entirely different when they are put down in cold black ink on the white pages of a diary, and read in the unromantic light of the early dawn next day.

Mademoiselle sat alone with me the other night under conditions recorded above. She sighed. I asked the reason why. She looked at me with those great big eyes of hers and said in her delightful broken English, " I tink you are what we call ' grand.' You go home to fight for France. You are one big, brave *homme*. . . . I love you. . . . I decorate you with my kisses for the brave deeds I know you will perform." This was receiving pay in advance with a vengeance. That was the start of the *affaire d'amour*. This war is turning out pretty good after all. I will be able to speak French by the time we arrive home. As I said good night, she whispered, " Je n'oublierai jamais." Neither will I.

August 20th.

One night we nearly ran into another ship. She was also steaming without lights. On several occasions the air has been simply full of German messages. They are all in code. The operator informed us that one night the sending ship was not more than ten or fifteen miles away. The signals came in so strong.

August 29th.

We left Lisbon this morning, after landing our passengers. Everyone is getting excited. We should see the shores of Old England in a couple of days.

Sunday, September 1st.

Just a hurried note as a reminder. We crept up the Channel and were " spoken " by several destroyers. Some of the youthful officers who command them, if you judge by their manner towards Captains of merchant ships (men old enough to be their fathers), seem overwhelmed with a sense of their own importance.

One of them was different. He told us about the naval scrap off Heligoland and gave a short, bitter laugh when we inquired, in all earnestness, if he thought the war would be over before we could get into harness.

He gave us to understand that all of us who had any training at all would be on active service *tout suite*. (I'm still strong on the French.)

To-day is Sunday. We are safely berthed in dock. As I have not been home for two years, I've decided to go home and see the folk. I wired the Registrar-General of

Shipping and Seamen, notifying him of my arrival in England, and told him I had gone home to await orders.

We could see the flash and hear the boom of guns on the Flanders coast last night as we passed through the Straits of Dover. We have had no real news yet. London seems just the same except that men are working night and day, and the general impression seems to be "business as usual."

The young Irishman went right off to enlist in the Army. He said there would be no bloody hand-to-hand fighting in the Navy. He is quite a character. He confided to me one night that he had often wondered what it would be like to drive a bayonet into a big fat square-head's guts. Well, he's on his way to find out. He is an extraordinary fellow, awfully nice, but crazy as a loon.

"ADVENTURE"

Dedicated to some of my companions on the Aragon

I'VE sailed the seven seas,
I've travelled o'er the land,
I've fought in revolutions,
And pay-dirt often panned.
I've known good luck and bad,
Had joyous times and sad,
In wars and strife, I've risked my life,
I've felt hot lead and the chilly knife,
I've had my loves, but ne'er a wife,
For my heart rebels at a quiet life.
I'm a born Adventurer.

In the mountains of Alaska,
Where the cold is sure intense,
I've searched for gold and silver,
I've known that great suspense.
I've felt the burning fever,
Mount up into my brain,
At the hope of mighty riches,
As I staked out many's the claim.

Way down in southern islands,
I've spooned with the native girls,
And joined their dark-skinned brothers,
As we've dived for lustrous pearls.
Then for the East I'd hanker,
And sail for the China Sea,
Till an earthquake or a blamed typhoon
Would near be the death of me.

But now I'm growing older,
And my days are nearly done,
Yet there's still one more adventure,
I know that's sure to come.
The ONE GREAT BIG ADVENTURE !
That no matter where you hide,
You can't refuse to tackle,
Ere you cross the great divide.

But I will never fear it,
For it appears to me,
Until you're safely anchored,
You're a derelict at sea.
Then why fear the last long journey,
Why let false terror ban,
The joy of that last adventure,
That opens heaven to man.

CHAPTER XI

September 3rd, 1914. Devonport Barracks.

We tied up to the London Docks 10:00 A.M. September 1st. There's no question about it now—there actually is a war on. Until I started home by train the war seemed unreal—a sort of nightmareish affair, but the sight of all those hospital trains rushing hundreds, yes thousands, of wounded towards the North of England, so as to make room for the tens of thousands more who are still to come, was a very convincing sight.

One fact which couldn't escape notice was the cheerfulness of them all. Some of them looked as if they'd just returned from hell and damnation, but they smiled.

Some of the poor devils were bleary-eyed and hollow-cheeked. They looked as though they hadn't eaten or slept for weeks, but they could still smile and smoke a fag. The newspaper reports are all cheerful and optimistic, but there is something in the appearance of those wounded men that makes me think going to war isn't exactly a picnic. The war isn't a month old yet, but nothing short of a month in hell could have changed those men from the happy-go-lucky Tommies they were such a short time ago into the haggard, pain-tortured, half-starved looking creatures I saw.

Another thing that impressed me greatly was the crowds of Belgian refugees one meets everywhere. Those who can speak English seem willing and ready to talk. A woman with her two daughters, the wife of some high official in the Belgian Government, travelled in the same carriage with me.

If she tells the truth, the newspaper stories of German atrocities are not exaggerated. I can't see the sense in that sort of thing. I believe brutality on the part of the enemy will only increase the determination of the Allies to win.

I arrived home at 10:30 P.M. Ye Gods ! Just imagine it taking nine hours to travel to Liverpool from London. We were side-tracked a dozen times to allow troop trains to rush south and hospital trains to rush north.

When I did get home, Mother was pleased to see me, but she wasn't what you could call surprised. I said, "Aren't you surprised to see me, Mother?" and she replied, "No, not in a way. I had a feeling that you would rush home to join up. I guess it's what your father would have done had he been alive."

I saw right there that it is the women who are going to pay in this ruddy war. Men have the excitement, the thrill, the adventure; women the worry, the anxiety, the sorrow, and often—the long weary years of a lonely widowhood.

We had supper and afterwards Mother gave me a telegram. It was from the Admiralty and read, "Report at Devonport Barracks for duty immediately." That was the reason Mother had not been surprised when I walked into the house. The moment my wire had been received at the Admiralty, they had, in turn, wired me to report for duty. The message had arrived ahead of me, and of course Mother had opened it. Yes, evidently there *is* a war on.

There is something wrong when you speak of war being popular—but this one certainly seems to be. After I left home to report in Devonport, I noticed that every vacant lot of land was turned into a drill-square. Hundreds of men of all classes, young and old, were sweating away, learning to be soldiers. Many places of business were closed, and signs hung in the windows, "Closed for the period of the war," or "Closed for the Duration."

The train journey south was a repetition of the one north; troop trains, hospital trains, and special freights all had precedence over passenger traffic. It is an astounding thing the way the whole population have accepted the fact of their lives being turned topsy-turvy.

I met a young fellow named Robinson and travelled down with him. He is an R.N.R. midshipman also, and is now in barracks with me in the same training squad. His father is a Colonel in the Regulars, and Robinson told me that things weren't going as well at the front as the papers led one to believe.

As we proceeded further south, more officers joined us, and soon we had a merry party under way. You may be able to think seriously when alone, but I'm darned if you can in a crowd—anyway, who wants to ? We're all in for the duration, so it's a case of " Eat, drink, and make merry," for to-morrow—— ? Who knows ?

While in Bristol on the way down I saw another incident showing the manner in which the war has affected England.

Owing to train schedules being knocked hell-west and crooked, we had two hours to wait for our connections in Bristol, so Robinson and I decided to have some dinner in the town.

As neither of us had been in the place before, and as we were both feeling happy after the hospitality of friends we had met on the train, we hailed a taxi and told the driver to take us to a good lively place to eat.

He took us at our word.

We dined and repaired to the bar parlour for a glass of port. There was a bunch of Territorial officers in ahead of us, and the pretty little barmaid was working her soles off to try and keep pace with the orders. One fellow suggested a little help and went behind the bar to give her a hand.

The boys persuaded her to have a drink, then another and another. Soon she was as happy as any in the party and did a step dance on top of the bar counter. She made a date with all of us and became so darn loving towards Robinson that I thought he was going to quit the war right there and then. However, we did manage to get him to break away and we left five pounds so that she could square her accounts, because I'm quite sure she collected no money for the liquor that was served during the last half-hour.

September 8th. Devonport Barracks.

Well, I'm an officer now in the King's Navy. It seems a bit strange, being all brass bound. I've come to the conclusion war is a strenuous game.

Morning divisions and prayers (God knows we need them), then drill, gunnery, etc., etc., till noon, lunch and more drill. After dinner, it's the Palm Court at the Royal in Plymouth, a show, and usually a party afterwards. Some find it hard to sober up in time to start drill again the next morning, but once on the parade ground, they soon sweat the liquor out of their systems.

Officers are congregated here from all over the world. The barracks itself is a wonderful place. The officers' quarters are palatial. The walls are hung with hunting trophies collected by past and present members all over the world. In the halls and on the landings are relics of every naval engagement that was ever fought. The very atmosphere makes you feel that such a thing as defeat would be impossible.

September 9th.

What a lark! An officer named J. B. P—— turned up at the barracks last night. He tried to enlist in the Army . . . did enlist in fact . . . but the authorities discovered he had sea experience and transferred him to the Navy. He's furious. He reported here in an Army uniform—that of the Irish Guards. The depot commander ordered him to report for duty properly dressed this morning. P—— will rank as sub-lieutenant R.N.R. in the Navy.

He reported for duty this morning, but he wasn't properly dressed . . . not by a long shot. He arrived on the parade ground in a naval monkey-jacket, army trousers, and putties. His cap was stuck on the back of his head and his "quif" curl stood from under the peak of his cap like the curl on a drake's rear-end. The thousand odd officers and men on parade nearly threw a canary fit. The Navy would have been wise if they'd left him in the Army. He'll give them more trouble than the whole of the German "High Seas Fleet." P—— feels he's been given a dirty deal.

He was ordered off the parade ground by the O.C. and told to go to his room. Later he was sent for by the depot commander and asked the reason for his "disgraceful conduct."

P—— simply told him the truth. "I was given orders to report for duty properly dressed on the parade ground this morning," he explained. "I went ashore to try and buy a uniform. I couldn't buy one to fit me and the tailors couldn't make one inside of a week. I did the best I could. I went to a secondhand store and asked the storekeeper if he had an outfit for sale. He said he had. He measured me and handed me a suit he swore was a perfect fit. The jacket I tried on wasn't so bad. I didn't try the pants on till this morning, and when I bent over to lace my boots, the stitching all parted. They were too tight.

"I waited in my room, not knowing what to do until an orderly came up and said I was to report on the parade ground with the R.N.R. midshipmen immediately. Well, Sir, you know the old saying in the Merchant Service, 'Obey orders if you break owners.' I obeyed. I did the best I could. It would have given 'em a bigger laugh if I had reported without any pants at all."

P—— told me the commander seemed quite sore when he explained. I don't wonder. This is going to be a real war now P——is fighting for the Navy. I hope we are appointed to the same ship.

September 10th.

Now I know we are going to be shot, but it won't be by the enemy. After last night's frolic at the Theatre Royal, it wouldn't surprise me if we were all court-martialled and sentenced to be shot at dawn every morning for a week. P——started the racket. If the "Brass Hats" ever find out who were responsible, there's going to be the devil to pay and no pitch hot.

About a dozen of us midshipmen went ashore together. We dined and got feeling pretty merry. Then we went to a show. We clubbed together and took two boxes, one over the other at the right-hand side of the theatre. Just as the show started, P—— decided he wanted to be in the lower box. He grabbed the curtain and, lowering himself down, swung himself into it as neatly as a monkey would have done. This was the start of it.

When a pretty actress made eyes up at his box, he climbed out again and swung himself down on the stage. There is something about P—— which, if it were properly developed, would make him a great leader amongst men. Instead of the management and the audience becoming hostile, he had them all eating out of his hand in about two minutes. He became the star turn of the whole show. Of course, R—— (he's another R.N.R. midshipman), who simply can't stand to take a back seat, and never was intended by Nature to sit in the front row of anything, had to barge in.

Different from P——, he was tight. He tried to climb

out of the box and shin down the curtain the same as P—— had done. The only difference was that when P—— climbed down the curtains, we held on to them. When Morgan began his descent, we didn't. The result was the curtain poles collapsed under his weight and he fell about eight feet and landed right on top of the taps and drum. One foot went through the drum, and his big fat head, in some inconceivable way, got jambed through the triangle. P—— tried to make out it was all part of the show, but he couldn't get away with that ... not quite.

After the show was over, we figured we might as well be killed for sheep as lambs. We stayed ashore all night.

Next morning, when I entered my room, I nearly threw a fit. It had been slept in and whoever had slept there had made about the worst mess I ever wish to see.

An hour later I was standing before the officer of the day, who demanded an explanation for the filthy condition of my room. I was trapped. I either had to admit that I had been ashore all night without special leave, or take the blame for the condition of my room. I gave the old brain-box a couple of shakes and then said:

"Please, Sir, I know I am in almost as bad a mess as my room is in, but I was absent without leave last night and did not occupy it and have no idea who did."

"Don't lie to me," he thundered savagely.

"I may be in the Navy, but I won't stand to be called a liar. What I said was the truth and I can prove it," I retorted, thoroughly aroused.

Instead of putting me under arrest, as I expected, to my utter astonishment he said, "I'm sorry for that last remark, but the room is certainly in a beastly condition. I'm afraid I'll have to report that you didn't occupy it last night, otherwise you will be blamed. There is sure to be an investigation. It looks as though you are between the devil and the deep sea."

I saluted and retired. I sought out P——. He came up to my room and surveyed the shambles and mess. Whoever was responsible had come up the back stairs. That was obvious. He had left his trail on nearly every step.

"It's that blighter, R——," P—— accused. He would credit R—— with anything.

"You shouldn't say that, P——. We can't prove it," I admonished.

"I could if I knew what he'd eaten for supper last night," he replied, and I burst out laughing.

"Page Sherlock Holmes," I suggested.

They certainly tried to get to the bottom of the mystery. Every midshipman who was ashore last night was called on the carpet and questioned, not only about the mess in my room but also with regard to the theatre incident.

I was one of the first. I told the depot commander the same story I had told the officer of the day.

"Why did you stay ashore without special leave," he demanded.

I remained silent.

"Were you with anyone else?" he demanded.

"Yes, Sir, I was with another officer."

"Where did you stay?"

"We stayed at the A—— Hotel. I signed the register. That should prove my statement," I replied coldly.

"Who were you with?"

"That is a question I would prefer not to answer," I retorted.

"I mean who was the other officer?" he replied.

"I am quite willing to take blame for my own misdemeanour, but I am no informer," I told him.

"Consider yourself confined to barracks until further orders. Incidentally, that order holds good for all R.N.R. midshipmen. It will remain in force until the culprits come forward, or I find out who was responsible," he told me coldly.

September 11th.

They might just as well try to dam the Niagara Falls as keep P—— in barracks. That limb-o'-Satan thought up a good one last night. He called some of the midshipmen into a conference. I think he is something of a socialist. "It is not fair to punish all for one offence," he argued. "I've got an idea. Let a bunch of us borrow the greatcoats of a number of senior officers and go ashore and raise Cain. To-morrow they will have another investigation. All the officers from the rank of sub-lieutenant upwards will be called into it. If we keep our mouths shut they'll never find out who is responsible."

It happened as planned. About a dozen of us went ashore. According to our greatcoats, we ranked all the way from subs to commanders. We hired taxicabs and headed for Plymouth.

The theatre was a wow! We all booked seats in the front row, early. We arrived for the show late.

P—— had arranged all the details. We had attended the show the previous night. When the chorus came on to sing a song and do a dance, we all got up and marched on the stage and coupled up with the girls. Some took it as a joke—others objected, and some didn't know what to do. It was all rather terrible. After about one minute, P—— gave the order, "Now beat it!" We dashed off the stage, left our borrowed coats behind the scenery in the wings, vamoosed through the stage doors, jumped into the waiting taxicabs, and returned to barracks. Everything went off without a hitch. P—— will make a great leader one of these days—that is, if he doesn't turn bandit.

At half-past nine the authorities were checking up to find the names of *all officers* who were absent ashore. We midshipmen were very much in evidence during the check-up. Some of us were playing billiards, some playing cards, and others industriously reading in the library. According to precedent, everybody from the commander down should be confined to barracks from now on until they find out who did it.

I hope nobody squeals.

September 12th.

P——'s ruse worked. The order suspending all leave has been rescinded.

September 13th.

Three possibilities seem to dominate our lives. We may be sent to the naval division which is in training for service in Flanders; we may commission H.M.S. *Tiger* which is fitting out here, or we may go to H.M.S. ——. Personally I don't care what happens, but I do wish it would happen soon, otherwise I'll be busted financially.

September 15th.

Hurray! I heard to-day that the *Carmania* sank the *Cap Trafalgar* in as nice and clean a stand-up battle as ever was fought at sea. Both ships were converted merchant ships, both carried about the same armament. It was a good scrap —all credit to the Cunarder.

We were all a bit crazy when we first arrived here, but we are beginning to settle down. Most of the midshipmen and junior officers are Reservists, and they don't knuckle down to naval discipline for the moment. I think we will all get licked into shape when we are appointed to ships. I personally would like to go with the Naval Division.

September 23rd.

We heard to-day that a German submarine sank three of our cruisers within a couple of hours the other day. They are the *Hogue*, *Cressy*, and *Aboukir*. We all feel as if the enemy were kicking us in the pants and that we are unable to retaliate.

September 24th.

Some officer died and we were given ceremonial drill by an instructor named Lynch. He is as Irish as you make them. He came to that part of the drill where you stand with arms reversed, rest the hands on the butts of your rifles, and rest your chins on your hands. Lynch said, "You will now reverse your arms. Rest your hands on the butts of your rifles and stand with bowed head, *for the corpse is about to march through the ranks.*" This finished any chance we had of remaining serious. They ought to provide someone other than an Irishman to teach us funeral drill.

September 25th.

There will be no Antwerp show for me. One of the midshipmen threw a six-inch shell on my foot instead of on the mat to the rear of the gun when we were practising gun drill yesterday. I am in bed and my foot is as sore as the devil. The sole of the foot is burst open and so is the skin between the toes.

October 25th. Onboard H.M.S. D——.

Just a month has gone by since I wrote. My foot is better. I was given seven days' leave and then I was appointed to this ship.

The whole world and living seems strange and unreal. The war maggot seems to have entered all our brains and we are doing the most extraordinary things, things we would not think of doing if we were normal. I'm at a loss to understand just where it is going to end. While I was at home I went to a dance. My foot wouldn't let me dance, so I sat out with a young lady I used to be sweethearts with when at school. It is only four years ago since both of us knew little, if anything. She had pigtails down her back. I was shy and awkward. The other night she drank punches like a man and volunteered to show me a nice quiet sitting-out place. Everyone seems to have grown up overnight, and changed.

The Antwerp show is all over. It was a complete wash-out from start to finish. If there was one redeeming feature about the whole thing it was the magnificent spirit of the men. Some ugly stories are circulating freely. I hear the brigade was badly equipped, poorly officered, and insufficiently trained. What is worse still, rumour has it that the 2000 men of the brigade who are now interned in Holland were deliberately led over the borders into neutral territory by men acting as guides, but who were in reality spies.

I had just got back from my week's leave when I received my appointment to H.M.S. ——. She is one of the county class cruisers. There are ten snotties, two sub-lieutenants, and one Captain's clerk in the gun-room mess.

Captain D—— read the Articles of War and gave the crew a fine talk about the justice of our cause and the traditions of the Navy. To sum up the whole thing in a word or two our duty, according to him, is to " fight the ship to the last gun and the last gun to the last man ; to hold inviolate the tradition ' Never to strike your flag.' " His arguments were simple and sound. He said, " A SEA FIGHT IS NEVER LOST WHILE THERE IS ONE SINGLE GUN LEFT IN ACTION AND ONE MORE SHELL TO FIRE. THAT LAST SHELL

MAY SINK YOUR ADVERSARY AND TURN SEEMING DEFEAT INTO VICTORY."

It was plain to see that the crew all agreed with him, so if a ship of the German " High Seas Fleet " wishes to lick H.M.S. —— they have got to sink her.

There is one thing I forgot to mention. While home on sick leave I went to Liverpool and asked Messrs. James Chambers if they would be kind enough to settle my account and release me from the balance of time my indentures called for. Mr. Chambers and Captain Lightholler, the marine superintendent, were extremely nice to me. I had quite a nice chat with Mr. Chambers. He questioned me quite closely about the Port Arthur incident when we fouled our propeller. I told him the truth. I don't know what Captain H—— had told the owners, but to my amazement I received £10 more than my settlement called for. Now I have finished my " time " and it is all over I begin to wonder if the kind of training I received during the past four years is not the best kind after all. If you can stand the gaff it will make a man out of you ; if you can't stand the gaff you will quit, and those that quit are probably no great loss to the Mercantile Marine. I am actually beginning to feel proud of the fact that I served under Masters like Captain Ben Smith. He is certainly one of the old school. He demanded that his word be law aboard his own ship and he was big enough in every sense of the word to insist on instant and complete obedience to his commands. When an officer or man questioned his authority or his ability to enforce it they were looking for trouble, and they usually found what they were looking for. The work was hard and the hours of labour long, the grub was scanty and the quality poor, but I want to be fair and admit that I have benefited from those four years in every sense of the word. I have grown until I stand nearly six feet tall and weigh 170 lbs stripped. If chipping rust and washing paint-work seemed irksome at the start I have finished my time feeling fully confident in my ability to keep a watch and know what a day's work really is.

When I entered the employ of James Chambers and Co. I didn't know them from Adam. I signed up to do four years with them as apprentice and receive £28 in return.

Twice I had the opportunity to do something a bit out of the ordinary, and twice they recognized the effort by promotion and cash bonuses. Everything considered I feel well satisfied. That chapter of my life is finished. Now there is a war on, so let's get on with the war.

CHAPTER XII

October 20th.

Some of us were disappointed after we got to sea and learned the news. We were detailed to make a preliminary cruise, put our crews through their drills, organize, and do gunnery practice. Most of us were wishing we would rush off to the war and get mixed up with some real fighting, but I guess those " Brass Hats " who hang out at Whitehall know their job after all. Our crew is composed of more than 75 per cent reservists. They hail from all over the place. Some from the Merchant Service, others from the fishing fleets on the east coast, but the majority seem to be fishermen from the islands off the west coast of Scotland.

They are about as unlike regular Navy men as one could imagine, but even if they are slow and deliberate in their actions, and untidy in their dress and deportment, they are proving themselves fine seamen.

Our Captain is a " nut " on gunnery. Perhaps that will prove a good thing if we ever meet the enemy, but after the last ten days, we are all agreed he is becoming a darned nuisance. It is general drill every morning, loading practice every afternoon, and during the night, when you least expect it, the alarm goes for " Night Action." The trouble is everyone has to turn out at the double, because nobody onboard, except those on the bridge, knows whether it is real or not until they are closed up at the guns.

I'm the midshipman of the after turret. We have two Mark VII 6-inch QF guns packed into an armoured compartment they call a turret. The ammunition and cordite cartridges come up on a miniature elevator out of the magazine below. There is just enough room in the rear of the guns to avoid being smashed up against the walls of the turret when they recoil.

The " Owner " (that's what the regular Navy call the Captain) thinks we should be able to get off at least twelve rounds a minute independent fire. We tried it. If Dante had waited and written his famous *Inferno* after spending a session in that turret, he could have made a real job of it.

Given the target and the order "Independent Fire!" Hell broke loose. It might sound exaggerated, but the din was so awful that one of the loading numbers had to keep his hand on the breech of the gun and yell out to the rest when it had fired. To add to the general discomfort of deafening noise, there were the stifling acrid fumes of burnt cordite and the sudden recoil of the guns to contend with.

Every now and again there would be a blinding flash as the breeches were thrown open to allow the bores to be swabbed out ready for the next load. This flash was from the unburnt cordite which was left in the cartridge chamber. It ignited when the draught reached it. They call it the "back flash."

A Scotch fellow with a beard got the nicest singe you ever wish to see. His beard caught fire from the back flash, and although he smothered it out with his hands before it really burnt his face, he was so scared he fainted. The Lieutenant of our turret seized the opportunity to carry out casualty drill. He is one of the cool kind. In casualty drill, the remainder of the crew carry out the duties of the disabled members in addition to their own. Scotty was dragged to one side and left to recover as best he might. The rest carried on.

But if general gunnery practice during the day was bad, "Night Action" was worse. After drilling the crew for nearly a week by having them called at all sorts of odd hours during the night, one afternoon we saw the carpenters constructing a target.

That evening, the officers in charge of the guns were informed that some time during the night the alarm would be sounded. They received orders to go to action stations and control their own guns. They were to open fire as soon as they "Picked up the Target" and continue independent fire until they heard the bugles sound "Cease Fire." The D—— carries fourteen 6-inch guns and several batteries of 12-pounders. I have often heard the expression "Bedlam broke loose," but what I saw that night was bedlam in reality. The alarm went at a quarter to two in the morning. The night was black, without moon or stars. We just reached our stations when the searchlights opened up. They threw out their beams of light and swept the surrounding darkness for the target which had been thrown overboard at three bells (1:30 A.M.).

The " Skipper " believes in doing things properly, so he had the target lowered at three bells, and then steamed away from it for fifteen minutes before turning the ship around and giving the alarm. We didn't pick the target up until it was almost abeam and about five hundred yards away on our starboard side. Eight of the 6-inch guns bore and most of the 12-pounders. They all fired split seconds apart and then reloaded and fired independently. After the first deafening crash, the noise was something almost indescribable. Add to the noise the blinding crimson flashes from the muzzles of the guns, the heavy clouds of black and yellow smoke, the spurts of flame immediately over, under, and both sides of you, while the clouds of acid vapours swirled around you like the breath of volcanic eruption, and you can perhaps imagine what it was like.

During all this bedlam, I tried to keep track of the fall of the shells from my particular guns. It must be remembered that all these guns which roared together were confined on a ship which was less than five hundred feet long. We were a green crew, but we came through that ordeal with only one casualty, and that was myself.

The gun-layer of the after 12-pounder gun forgot what he had repeatedly been told—that was to see, before firing the gun, that the training " stop " was in. This " stop " was to prevent the gun being trained too far aft so it would not actually shoot over the after turret. When the ship altered course to give the guns on the disengaged side a chance at the target, the gun-layer of the particular gun I refer to was so intent on " following the target " that he didn't realize the ship was rapidly altering course, and he pressed the trigger just as the target passed astern. The blast from the charge blew me off the top of the turret and burnt all the hair off the back of my head. The gunner thought he had blown me into Eternity. He remembered his neglected duty and ran from his gun, horrified. He was found an hour later hidden in one of the hammock nettings moaning in his mental agony.

I never met anyone before who seemed so worried about my personal welfare. He was let off with a caution. I suffered nothing worse than a bad shaking, partial deafness, and a sprained shoulder. I fell onto the barrels of the two 6-inch guns when I disappeared off the top of the turret; it was a comparatively small fall to the deck when they shook me off as they recoiled with the next round they fired.

It was quite evident the permanent naval officers and men who formed the nucleus of our crew altered their opinion of the reservists before they had been shipmates very long. It was really astonishing the way these men adapted themselves to their new duties. They actually beat the other ships of the fleet with the speed with which they " coaled ship."

The first real job we got was to proceed and meet the first Canadian contingent and escort them to Plymouth.

It was originally intended they should disembark at Southampton, where all facilities were available, but information was received to the effect that the enemy had detailed some submarines to give them a warm reception. The effectiveness of submarines had been only too clearly demonstrated when the U 9 sank the *Hogue*, *Cressy*, and *Aboukir*. The plans for landing Canada's contribution to the Empire's forces were altered and we took them into Plymouth instead. The morning before we met the fleet of transports, we were almost torpedoed ourselves. It was a beautiful day and everything seemed so calm and peaceful. Suddenly one of the look-outs yelled, " Torpedo on the port beam."

I was standing on the shelter deck by the 12-pounder guns and the track was plainly discernible as the " tin fish " rushed through the water towards us. The torpedo was well aimed, and nothing we could have done would have prevented a hit. By some miracle, the thing stopped about a hundred feet short, bobbed to the surface, and then sank. Perhaps it was because Fritz had tried a long shot, and the supply of compressed air, which propels these engines of destruction, failed before it reached us.

The experience was a valuable one, for it made us all more alert. We realize now that danger can lurk hidden in the most peaceful surroundings. We are really at war.

It was a wonderful sight to see the thirty transports come into view over the horizon. Transports that carried a completely equipped army of thirty thousand men. As we steamed towards them, our makeshift band played " The Maple Leaf Forever," and the Canadians responded by singing at the tops of their voices " Rule Britannia." I got a real thrill when I heard the two tunes played. I know it affected everyone else the same way. It was a touching scene, these sons of Britain returning home to defend the Motherland.

Sunday evening found them all safely moored or anchored in the harbour. The people of Plymouth certainly gave them a right royal reception.

One fellow got into trouble for jumping overboard and swimming ashore. He explained afterwards that he only wanted to be able to claim he was the first one to land.

December 1914.

" Well, we belong to the bleedin' nivy at larst," as the Cockney seaman so aptly put it. We dropped anchor in Scapa Flow yesterday. We are a unit of the 7th C.S. (Cruiser Squadron) attached to the Grand Fleet.

I intended to write this diary every day, but so much has happened that a summary must suffice. Rumour had it when we left Plymouth that we were destined for the chilly North, but we headed South instead. We were sent to chase German raiders. We dashed about here, there, and everywhere, looked the Canary Islands over, then the Azores, but we couldn't catch anything other than colds. We just missed capturing an enemy ship which was, or had been, acting as a collier to the *Karlsruhe*. She managed to reach neutral waters just before our shells reached her. The enemy cruiser was sinking ships right in our vicinity, but our luck was dead out. We were on our tip-toes night and day expecting trouble. We often chased smoke, but nothing happened. Our biggest job in this man's war is coaling ship. We are at it all the time, both at sea and in port.

We visited Sierra Leone . . . and coaled ship. The temperature was 110 degrees in the shade. The only shade was where the thermometer was hung. If Hell is any more uncomfortable than coaling ship in Sierra Leone, I'll seriously consider improving my ways.

We managed to go ashore and stretch our legs for awhile.

Some of the troops developed such a thirst coaling ship, they tried to drink the place dry. There was plenty of work for the patrols. Strong liquor and tropical heat don't agree with the average constitution.

We stopped cursing when we heard that the coal we'd stuffed in our bunkers was to take us south to join Sturdee. Cradock has to be revenged and Admiral Sturdee is the right man to do it. We started cussing all over again when, after racing south for several days, we received the news that he'd polished off the enemy without waiting for our assistance. I don't know just how to describe the feelings of the men, but I honestly think they are mad enough to fight all Sturdee's squadron should we meet. They feel like people do when they've rushed down town to see a show, only to find the seats are all sold out before they arrived.

If the "powers that be" were wise, they'd land this outfit in France and give them about two weeks in the trenches so they could blow off steam. Keeping the crew cooped up aboard a ship after so many disappointments makes me feel as if I was sitting on top of a volcano just before it is due to go off. Turning the ship around and sending her straight from the tropics to this hell-hole of cold, mists, and gales hasn't helped sweeten the tempers of the crew in the least. What happened when we arrived here put the climax on everything.

We had the colliers alongside almost before the anchors were down. We started to coal ship. It wasn't long before we realized that we were junior ship of the squadron. We finished coaling ship about eight bells in the afternoon watch (four o'clock). We washed down and had just started to eat our dinners and read our mail when we received orders to "put to sea and report on the weather." That is what it means to be junior ship of a squadron.

Just as darkness was shutting out as dreary a scene as it is possible to imagine, we steamed between the anti-submarine nets, out past the barren headlands, into the Pentland Firth.

The wind had risen until it was blowing a full gale from

HELL'S ANGELS OF THE DEEP 151

the north-west. Our task was to patrol around the Orkney Islands and report the condition of the weather every hour. Why? God alone knows.

The sky was black and murderous-looking. The wind shrilled and shrieked through the rigging. It sounded as if the very elements were giving us the "horse laugh." As we left the protection of the harbour and made the eastern entrance of the Pentland Firth, we passed, in less than five minutes, from waters which were comparatively calm into a raging maelstrom. The wind and the sea were against the tide, and the waves were so confused that they piled aboard from every direction.

The whirlpools threw the armoured cruiser around as if she had been a dory. I was sent aft to read the log just as we straightened away from the "Barrel of Butter."[1] I had made my reading and turned to race for'ard when the old tub buried her stern right down into a beauty. Instinctively I threw myself flat and held tight to the after companion ladder, which was lashed to the quarterdeck. It was lucky I did. The cold waters surged up and over me to the depth of several feet. I could feel them tugging at me like arms of giant strength. I held on grimly. I experienced no confusion of thought. I remember thinking that I must hold my breath until I felt the pressure of the water growing less. I even struggled to force my legs between the rungs of the ladder so as to keep the water from lifting them above my head. I opened my eyes, but everything was dark. Just as I felt it was impossible to hold my breath a second longer, the stern rose clear again and I felt the propellers racing clear of the water. The wind took hold of my oilskins and turned them inside out. I heard a voice yelling, "Man overboard." But I wasn't. I scrambled to my feet and raced for the shelter of the after-bridge, proud of the thought that I still remembered the log reading. I informed the sentry who had given the alarm that I was still one of the crew and made a similar report to the fore bridge.

The ship trembled from stem to stern as she bucked the wind and seas all night. About 3:00 A.M. the fore-topmast went by the board; we were reporting the weather by W/T

[1] A light marking the entrance to Scapa Flow.

as ordered. Fortunately none of the crew was killed. She had rolled her " Sticks " out of her.

We reduced speed and hove-to until we had cleared away the wreckage. We worked in water waist deep. The wind howled the louder, as if gloating over the damage done. It was like a concert in Hades. Men tugged here and chopped there ; they cursed and swore as only seamen can. As the last wires were cut and the wreckage floated clear, we resumed our course and proceeded into harbour. The first signal we received was—

" Flagship to D——— :

" Explain why you stopped sending signals ? "

Ain't war Hell ?

January 1915.

We were nearly in action since I wrote last time. We finished coaling and "stepped" a new topmast, when we were ordered to sea with the whole of the Grand Fleet. I never saw a more impressive sight.

On the evening of December 15th we received the message which put life into the slumbering might of the British Navy. One moment those hundreds of ships looked like big lazy cattle, fast to tethering chains in a pasture ; the next they were like greyhounds, straining at their leashes, and a moment later they were a pack in full cry.

We must have a wonderful secret service. Some extraordinary messages come through. I am acting decoding officer for awhile and I saw messages which told how many hours' notice the enemy fleet were at. One message in particular told of a certain German Admiral going aboard another ship to dine and mentioned that the fleet reverted to two hours' notice following the visit. When that happens, we usually go to sea. We try to be one jump ahead of the enemy all the time.

This sweep down the North Sea initiated us into our duties with the Grand Fleet. The old heavy cruisers of our class are called " Mine-bumpers." We are of deep draught and we spread ourselves out ahead of the fleet. If there is any trouble in the way, such as hidden minefields, submarine ambushes, etc., we find it.

To be at the head of anything is deemed an honour. Ours

MY GUN CREW AT THE
OUTBREAK OF HOSTILITIES

seems to be a path of glory, but it leads most surely to the grave . . . a watery one.

Perhaps if we are allowed to live long enough we may adjust ourselves even to this sort of life. I have already experienced the worst feeling a human being can possibly be subjected to. I refer to the infernal wait . . . wait . . . wait, waiting for something to happen. What an awful sensation it is. I don't know how to describe it, but it isn't fear.

While we were waiting for the enemy to appear this last time, I tried to analyse that feeling. The nearest thing I can liken it to is an experience I once had standing outside the headmaster's study door, not knowing the nature of the visit. I stood there, waiting and wondering, not knowing if I was to receive praise or punishment. It is the same thing at sea. It is the suspense—the uncertainty—that " gets " you . . . not fear. It is the fact that the enemy is unseen ; their plans unknown ; the deadliest dangers hidden. I would, and I know every jack man aboard this ship would, glory in a real honest-to-goodness scrap. Out in the open, ship to ship, man to man if it were possible. I don't think I'd mind dying in the open. It would be better than dying in bed with a lot of relatives sobbing and weeping all around you, but one hates to be blown to Eternity in a second without knowing what blew you there and with never a chance of taking the other fellow with you. The whole situation is unreal—nightmareish—if there is such a word.

What a night of tenterhooks that was ! We chased down through the pitch darkness with the engines going " all out." Down below the " black-gang " piled on coal until the funnels were literally red hot and stood out of the darkness like ghosts. What a wonderful and yet weird experience it was to feel this ship vibrating from stem to stern under the powerful impulse of her engines ; to feel her screws grip the water and pull her stern down deeper as they increased their revolutions until she was going three knots faster than her builders ever intended, or her boilers were tested to stand. " Hell bent for leather," or " Hell bent for election," is how the men put it.

Then also there was the knowledge that the enemy was

somewhere in the darkness ahead. We knew the raiders would be speeding towards some town on the east coast, timing their arrival, most probably, for daybreak. We knew they would shell the chosen place and then race home again. It was our task to intercept them and prevent the raid, if possible, and if we failed in that, to cut them off and fight them next day.

We stood closed up at the guns all night, every man alert and ready, ready for night action in an instant. Not a light was showing except the tiny guide light housed in the stern of the next ship of the line ahead—this to keep station by.

The dawn broke dull and dismal, with fog-banks and low visibility. What any of those fog-banks held nobody could tell until we were through them.

During the afternoon we were told the enemy had shelled Scarborough. About noon the climax came.

The light cruisers scouting ahead reported sighting the enemy. A message flashed back warning them that a squadron of our own ships were expected to join us from the south. Back came the signal telling the number and class of the enemy. Then came the range—18,000 yards. Range dials were set; the guns swung round; the muzzles climbed to greater elevation.

Then came what? ... not action ... but fog. Fog which was thick and enveloped us like a blanket. For one unforgettable hour we raced blindly in the direction taken by the enemy. When the fog lifted, they were nowhere to be seen. We continued the mad race for the enemy coast. The squadron joined us from the south. We altered course and joined the Grand Fleet. Then the whole vast array of Britain's gigantic Navy deployed into battle formation and steamed majestically on, stretching from horizon to horizon, powerful giants of destruction, whose strength and effectiveness was yet only a matter of conjecture.

Night closed down once more as we neared the enemy minefields. With feelings of utter disgust we altered course and turned sixteen points.

While we were at sea an enemy U-boat, showing more initiative than others, managed to sneak into Scapa Flow. She is reported to have made a tour of the harbour and found nothing. On her way out her periscope was sighted by a drifter carrying meat to the ships of the fleet. The drifter was so close to the periscope when it bobbed up that the skipper took a swipe at it with an axe which stood handy. He smashed the top mirror, and rendered it useless.

The U-boat, one of the older type, having only one eye, floundered about scared to come up for fear of the fire of the forts. Finally she ran ashore trying to feel her way blindly through the channel. She was captured intact.

It is a hell of a life up here. The senior officers keep us busy. Every now and again we have general drill for the whole squadron. The other day we " exercised " abandon ship stations and none of us has recovered from the ordeal.

" Jock " pulled his latest gag. We have done nothing but laugh ever since. I hear he is to be court-martialled.

Jock is the sub-lieutenant who joined us from the Army when in barracks, and the truth is that by nature he can't stand inactivity. He is much the same type as Mickey, only he is Scotch. You might as well capture a full-grown lion and train it to watch a mouse-hole in your house and expect it to be happy, as shut Jock up in an outfit like this. He is not happy and he is determined to break away from this ship. He certainly helps cheer us up a whole lot. He is continually acting the fool " trying to work his ticket." It takes a lot of courage to do what he did the other day, and yet there are some on board this packet think him crazy. If he is crazy, I am first cousin to " Mad Harry." But to get back to the general drill.

One of the evolutions we were ordered to carry out was " Abandon Ship." All those who have been detailed to boats (about 10 per cent of the crew) go to them as soon as the order is given. The rest of the ship's company stand-by and assume as comfortable a position as possible to drown in. I have charge of the first cutter and Jock the third. Just as we manned our boats, the signal was given from the Flagship, " Away all boats, pull around the Fleet." This is a good stunt. Every boat in the Fleet tries to be first back. The honour of winning the evolution goes to the ship which is first to hoist her boats to her davits again.

Away roared the boat falls. Splash into the water we went . . . and away. Not so Jock's boat. In some manner his after falls fouled. The bow of his boat went down, the stern stayed up. Most of his crew were shot into the water. Jock cut the falls and the stern went down with a thump. The boat righted herself, but she was half-full of water.

What happened next I'll remember if I live to be a hundred. The half-drowned crew scrambled back into their water-logged boat. Jock cursed them for a bunch of good-for-nothing imbeciles. He called them for everything he could lay his tongue to, and Jock can swear. He holds the gun-room championship. He swore for fifteen minutes during the last contest and never repeated himself once. That is one of the rules. If you repeat yourself while competing, you are disqualified. Jock first joined the Army and he benefited by his short experience listening to a regimental sergeant-major when he was on parade. In that manner he gained an advantage over us sailors. But to go on with the story.

He stood capless in the sternsheets and ordered the crew to their oars, then he tore off his monkey jacket and started to bail the water out of the boat. Senior officers stood speechless in amazement and paralysed with rage.

Jock was unconcerned. What others might think of his *conduct* was the last thought to enter his head. His mind was made up on one thing. He would drive that crew of his and arrive back first or one of the first. He would retrieve his honour. He thought nothing of naval dignity or procedure. Everything was shut out of that extraordinary brain of his except his determination to win.

Having bailed the water out of the boat, he coxed his men and speeded up their stroke. He was a comical-looking sight as he stood without cap or monkey jacket in his dirty wet shirt, waving his arms, coaxing, threatening, pleading, driving his crew of half-drowned men until his boat flew through the water as if it had an evinrude motor hidden in its stern. My men, and the crews of all the other boats (in a position to see the Sullivanic Opera stunt) laughed until their sides ached. They couldn't row. As Jock flashed past us, he was singing at the top of his voice :

"Pull, boys, pull, boys, pull for the shore,
Pull li-ke bloody Hell but don't break the oars."

Everyone was in convulsions ... either of rage or laughter.

One of my men collapsed with merriment and fell off the thwart. "What's the bloody Nivy come to now?" he gasped, as he huddled there, holding his stomach. What indeed? Many asked that.

Jock arrived back first. His antics all around the Fleet had much the same effect as laughing gas would have on his competitors. He rushed up the companion ladder and saluted the quarterdeck. The Commander was waiting to receive him. His stare was sufficient to have turned Vesuvius into an iceberg.

"Read that!" he thundered, thrusting a signal pad under Jock's nose. It read:

"From Admiral B——. To D——.

"Report immediately the name of that asinine fool in charge of your third cutter. Stop. As he only appears happy when making a hideous spectacle of himself, order him to pull round the Fleet again."

Jock read the signal in silence. His face flushed. Beckoning to the signal rating, who was standing at a respectable distance, he said, "Did the Admiral send that?"

"Yes, Sir!"

"Then take this signal."

"Sub-lieutenant P——. To Admiral B——.

"Replying to your signal. You are a blankety blank blank old fossil."

The Commander threw his arms in the air with horror. Never in the history of the Navy had such a thing been heard of. Jock was ordered into his boat. He pulled around the Fleet again. I think he has worked his ticket all right this time. The funny thing is everyone likes him. He's a hell of a fine fellow. The ship will be dead when he is gone.

January 15th.

Jock has gone. We gave him a farewell party. It should go down in naval history. What a night *that* turned out to be.

The party was held when we went to forty-eight hours' notice for cleaning boilers. That meant we could not be sent to sea for two whole days.

We needed the forty-eight hours, but it wasn't for cleaning boilers.

The steward went ashore and begged, borrowed, or stole everything we needed for a slap-up banquet. We were just about feeling " right " when dinner was announced. After the King was honoured, we started to go through the toast list, which was a yard long. It was " bottoms up " every time. By the time we reached " Sweethearts and wives " the oldest member of the mess could hardly respond. He was to say, " May they never meet," but what he wanted to know—" Wash-do-we-care-ifsh-they-do-meish." He was feeling very brave.

One sub-lieutenant jumped on top of the table to sing, " She was pure and she was simple . . . victim of a rich man's wiles." He forgot the deck-head is low and passed out of the picture. It was a rotten shame because I'd always wanted to hear the words of that pathetic little ditty.

Jock volunteered to sing and went to the piano. As he sat down I thought how often we had nearly lost our piano (every time we chased the enemy, the piano had been carted on deck, ready to be pushed overboard. Everything which will burn is dumped as soon as a ship goes into action so the fires can be more easily controlled). Jock struck some notes which sounded like a cross between a train coming to a sudden stop and a triple expansion engine which has developed hot bearings. He threw his head back and started to sing in a high nasal falsetto. I never heard anything so terrible. We all burst out laughing. Jock was singing in Chinese.

Suddenly the singing stopped. He whirled around on the piano stool. His face was serious as an owl's.

" Gentlemen, why do you laugh ? Don't you understand ? That is a most beautiful song. It is a Chinese love ditty thousands of years old. No English composer has ever compiled anything like it," he informed us, evidently quite hurt that we should think it funny.

Someone was heard to whisper, " Thank God." This made Jock mad . . . or sad. I don't just remember which. However, we allowed him to continue. He sang his song. He was tight as a Victorian corset and so were we all.

We smothered our faces in our handkerchiefs to drown our laughter while Jock wailed out the story of the Chinese Romeo and Juliet. When he turned round at the finish of his song, the tears were streaming down his face as they were down ours, but his were from emotion; ours from suppressed hilarity.

Jock had been brought up in Zululand when a child. I had heard him say he could dance the Zulu war dance and begged him to do it. When happy, he always becomes very thorough. He insisted on being a proper Zulu. We had to strip him and blacken his body with burnt cork and vaseline. This operation was done in a cabin, and every time we applied the cork without giving it time to cool off properly, Jock did a rehearsal of his war dance.

I never laughed so much in all my life. He was black and shiny. We had fixed him up with a fringe of a travelling rug for a loin cloth, a large serving tray for a shield, and one of the Captain's golf sticks for an assegai. The Chief Bos'on manufactured a head-dress while we were dabbing him with burnt cork. He looked a good Zulu or a bad one. It all depends which way you considered the question.

Finally we rushed him out into the half-deck. He crouched outside the gun-room door, waiting for the signal. To make sure that his entrance should be sudden and dramatic, one of the midshipmen stood behind him, and, when the word was given, jabbed him in the stern-sheets with a sail needle.

Jock bounded forward like a frightened deer and let a yell out of him which would have turned any real Zulu green with envy. He reached the centre of the gun-room in one bound. Then he started to dance and chant.

"Um-talla-um-talla-um-talla, etc., etc."

He danced slowly around his supposed victim, his step became faster, his chant louder and wilder. When he reached the climax, he hurled his spear in what would have been the death thrust.

Unfortunately his hands were slippery from perspiration and grease. The spear, or rather golf club, slipped out of his hand and crashed into the senior Sub's tummy, doubling him up for the moment with pain. If it is possible, Jock was more funny when he tried to apologize to the Sub, dressed up in his war-paint, than he was while singing his Chinese love ditty at the piano.

The doctors worked over me for two hours before they could make me stop laughing. I had them worried. They thought they were going to witness one instance where a fellow actually did kill himself laughing.

And now Jock has gone. Both he and I nearly made fools of ourselves when we said " Good-bye."

CHAPTER XIII

February 1915.

The last days of January brought with them another of those nerve-racking sweeps through the North Sea. We played another game of " Blind Man's Buff " with the enemy. We went off chasing " something "—" somewhere." We put in another day and a night of anxious waiting, petty grouching, lurid swearing, but at the finish came action. Short, brief, incomplete, but all the same it was some recompense for our time of waiting.

It is the damnable policy of secrecy which upsets the men's nerves more than anything else. They are never told anything. They do not know where they are, where they are going, or what they are doing. They surmise the enemy is out, but they don't know for sure. The " stunt " may be the " real thing " or it may be nothing but manœuvres.

They feel the ship shiver and shake as she is driven along at full speed. They spend hours closed up at action stations or sleep alongside their guns. They have heard the cry " Wolf . . . Wolf " so often they begin to grow indifferent. It is wonderful that the morale of the men remains as good as it does. If it were only possible to take them into one's confidence and tell them something of what was expected or what was planned, it would make a big difference.

This sweep ended different for some of the ships. It wasn't so much a battle as a game of hare and hounds.

The battle cruiser squadron intercepted the enemy raiders as they raced home. They engaged them in action. We received the news and raced on, hoping to become engaged in the battle. At noon the enemy cruiser *Blücher* was reported out of action and sinking, but then we heard the *Lion*, Admiral Beatty's flagship, was also hard hit and out of the action. Now we are back in harbour, queer rumours are flying about. In my opinion they should be confirmed or denied. Some say that after the *Lion* was knocked out of action, another Admiral ordered the battle cruiser squadron to turn sixteen points. Beatty, seeing this manœuvre, ordered them to turn sixteen points again, but it was too late. The range had increased too much. The rest of the enemy fleet escaped.

The other rumour is to the effect that as Admiral Beatty transferred his flag from the *Lion* to the *Princess Royal*, he ordered his signal staff to make the signal " closer action." It is said that this order was misunderstood and interpreted as " Close action." I don't suppose the truth of the case will ever be made known. Whatever the truth is, the fact remains we had the Germans where we had often tried to get them, and they got away with the loss of one ship.

The *Blücher* put up a splendid fight. Disabled, outgunned, out-numbered, she fought to the bitter end. According to reports, she hit the destroyer *Meteor* right in the boiler-room with the last round she was able to fire, and she only just missed one of our light cruisers with a torpedo a moment before she rolled over on her beam-ends.

She was on fire fore and aft and actually sinking when she fired these last rounds. Her crew behaved magnificently. They lined up on the slippery side and held hands after she rolled over on her beam-ends. She went down defiant to the very last, flags flying. When you see this kind of thing, it makes you wonder if newspaper men are just naturally born liars or if they are working for a purpose. As far as I can see, the Germans are darn good sailors and courageous as the devil. They don't lie down till they are knocked out. What I can't understand is the policy of the Zeppelin and the Taubes which bombed our ships and boats when they were attempting to rescue the survivors of the *Blücher*. I wonder if these things will be thrashed out after the war?

I hate to admit it, and yet I personally agree with the policy of the Hun. There is only one purpose in going to war, and that is to bring the other power to submission by inflicting the greatest possible losses in the least possible time. Chivalry has no place in war to-day. It is just plain scientific killing, cold, calculated, bloody murder. It is, more so now than ever, what Sherman called it—Hell. To look for sentiment or virtue in Hell seems ludicrous. To employ half-measures in battle is only prolonging the agony. War has so vastly increased its scope that it includes the whole population of warring nations. Are not the miners,

HELL'S ANGELS OF THE DEEP 163

ship-builders, munition workers, both men and women, as dangerous to the enemy as the man with a rifle at the front? Is there any reason why it should be considered quite right and proper to shell Army Service transports when within a few miles of the front line, and consider ocean transports as non-combatants and only subject to capture after visit and search because they are a few hundred miles further away from the recognized scene of action? The whole thing savours of nonsense to me.

I was sitting up in the fore-top last time at sea, and I tried to define the word "war." The dictionary calls it, "A contest between nations," "the profession of arms," "Art of war." I thought of a better definition:

"War is the self-inflicted punishment suffered by humanity because they have refused to settle their differences according to the precepts of Christianity."

March 26th, 1915.

I didn't write much last month, but what happened yesterday gave me fresh ambition. It was Sunday, Easter Sunday, and while most of the folks at home were still in church, I witnessed one of the most thrilling dramas possible to imagine. I saw the sinking of U 29. Report has it that she was commanded by Lieutenant Otto Weddigen, who sank the *Hogue*, *Cressy*, and *Aboukir* last September.

What happened was this. We were doing manœuvres. The Admirals were exercising their brains instead of allowing us a nice quiet Sunday to exercise our souls. I'm that august person known aboard the ship as "Captain's doggie." The term requires little explanation. I'm the midshipman who runs here and there to do the Captain's bidding. I carry his personal messages and orders to those they concern.

Not having anything to do on this particular occasion, I was trying to shoot some pieces of pitch down the neck of the midshipman of the watch. He was on the lower bridge while I was up on "Monkey's Island" with the Captain. The Captain couldn't have been keeping a very good lookout for submarines, for he "twigged" what I was doing and ordered me to the mast-head for punishment. Thanks to his lack of humour, I had a bird's-eye view of all that happened during the next half-hour.

A signal came through from some ship well ahead of the Fleet saying she *thought* she had seen a submarine's conning-tower on the horizon, but it had disappeared. That was sufficient to put everyone on the alert. I know some pretty rash promises were made to our crew by the Captain. He said that the first man to sight the enemy's periscope would be given a decoration, an extra tot of rum, and as far as he was concerned, he could marry a wife in every port for the duration of the war. Naturally everyone was "on their toes," so to speak.

I was perched up as near to Heaven as ever I'm likely to be, and it was cold enough to freeze . . . well, you know what sailors say.

The 7th Cruiser Squadron were stationed on the port side of the battle fleet and a little in advance. Destroyers and light cruisers were outside of us again. We were screening the capital ships from attack. Look-outs were doubled. Thousands of human eyes were looking for the one single artificial eye of that submarine. Suddenly it bobbed up right close to the first line of battleships . . . too close. U 29 had overrun her distance.

The *Dreadnought* turned out of line. Her ram ploughed under and into the "Fritz." The submarine was lifted up and right clear of the water. She seemed to literally roll up the bows of the big battleship. Many of us could see the number—U 29—painted on the conning-tower. She seemed suspended for a moment, then she broke in half and sank, one half either side of the bows. There were no survivors. So died Weddigen and his crew. It was this officer who, when in command of the U 9, sank the *Hogue*, *Cressy*, and *Aboukir*.

He had made a daring attack, one which might have caused us severe loss had it not been that he overran his distance by a few hundred yards. If he had come up outside the escorting cruisers, it does not seem possible that he could have missed hitting some of the ships. He was the type who was willing to take chances when the prize was big enough. He tried to make certain of a battleship and luck was against him. I guess his motto must have been "Aut vincere aut mori."

April 1915.

The whole ship's company are wild with delight . . . delirious with joy. We can't believe our good fortune. As I write, we are steaming south, bound for Plymouth. The news came unexpectedly. Out of all the hundreds of ships attached to the Grand Fleet, this old tub has been singled out for special duty. Nobody seems to know just what it is and nobody cares. The main thing is we are away from that awful spell of the dreary North. We have broken, even if only for a time, the terrible monotony. We will exchange, if only for a single day, the cold damp mists and the bleak cold winds of the North for the warmth and sunshine of Devon's Spring days.

April.

It is less than a week since I wrote in these pages. Things happen quickly in this ruddy war. One hectic, glorious evening with my friend Miss S—— in Plymouth, and now we are at sea again bound for Halifax, with 5,000,000 pounds in gold to sweeten our credit with the U.S.A. That is what we went to Plymouth for. Uncle Sam required another little anti in this game of war.

Afternoon tea in the Palm Court of the Royal, one glorious hour on the Hoe, sitting together where midshipmen of two centuries ago sat, telling the same old story to the girls who bade them " God Speed " when they set out to challenge the might of Spain ; early dinner, the first house at the show . . . then we went to the Royal for supper. How I hated to tear myself away, but we were due to sail at noon and I was down on the duty book for the forenoon watch.

May 1915.

We are back at Scapa Flow with the Grand Fleet. Our trip to Halifax is a thing of the past. It was accomplished without incident. The only thing which happened was the fact that the *Lusitania* was sunk in our vicinity on our way across. We were ordered to remain on our course. It is evident the enemy mean business with their submarines.

I got myself very much disliked in the mess because I took the stand that the enemy were justified in their policy of sinking all ships they found in the blockade zone. I feel that times and conditions of war have changed. It is no longer possible to fight a war like we were taught to play cricket. In the old days, victory was decided when the Army or Navy of one country or combination of countries beat the armed forces of the other group. Nowadays everyone is involved in the war. Women and girls make munitions in the factories. It seems a lot of nonsense to say that the enemy must wait until those shells are over in France and actually being fired before they can try and destroy the "dumps."

It is the same thing with ships. The *Lusitania* might have been carrying passengers this trip as claimed, but she could be sent to sea as an armed cruiser next trip, or as an Army transport. Hundreds of other passenger ships have been turned into armed cruisers. They are the very ships used for blockading Germany in the hope that we can starve her into submission the same as she is trying to starve us.

It is the same old grind all over again. The monotony is becoming awful. There is just one ray of hope, that is the chance that we may be down for refit. The ships are beginning to go to dockyard in turn. They are away about two weeks. Then again there are possibilities of changes in our mess. We are all about due for promotion. I wonder where Fate will move me to then?

We do what we can to keep cheerful. We even played a game of rugby the other day. It was played on the island. Grass had never grown there. The "field" was covered with broken-down heather and thick with mud. I'll never forget that game. I hear they are using gas at the front. The troops have my sympathy. I think all the opposite side, mainly composed of stokers, had forgotten to shave and they most certainly had eaten onions for lunch and washed them down with issue rum. No gas attack could have been nearly half as bad as those scrum-downs. What a life!

About the only branches of the Naval service which seem to see any real action are the men who serve in destroyers or submarines, but they say the losses suffered in our submarine service are terrible. Everyone admires the feats these vessels have performed in the "Bight," in the Baltic, and in the Sea of Marmora, but they call it the "Suicide Club."

HELL'S ANGELS OF THE DEEP 167

I receive letters regularly, but it is impossible to write much of a letter in return when every line is read by the ship's censor and he happens to be the "Sky Pilot." That's why I write in my diary. It is a great pleasure to write one's thoughts and it passes away many weary hours.

Life here in the Grand Fleet has settled down to a round of drills, patrols, football, and binges. It's a wonder the morale of the officers and men stands up to such conditions, cooped up as they are, day in and day out, on the same ship, seeing the same faces, hearing the same voices, talking the same tommy-rot. It is no wonder some of them go mad. A sentry on board the *Hampshire* blew out his brains last night while doing duty on the after shelter deck.

September 1915. *Somewhere up North.*

I have neglected to write in this diary for several months. To tell the truth there has been little to write about. I'm fed up. Drill . . . drill . . . drill . . . patrol . . . patrol . . . binge . . . binge . . . binge . . . the whole damn world's gone crazy.

January 1st, 1916. *In Cromarty.*

Christmas has gone, and so has H.M.S. *Natal*. The Powers-that-be do try and give us what relief they can from the monotony of life in the Grand Fleet. They send down different squadrons and base them here for a few weeks at a time. We go route marches, have sham battles, and play football.

When not engaged in anything more strenuous the officers congregate in the local hotel and make love to Dodo. She should go down in history as the most courted girl that was ever born. Dodo is an extremely nice girl and would make a wonderful diplomat had she been a man. She is pretty, and Scotch, and she manipulates the handles behind the bar of the Cromarty Hotel. What is more, she governs the domain over which she rules with a quiet, dignified discipline which is truly marvellous. She holds court every day and receives the advances and homage of hundreds of men, some of whom have not seen or mixed with the opposite sex for months at a time, and she handles them just as if they were her humble subjects. It is rather amusing to watch the rivalry which exists between some of the hotter young bloods. Just about the time jealousy is ripe to run riot, Dodo will look at the clock and remind them that the duty boats will be alongside waiting to take them off to their ships again. Thus a serious situation is saved until the next occasion.

I met an old friend of mine, who is now assistant paymaster while here. Through him I met the Georges and their two very charming daughters. We spent many happy afternoons at their house.

The real high light of our visit to Cromarty was the "Battle of the Firth." Somebody sighted a submarine's periscope in the harbour. Of course, it wasn't a periscope, but the report of such a thing was sufficient to cause all kinds of excitement. The first thing that happened was a big " B-A-N-G." A gun-layer, with visions of earning a medal and a week's leave, fired his 12-pounder at what he thought was the submarine's periscope. In reality it turned out to be an empty whiskey bottle floating in the harbour. But shells have strange habits. The one he fired ricocheted off the water and ploughed through the roof of a cottage ashore. In the cottage a babe was sleeping peacefully, and it was still asleep and unharmed when the horrified mother returned to find the cottage in ruins.

While this was going on, the midshipmen of all picket-boats and steam pinnaces had been ordered " to sea." Golly, what a thrill I got when I went to war on my own for the first time in command of the *D*——'s picket-boat. We had a little pea-shooter of a gun mounted for'ard and some cans of gun-cotton aft, but I doubt if Admiral Jellicoe felt prouder when he was given command of the Grand Fleet than I did that day.

Off to sea we went, dashing madly for the harbour entrance, through the anti-submarine defences we swarmed like a pack of hounds hot on the trail of their quarry. But once through the gates, we were ordered into proper formation. It was a sight to see those picket-boats obey the signals and form into sub-divisions, line abreast and spread out over the whole surface of Cromarty Bay. We went ten miles out to sea and then turned sixteen points and returned to harbour, keenly alert for sign of that " Fritz." We were doomed to disappointment.

HELL'S ANGELS OF THE DEEP 169

The senior officer, being a good sport, ordered us each to lower a depth charge and explode it as we converged on the harbour entrance. Over went the cans, the electrical contacts were made, and boom went the gun-cotton charges. The depth charges stunned all kinds of fish and brought them floundering to the surface. We all circled and worked like galley slaves for fully ten minutes. My picket-boat's crew secured enough fish to supply the officers' mess and the messes to which the men in my boat belonged, with a good meal.

But close upon the fun came tragedy. Christmas came, and as always happens, we went to sea on patrol. When we returned, we celebrated. The officers onboard H.M.S. *Natal* (which ship had incidentally just returned from refit), in order to show their appreciation to the citizens in Invergordon and Cromarty for the kindness and hospitality they had shown to the men of the Fleet, invited them onboard with their families to afternoon tea, after which a moving picture was to be shown. The party was held yesterday, December 30th.

The guests were all aboard. The liberty men from the ship had been landed, when suddenly we heard the bugles sound and the bells ringing for " fire stations " aboard the *Natal*. All eyes turned on the ship. Sooner than it takes to relate the stern seemed to open right across. A flash of flame shot straight up into the sky. The *Natal* rolled over and sank before our eyes. All boats went to the rescue, but the only members of her crew who had a chance were those on the upper deck. The vast majority were imprisoned down below. And in the half-deck were nearly a hundred women and children and some nurses from one of the hospital ships. They died where, a moment before, they had been laughing heartily at a comic moving picture.

All kinds of rumours are rife as to what caused the explosion. Some claim it was the work of spies ; others say a working party was down the after magazine and that the fire originated there. I don't suppose we will ever learn the truth. My task as midshipman of the second cutter is to get up at daylight and search the harbour for bodies which might escape from the steel tomb in which they are imprisoned.

Divers went down to try and remove the bodies. One man actually made his way into the half-deck and then discovered his lines had fouled owing to the strong tide and current. He was imprisoned with the bodies for nearly four hours. When he was finally rescued, he was nearly out of his mind.

It must have been a terrible and nerve-racking experience to be tangled up down there as helpless as a fish in a net, while the bodies of dead men, women, and children floated towards him out of the murky semi-darkness. One of the divers who took part in the rescue explained that when the gases formed inside the victims, they rose as high as they could, and failing to find an exit, drifted around under the influence of the tide. He told me that while he worked to clear the other diver's air-line, a woman in a nurse's uniform came floating towards them. She was practically in a horizontal position, her hair a tangled mass in wild confusion, her hands outstretched as if dumbly pleading for aid. She moved slowly under the gentle influence of the tide and currents which found their way through portholes. She came closer and closer until her body brushed against theirs, and the imprisoned man struggled to fight it off. A truly gruesome and horrible experience. It is hard to realize just what an awful catastrophe the sinking of the *Natal* was to the people of Inverness, Invergordon, and Cromarty. In some cases nearly whole families were wiped out.

April 5th, 1916.

Three months have elapsed since last I wrote in these pages. A year of dull monotony, soul-destroying inactivity. I have taken up boxing to keep from going insane. To-day I received news that I had been promoted to Acting-sub-lieutenant-acting. The date of the promotion was April 1st. All Fools' Day. Perhaps that is why there is so much of the acting-acting.

Because we have been at war (I write of the permanent officers of the Royal Naval Reserve) midshipmen have not been promoted, owing to the fact under the conditions of warfare we have been unable to comply with the regulations and pass the necessary Board of Trade examinations. On the other hand, men who were junior to us in the

Merchant Service are now in the Navy as sub-lieutenants and acting lieutenants because they stayed where they were until they had passed the B.O.T. examinations. We put in a petition, pointing out the injustice of the whole thing, about a year ago, but it has only taken effect now. We have a midshipman aboard who has served as Second Mate on passenger ships of the B.I., and I think he is the one and only grey-headed midshipman in the whole naval service. His name is Sanderson. Now we have all been made Acting-sub-lieutenants-acting. Whatever that is ? We understand it means a rise in pay.

However, we all feel like the Israelites must have done when they were delivered from bondage. It is funny, but I had just succeeded in working my ticket when the promotions came through. I am being sent down to the Naval Hospital at Haslar for an operation on my nose. I have been suffering from catarrh for more than a year. I don't think the crack I got from the German sailor when I was serving aboard the *Dacre Castle* did my nose any good.

May 1916.

I have had my operation. I feel fine. I am back in barracks awaiting disposal. I heard to-day from Lieut.-Commander Addison (disposal officer) that I was booked for the *Virginian*. I don't want to go to her. She is an armed merchant cruiser up North on blockade patrols. I want to get into submarines, or destroyers, or mystery ships, anything so long as it promises some excitement. I told Addison so. I would far rather be a dead corpse than a live one.

May 1916. *Aboard the* Virginian.

It was no good. I am here. She is a fine ship and all the best accommodation is still intact. I have a fine cabin, with the first decent bunk to sleep in since I left home in 1911.

From what I hear, the hardest job anyone has aboard this ship is to keep wine bills within the five pound limit, as laid down in the regulations. We do six weeks at sea, up North, and two weeks in port, Liverpool. I feel like a prisoner just released from jail. When at sea, I understand I will keep watch with a midshipman on one of the guns until it comes my turn to go away with an armed guard. We send in all ships we meet for examination if they haven't what is known as the " green clearance form."

I hear a lot of yarns about this armed guard business. Some of the neutral ships have been intercepted by U-boats after the armed guards were placed onboard. The armed guards were taken prisoners. Other ships' crews overpowered the armed guards and took them to Germany, irrespective of whether they liked the idea or not. On the other hand, I have also heard of some good stunts pulled by our own men who took their ships into port under hardships almost unbelievable. Three small fishing boats were captured off the coast of Iceland. They were German with German crews. They were sent to Lerwich under armed guard. A midshipman named Lea (if I have it right) was on one of the smacks. They ran into bad weather. Two of the boats foundered. The other managed to make port, but what a harrowing tale of hardships the crew had to tell.

They were short of water and food for nearly two weeks. They had to limit the supply of drinking water to a cigarette tin lid per man each day. They had salt herring on board, but to have eaten them would have driven them crazy with thirst. Finally they used the herring as bait and lured some gulls within range of their rifles.

I have a hunch that my luck is going to turn and that I am going to have an adventure or so before long.

June 6th, 1916.

Stirring events have happened since I last wrote in these pages. I wonder if England in her whole history has experienced such a chapter of catastrophes in so short a period of time ? First there was the battle of Jutland. According to the official statement issued by the Admiralty the enemy put it all over us like a blanket during the scrap. Personally I don't believe a word of that message. It was either a hoax or a damned lie. If it is neither a hoax nor a lie then it is a deliberate plan calculated to remove Admiral Jellicoe from his command. I don't know and I can't figure the matter out. Neither can anyone else aboard this ship for that matter. There is only one ray of sunshine in the whole dark picture, and that is the faith all officers and men have in Admiral Jellicoe. They refuse point-blank to believe our fleet were given the worst of the argument.

The dastardly report issued by the Admiralty might well have destroyed the morale of the entire Navy. It would have done so, if the officers and men had been made of less stern stuff. The person who was responsible for the sending of that signal should be shot, nothing an irresponsible nincompoop might have done could have played more surely into the hands of the enemy.[1]

I was on duty about midnight when we received the wireless message. I read it and was absolutely flabbergasted. I took it to the officer of the watch and kept the bridge while he went into the chart-room to read it. I'll never forget his remark when he came out of the chart-room. He was furious.

"If that's your idea of a joke G—— D—— your soul I'll . . . I'll . . ." But he couldn't finish what he wanted to say.

I assured him that it was no joke, but was the actual message received over the air. The O.O.W. sent for "Sparks" (the wireless operator). He fumed and he raved but Sparks assured him it was no hoax. Still he didn't believe the message was real, and to test us out he ordered me to take the message and show it to the Captain, who was asleep in his cabin. I did as I was ordered.

When I woke Captain S—— and handed him the signal he blinked and rubbed his eyes and then read it again. It was plain to see he was trying hard to believe he was dreaming. He read it over again and muttered aloud: "The Grand Fleet met and engaged the enemy High Sea Fleet off Jutland. The enemy retired after inflicting heavy losses." He read out the long tragic list of our losses. There was not a word about the enemy losses. Some of their ships had apparently been damaged, but according to the wording of the message only one inference could be drawn. The Navy

[1] I still feel the same way about this message which was sent out by some official at the Admiralty. It was worded so that it could only be understood to mean that the British Navy had suffered a severe defeat at the hands of the enemy High Sea Fleet. History has proved it to be wrong. Admiral Jellicoe stated personally at a recent naval banquet which I attended that he was never informed that the enemy fleet were passing to his rear. He stated definitely that had he received this information, Jutland would have ended differently.

... the British Navy ... the pride of the Empire ... had been beaten in battle by a vastly inferior fleet.[1]

Right on top of this ghastly piece of news came the signal reporting the loss of H.M.S. *Hampshire* with Lord Kitchener aboard. My ship was on patrol north-west of Orkneys that particular night. We were particularly interested in the *Hampshire's* course and speed because she was routed to pass near us in the dark hours of the night. The weather was stormy, but it was not so bad that boats could not have been launched had there been time. The officer who was on watch from midnight to four in the morning is of the opinion that the *Hampshire* went down after striking the North Shoal Rocks. We have no definite news as yet, but he seems convinced of this fact. He gives three reasons for his belief. First he argues that the weather was too rough for a submarine to have attacked her with a torpedo. No torpedo could have been expected to "run" in such a sea. Secondly, he claims that the water is too deep for moored mines. He claims that the enemy would never be so crazy as to attempt to moor mines in water more than a thousand fathoms deep. Drifting mines are harmless unless strung together, and the chances are that a string of floating mines would have blown up owing to being bumped together in the heavy sea.

His contention is that there would be an extraordinary set of both tide and current due to the weather conditions we had experienced during the days preceding the tragedy, and that if set and drift due to these extraordinary conditions were overlooked the *Hampshire* could easily have been wrecked on the North Shoal Rocks.

These rocks are a phenomenon of nature. They are situated off the west coast of the Orkney Islands and they don't show above the surface of the ocean at all when the sea is calm. In stormy weather all one can see is broken water in their vicinity. They are a very real danger during the hours of darkness during a storm. These rocks rise straight up from the bed of the ocean like church spires. The water all round them is a thousand fathoms deep.

---

[1] It is only fair to say that the loyalty of the officers and men was such that they refused to believe the message, and history has proved them justified.

Every officer aboard has figured out what allowance he would have made for set, drift, and leeway under the extraordinary weather conditions which had prevailed just prior to the loss of the ship. The officer who first voiced the opinion that the *Hampshire* might have been wrecked on the North Shoal Rocks proved his contention to my satisfaction when he received news that a number of her crew had been washed ashore on the island of Horta on a raft.

As soon as we received this news he worked the problem backwards to find out where the raft must have started from to drift ashore at that particular time with nothing to propel her but the wind and current.

It was an interesting experiment. He knew the exact time the raft was washed ashore, he also knew the exact position. He applied the same allowances for set and drift of tide and current which he had allowed in working out what, in his opinion, would have been the *Hampshire's* position had she steered the course reported to us by wireless. In other words, his contention was that the navigator of the *Hampshire* had not allowed sufficiently for the set and drift of tide and current which might be expected owing to the peculiar weather conditions experienced for the five days preceding the loss of the vessel. The raft having no means of propulsion was at the mercy of the wind and sea. The officer in question took the time which had elapsed between the time the *Hampshire* stopped using her wireless and the time the raft was washed ashore. He took what he considered would be the set of the tide and the drift of the current, he then applied the leeway due to the direction and force of the wind, and using this as the course and speed of the raft he applied it backwards from the position it had arrived ashore. Incredible as it may seem the position this gave him on the chart was near enough to the North Shoal Rocks to remove any doubts I personally may have had in regard to his theory at the beginning of the argument.

With the sinking of the *Hampshire* I lost many personal friends. She was one of the ships of the 7th Cruiser Squadron in which I had served while attached to the Grand Fleet. The nights the *Hampshire's* officers had dined aboard my ship or the officers of my ship had dined aboard the *Hampshire* stand out in my memory as red letter days. Now they have all gone to the port of missing ships. . . . Lord Kitchener, the strong man of the Empire, is dead. . . . It is my firm opinion that the double tragedy is due to an error of judgment and not an act of the enemy. The last few days have seemed more like a horrible nightmare than the cold stern realities of life . . . and death. The boarding boat's crew has just been piped away and it is my turn to take charge of the armed guard.

July 5th, 1916.

The ship I got was all right but her Captain was a Tartar. He was absolutely pro-German and I had to put him under arrest and bring the ship in myself.

I had hardly lost sight of the *Virginian* when he told me he was not going to stand for any interference from me in regard to the navigation of the ship. I had told him to slow down so that we could proceed full speed through the Fair Island Channel and make Kirkwall just about daybreak the following day. Submarines had been reported active in the Channel and it was foolishness to enter the narrow water during daylight when we could take our time while out at sea and speed through the danger zone under cover of darkness. I didn't tell him the why and wherefore. He was supposed to obey the instructions of the officer of the guard or refuse definitely to do so, in which case the officer of the guard assumed command of the ship.

After some argument, he gave the engine-room the necessary orders to reduce speed. It is customary for the officer of the guard to eat in the saloon of a neutral ship with the Captain. Naturally, when he enters the saloon to sit at the table, to break bread with him, he takes off his side arms and leaves them in his sleeping quarters. At the same time, for the sake of precaution he leaves his petty officer and one man as sentries on the bridge.

I had hardly sat down when the Captain of the oil-tanker said: " Tell you what—there's too much God damn red tape about you Britishers. You think you can do as you like, but mark my words, you're in for a trimming, and I hope to God you get it good and plenty. I wonder what the hell they think I am ? Do they think I'm going to stand for them sending a kid like you aboard my ship to tell *me*

H.M.S. *HAMPSHIRE* SUNK WITH
LORD KITCHENER ON BOARD

what to do. As far as I'm concerned, you don't exist. You hear that, Mister Mate? Neither you, nor any of my officers, take orders from this kid. You understand."

The Mate looked mighty uncomfortable. My blood began to boil. Angry words came to the tip of my tongue. Then I saw through the plan. If I quarrelled I was unarmed while at the table. If anything happened, the Captain would have several witnesses, I would have none. I stood up. I spoke as calmly as possible. " I am sorry, Captain, that you should see fit to act as you have done. Under the circumstances, I must decline the offer of your hospitality. Please excuse me." Saying which I left the table and went to the cabin allotted to me.

I buckled on my revolver, placed some ammunition in my pockets, and went on the bridge. I checked the course, told the petty officer what had happened, and waited. I placed one man behind the helmsman, one in each wing of the bridge and stood by the binnacle with the petty officer myself.

The Captain finished his meal and then climbed onto the bridge. I took the initiative. " Apart from your personal insults, do you intend to obey my instructions or do you not ? " I demanded.

" You can go to hell as far as I'm concerned," he replied, as he rang the telegraph to full speed ahead.

" You will go to your cabin. Consider yourself under arrest," I informed him, and added, " Should you or any of your crew attempt to resist, I will use what force I have at my command to overcome that resistance. Please consider carefully before you cause further trouble. Will you accompany me down to your cabin, or shall I have you removed forcibly from the bridge ? "

I never saw man so completely taken aback. He opened his mouth to speak, but words wouldn't flow. I did expect open resistance, but instead, when I took him by the arm, he went with me like a lamb. It was only when I closed the door of his cabin and turned the key in the lock that I heard him muttering threats about what his country would do when he reported the outrage to the authorities. I was past worrying over him. I placed a sentry on the cabin and took the bridge myself. Next morning we were in Kirkwall.

I landed with my prisoner, and when I marched into the

headquarters of the S.N.O. he greeted me cordially. I explained what had happened and reported the action I had taken. I will admit I was a little bit worried for fear I had exceeded my authority, but my fears were groundless.

"So, Captain, you've landed where I always thought you would one of these days. Every officer in charge of an armed guard who has had the misfortune to be placed aboard your ship has complained about your foul tongue and insulting behaviour. Now this officer has seen fit to take action. I am going to back him up to the limit. You will be sent to Edinburgh Castle. That will allow you time to cool off."

We found three Germans masquerading as Dutchmen aboard the ship when we examined the crew. They also were interned. They had faked passports and false identification papers, but they were easily trapped. They trapped themselves. They were asked where they lived in the States and where they lived in Holland before they went to the States. They were asked in a nice, friendly way the name of the street and the number of the house and many more questions besides. They each and everyone answered them promptly and without hesitation. The trouble was, they forgot what answers they had given the first time. When we started to ask the same questions all over again, they became confused and contradicted themselves.

Once you catch a man lying, it is strange how flustered he becomes and how easy it is to break him down and obtain the truth. When you tell him he can have the option of being interned as a prisoner of war in an internment camp or of being locked up as a suspected spy in the local jail, he usually comes across without much trouble.

I left Kirkwall for Scapa and from there went up to Busta Voe which is a base in the Shetlands. I stayed aboard the depot ship one day and went to sea on the *Alanza* the next. I was transferred back to the *Virginian* with my armed guard when we met at sea.

I had hardly arrived onboard before I was ordered away again. This time I picked a peach of a ship. She was a big Swedish vessel and she carried stewardesses. The Captain was as jovial an old sea dog as you ever wanted to meet. He was a real host, and there was nothing onboard too good for my guard and myself. We made a quick run into port and I was sorry to leave him. When I reported I was ordered to take my guard down to Liverpool and join my ship when she arrived.

"I KNOW NO FEAR"

To my Wife

LIKE the cold mists
  That on the waters lie,
Melt as the sun
  Bursts through, and clouds roll by;
All trembling doubts
  And fears that lurk the while
Soon disappear
  In the mem'ry of your smile.

I know no fear,
  For I can do no wrong,
While in my heart
  Love's flame does burn so strong,
Though sorrows come,
  I'll shed no tear,
But trust in thee,
  And know no fear.

And when the tempests,
  Raging wild and free,
Wreck fondest hopes,
  In the turmoil of life's sea,
I'll know no fear,
  It but awakes in me,
The burning passion,
  I do hold for thee.

And when shy moonbeams
  Fall in silv'ry spray
On the calm waters
  I will kneel and pray,
And hear, in the
  Soft whisp'rings of the breeze,
Thy loving answer
  Borne far across the seas.

CHAPTER XIV

WHILE waiting for the *Virginian* to arrive in port, I met quite a number of officers who had arrived with their armed guards. Amongst them was a sub-lieutenant who had quite a thrilling experience. The ship he was taking into port was stopped by a U-boat. The German submarine came close alongside, and her commander asked the Captain where the ship was bound, the nature of her cargo, if she had met the British patrols, and if he had an armed guard aboard!

The neutral Captain gave him answers, but they could hardly be called truthful. He was bound for Norway. He carried a general cargo. He had *not* met the British patrols. He did *not* have an armed guard onboard.

The German commander called back, "Throw over a ladder, I am coming onboard."

The Captain remained calm. He ordered the British sailors to discard their uniforms, climb into old jumpers or anything they could find which would fit them. They did as they were bid, and after dirtying their hands, wiped them across their faces to make themselves look more like the members of the neutral crew.

Aboard came the U-boat officer and he walked up and down the line of men. My informant told me his heart was literally in his mouth. Would every man amongst that crew stand by him? Would not one of them be pro-German and give the show away? In a kind of a dream he heard the Captain say to the U-boat officer, "If you wish I will line all the crew up properly, Mister Officer, so you can examine them. I must apologize that I no speak German, but only the Norwegian and the English."

This last show of confident indifference apparently assured the submarine commander that all was as it should be, for he climbed the rail and went down over the side to his boat again. It only needed one man aboard that ship favourable

HELL'S ANGELS OF THE DEEP 181

to Germany and the officer and his guard would have been prisoners of war. I record this incident to show how universally disliked Germany is becoming owing to the unrestricted nature of her U-boat campaign.

I do not want it to be thought that all Germans are inhuman, or, for that matter, that all her U-boat commanders are first cousins to His Satanic Majesty. Some of them are and some of them are not.

One of the 10th Cruiser Squadron picked up a ship's lifeboat the other day. There were five men alive in it and six dead. The rest who had left the ship in her had gone mad and jumped overboard and drowned themselves. This tragic group of survivors had been tossing about on the broad bosom of the North Atlantic for three solid weeks. Their ship had been torpedoed without warning hundreds of miles from the nearest land. When they were rescued, their tongues were black and swollen, their cheeks haggard and drawn, their minds on the verge of insanity. For one of the men, this was his third experience of U-boat warfare, having had two previous ships sink under him. It is to the eternal credit of the Merchant Service seamen that they carry on under such conditions of hardship and danger. If they refuse to carry on, the war is lost and the Empire is doomed. The outcome of this war rests in their hands. Should their courage weaken, the population of Britain will be without food in three weeks, the Navy without oil, the Army without food and supplies.

On the other hand, there is a jovial old pirate commanding one German submarine who looks his victim over and then comes up and warns the crew that they are his meat and must take to their boats. He then sinks the ship and sends a wireless message couched in these terms:

" U-. . . to all Allied ships on patrol:

" Sank the S.S. . . . in position so and so. The crew are in their boats. Hurry, you laggards. It looks as if it is coming on to blow."

He is a nice gentlemanly sort of pirate with a sense of humour. I wonder if he will retain his sense of humour if, one of these fine days, he runs up against one of our Q-boats? Personally, I don't think he will.

I have found out if you want to find any officer in Liverpool there is just one thing to do, and that is to follow the " Stations of the 10th C.S."

From the " Oriel " you go to the " Angel," from there to the " Three Feathers " and then on to the " St. George," the " Bear's Paw " and back to the " State." If you don't find him in one or other of those hotels and restaurants, you might find him in Bill Wakeham's office in the " Oriel " alleyway. Failing that, he must have a date with a lady friend and have gone off on his own.

Talking of lady friends, I have met an extremely nice girl. I have only one fault to find with her up to the present ; she is too popular with the officers of the 10th C.S. Rivalry is keen. I told Lieutenant J—— that I was going to eliminate all contestants for her favour and marry her. She is a nice girl and a thorough good sport. Miss Wright is her name and it brings the old song back into one's mind. It ran something like this, " When Wright married Wrong and Wrong married Wright."

We had a great time together at the " State " and the " Empire " each time I have been in port since I joined the *Virginian*.

My ship is familiarly called the " Virgin " by the officers of the 10th C.S. and their friends ashore, but every time I hear the ex-Allan liner referred to in this way, I think of the two little urchins who stood with their noses pressed against a window behind which were displayed some rare paintings. One was " The Virgin and the Child." The youngest urchin said to the other, " What is a virgin, Bill ? " The other replied, " What, yer don't know what a virgin is ? Why a virgin is a woman what hasn't got a husband." " Go on, yer don't mean ter tell me. Why, then, me mother's a virgin," replied the other proudly. I think the *Virginian* was just about as much entitled to the name " Virgin " as the poor woman whose love had exceeded her caution.

December 1916.

I have been negligent. All kinds of things have happened. The most important event was my marriage. I am going to submarines, and I didn't want to lose the companionship of Miss Wright. So we were married and she is going to Harwich with me.

Next in importance is my trip onboard the *H*——. She was a big fine sailing ship, once British owned, but sold to the Norwegians. She is as old as the hills. We intercepted her to the west'ard of the Shetlands and I was sent onboard to take her into Lerwick. My armed guard consisted of two stokers, two R.N.V.R. seamen (counter-jumpers before the war) and a good solid hard-boiled petty officer. One of the stokers was as round as he was tall. He was a good enough fellow, but he waddled like a duck, and was about as much use aboard a sailing ship as a fifth wheel to a coach.

It was November and blowing big guns that particular night when I heard " Away boarding boat's crew ! " The boarding boat's crew, incidentally, was about as tough a bunch of Newfoundland fishermen as ever were collected together. They were conceived and born in boats, and the rougher the weather, the better they liked it. They were proud as Lucifer of their record. They had never failed to board any ship the *Virginian* had met up with, irrespective of the weather conditions prevailing at the time. I made some trips with that crew of human seals, compared to which a ride on an unbroken broncho, or a flight with a stunt pilot in an airplane, would leave one cold.

This particular night the waves were mountains high. I never expected to see the boat get away from the *Virginian* without having its side stove in. When we neared the sailing ship, which was hove to, the problem was even more difficult. A steamer can make a lee. With a sailing ship it is different in that kind of weather.

One minute we were fifty feet up in the air looking down at the sailing ship, the next she was towering above us while we were down in the trough. No seas off Cape Horn were ever bigger than those we had North of the Shetlands that night.

The cruiser played her searchlight on the wild scene.

" I'm going to put you alongside. Heave your dunnage aboard and jump when I give the word," warned the coxswain of the boarding boat.

He gave the necessary order and steered closer. We were within a few feet and, for the second, level with the rail.

Everyone threw their bag. Up in the air we went, then down again.

"You hang on to your grip and wait, Sir. I can't put you all aboard at the same time," advised the coxswain.

"When I say 'Jump!'—jump," he warned the guard once more.

With great patience and skill, he worked the frail boat alongside and watched his opportunity. Suddenly it came. The boat rushed in, swept alongside level with the bulwarks, and the coxswain yelled "Jump!" Four men landed all of a heap aboard the deck of the sailing ship. "Tubby's" heart failed him at the last moment. He was still in the boat as we swept away to prevent being crushed under the keel.

"I'm going to do it again. When I say 'Jump!'—jump. You understand?" There was an ominous tone in the coxswain's voice, as he addressed the fat stoker.

He went through the whole manœuvre again. We swept alongside once more. I helped to hold Tubby on his feet. Up we went like a soaring pigeon; down we fell like a ton of bricks; then for one split second we wavered level with the rail.

"Jump!" yelled the coxswain, and Tubby jumped. He sailed through the air far and high. It was a wonderful jump. My only regret was that Tubby couldn't claim it for a record standing broad jump. It was a jump which has never been equalled in history. I was amazed, that is until I saw the end of a large-sized sail-needle protruding between the thumb and forefinger of the coxswain's left hand. He had given Tubby a firm prod in the stern-sheets when he gave the order "Jump!"

Now came my turn. I was clothed in oilskins and sea boots. In my grip was a change of clothes and a good uniform. We closed the sailing ship once more. Over went my grip. It fell short, hit the rail, and tumbled into the ocean. As we swept by, I made a frantic grab for it. I lost my balance and into the "ditch" I went also.

My first thought was that I would be knocked unconscious by the boat as she came crashing down on the next sea. I felt my feet against the side of the sailing ship. I was deep down under the water. I bent my knees and obtaining a good purchase with my feet against the side of the sailing ship drove myself upwards and outwards with all my power and strength. I rose outside the boarding boat and was quickly pulled back into her by the coxswain. I was furious. It was no time to play this comic opera stuff before a crew of neutrals. The next time I jumped, I landed on deck and to my keen satisfaction was able to keep my feet after I had landed on the slippery decks.

I made my way to the poop. The boarding boat pulled back to the cruiser. I informed the Captain of the *H——* that we would try to make Lerwick. His first question showed me he was antagonistic.

"Will you help me to make sail? I am short-handed and have three men sick in the fo'c'sle. Britishers are good seamen. I am indeed fortunate in having you come aboard."

I felt very small, indeed. I had always wanted to go in sail. If ever a man needed knowledge of sailing ships I needed it then. I knew that not one member of my armed guard would dare go aloft in weather like we were experiencing. I knew that if they went aloft they would only be in the way. They would have been just as completely lost up amongst those creaking yards and riggings as they would if they were turned loose in a jungle.

I told the Captain that my guard was not put on board to work the ship but to see she was navigated into the port of Lerwick.

I looked around for the *Virginian*. She was nowhere to be seen. She had been swallowed up by the darkness; we were alone on the ocean amongst mountainous seas.

I waited until the crew had made sail, then I took charge of the poop. I placed a sentry on the wheel and ordered the helmsman to steer due east. The Captain wanted to know what my intentions were. I didn't mince matters. I told him that if he refused to sail the ship into Lerwick I would sail her before the wind and pile her up high and dry on the rocks of Norway. I told him that she would never arrive in Germany until after she had been cleared from Lerwick by the proper authorities.

We drove on until we were perilously near the rocky coast of Norway. When the Captain saw I was determined in my threat, he weakened.

"You win," he told me, and held out his hand. He called the crew. All hands raced aloft, and to show there was no ill feeling, I went aloft also to give them a hand. What a condition that ship was in. The ratlins and gear were so old they were rotten. It wasn't safe to rest your full weight on anything above the decks. An hour later we were headed back for Lerwick.

The Captain turned out to be a real good sport. He had made a bid to get his ship and her cargo through the blockade. When he failed in his effort, he submitted in good grace just like a good sportsman should.

Several times on the way back he would pucker his forehead and muse, " I wonder if you would have wrecked the ship rather than let her go through ? "—" You're darned right I would," I told him with a smile, but I wonder just what I would have done if the test had been carried right to the limit. I do know this, if we had piled up, none of us would have had the ghost of a chance of being saved. I often feel glad it all turned out the way it did. I did not make any adverse report to the S.N.O., but that gentleman gave me one of the worst dressings down or " straffings " it is possible to imagine. It was all on account of my dress.

My uniform was coated with white brine. The buttons were green with rust and turning brown. I hadn't shaved for more than two weeks. I wore a muffler instead of the conventional collar and tie.

"You are a disgrace to the uniform you wear and the Royal Navy. What do you mean by appearing before me in such a disgraceful condition ? I'll have you cashiered. . . . I'll. . . . I'll . . ." he fumed, and tried to think of some other more drastic punishment he could inflict.

I was tired. I had hardly had any sleep for two weeks. I had not eaten a decent meal. I was filthy and craved a bath. I was fed up. I don't know exactly what retort I made, but I was ordered to go to my room in the hotel and consider myself under arrest.

I went to my room, ordered a bath and a real good meal to follow it and then I turned in and slept like a log, little worried by the thoughts of courts-martial, etc. I awoke to hear the S.N.O.'s orderly pounding on the door. I let him in.

"The S.N.O.'s compliments, Sir, and he invites you to dine with him at his home to-night. He told me to tell you not to worry about your clothes. It would be perfectly all right to come as you are."

I am still at a loss to know how he came to find out exactly how and why I appeared before him like a tramp, but he evidently had heard the story from somebody, probably one of my men. It may have been from the Captain of the sailing ship.

I enlisted the aid of the S.N.O.'s orderly, sent him to buy a new collar and tie, did what I could to clean my uniform and make myself as presentable as possible. I dined with the S.N.O. and met his very charming wife and daughter. Just before I left he informed me that he was going to place a midshipman and his guard of four men under my command and send me down to Fleetwood in charge of another big sailing ship which had been condemned as a prize.

We made the trip in the prize, but not to Fleetwood. We were ordered into Stornoway and I was sent out to sea again to join my ship.

I went to sea on the *A*——. Onboard her, serving as a seaman, was one of the few survivors from the *Hampshire*. I know the Admiralty say she struck a mine, but after talking to that man I will personally never believe she did. I am more convinced than ever that she was wrecked on the North Shoal Rocks. The reason I believe this to be the case is because the man told me he was aware of no explosion whatever. He said that he was in the for'ard mess deck when the accident occurred. The ship seemed to strike something, then she stopped and shivered and trembled all over. There was a series of sickening bumps. He was conscious of being thrown to the deck as he rushed for the companion way leading to the upper deck. He said this was more like heavy bumping than the effects of an explosion.

He told me that when he got on deck he went aft to his abandon-ship station, which was the raft on the shelter deck. He described the sea as being " a mass of foam and broken waves which washed aboard from all sides at once." The ship gradually settled. Contrary to other stories, he said he never saw Lord Kitchener. He saw an officer rush aft along the flying bridge, but that was all.

I asked him why the cutters were not lowered. He replied that the sea was so confused and such " a smother of foam " that they were unable to live in it. This very important statement goes to prove that the state of the sea where the *Hampshire* sank was very different from what it was a few miles away, even a few hundred yards away.

I was at sea that night and not far from where the *Hampshire* sank. It was rough, but not so rough that it was impossible to lower boarding boats. If the records and logs are searched, it will be proved that boats were lowered from ships of the 10th C.S. that night.

More significant yet was the statement of this survivor who said, " When the raft was washed off the shelter deck, I was clinging on to it for dear life. At first, we were in a smother of foam which tossed us about all over the place and made it so we could hardly see anything. *After awhile we seemed to float clear from the terribly confused seas into waves which, while fairly high, were more uniform and much less broken.*"

This is all very interesting. When I returned to my own ship, I told the assistant navigator what I had heard. He made this extraordinary statement : " I checked back the set and drift of the raft from where it was washed ashore to where it should have been when the *Hampshire* met her doom. Allowing for nothing but wind, tide, and current, it gave me a position right on the North Shoals Rocks. The less you say about this the better. Conditions are bad enough as they are."

These things make one think seriously Lord Kitchener was never killed by the work of a spy, for the *Hampshire* had only just arrived back from Jutland, and according to reports, nobody knew which ship he was to sail on until just prior to the time he left.

If the enemy had been waiting for him outside, they would naturally have laid their trap outside the eastern entrance. The Fleet rarely went to sea and turned west. The only occasion I remember them leaving Scapa and going west about through the Pentland Firth was when we went out for battle practice and manœuvres. The water to the

HELL'S ANGELS OF THE DEEP 189

west of the Orkneys is too deep to lay moored mines. If floating mines were laid, they would be strung together and in weather like we experienced after Jutland, the chances were that they would have bumped together and exploded due to the wave motion. If they had survived the action of the waves, and floating mines were the cause of the *Hampshire's* loss, then why did the others not explode when those which wrecked the ship blew up? And if mines did explode, why did a man, who was actually in the fore part of the ship down below decks at the time, have no knowledge of the explosions?

The theory that a submarine sank the *Hampshire* by torpedo can be dismissed. Under the conditions which existed that night, the submarine would have had to attack her from the surface, and no torpedo would have " run " true in such a sea.

If the Germans had had any hand in the sinking of the *Hampshire* and Lord Kitchener's death, wouldn't it have seemed more reasonable that they would have made the most of their success and broadcasted the news throughout the length and breadth of the world? Did they do this? They certainly did not. The news of his death was as big a surprise to them as it was to us.[1]

I hear H.M.S. *A*—— was torpedoed soon after I left her to rejoin my own ship. I wonder if the man who served on the *Hampshire* was lost or saved?

It would be a dull old war if there were not some humour at times. After wandering around the North Sea in the *H*—— I was sent to Stornoway with the prize, then I was sent North to try and catch the *Virginian* onboard the *A*——. I missed her, and it was nearly five weeks before I slept in my own bunk again. After submitting my expense sheet, I submitted a claim for the loss of my grip, a uniform suit, and the other contents. Imagine my surprise when I received word that my claim for lost equipment could not be considered because it had not been made within the time

---

[1] Since these pages were written, one of the big German leaders, I believe it was Ludendorff, said " Lord Kitchener was neither lost by a mine nor a submarine, but by the power of God, who wouldn't allow the Russians to be reorganized." What is more significant still, the British Admiralty have never made known the evidence submitted to the Court of Inquiry or given a clear statement as to the findings.

limit as set forth in articles so-and-so, page so-and-so, of the King's Regulations and Admiralty Instructions.

This was bad enough, but when I received my expense sheet back a few days later, it was worse. The brainy individual in the Paymaster-General's office who sent that sheet back should receive the O.B.E. He wrote: " I have returned this expense sheet for correction. I would draw your attention to article so-and-so, page so-and-so, of King's Regulations and Admiralty Instructions, which distinctly sets forth that officers are expected to pay for their own luxuries." A big blue cross was marked against the item on the bill, given by the proprietor of the hotel at Lerwick, " Bath . . . £0 1s. 0d."

I immediately wrote back and said that as I had not even had a wash during the whole two weeks I was aboard the sailing ship *H——* I did not consider a bath a luxury, but an absolute necessity. Much to my amazement, the bill was paid. I have not been reimbursed for the loss of my uniform and grip.

I cannot vouch for the truth of the story, but when I mentioned the incident of the Accountant General Department questioning the item of one shilling for a bath, another officer, who acts as King's Messenger, said that he had once submitted an expense sheet and had put: " To taxi from station to hotel, 2s. 6d." This item had been questioned and his attention drawn to the article which said: " Officers on duty are required to travel from one place to the other by the cheapest method of conveyance possible." At that time cab fare was cheaper than taxi hire.

Remembering this, the next time he put down: " To cabbage, 1s. 6d." The expense sheet was returned with the comment that 1s. 6d. was thought an excessive price to pay for a vegetable.

Thinking they were trying to be smart with him, on his next trip to a seaside resort, his expense sheet read: " To hire of moke from station to hotel, 6d." He received that back with the mention: " It is felt that no officer would so far forget his dignity as to ride a 'moke.' " All of which goes to prove that no matter how you try you cannot put anything over on the A.G.D.

I know some officers who have done so, however. When

a certain ship was lost at the beginning of the war, they salvaged several books of railway vouchers. Ever since then while on leave they have travelled where they wished and it has never cost them or the Admiralty a penny. They simply made one voucher out so it read, say, "From Plymouth to London and return"; they made another out to read "From London to Plymouth and return." By showing the first when they arrived in London, they were given it back as they required it for the return journey. When they arrived at Plymouth, they presented the voucher which read "From London to Plymouth and return." In this way, they never handed a voucher in and they were never checked up.

We were in port early in November when we experienced one of the worst fogs in the history of Liverpool. The *Virginian* was in dry dock that particular night and the fog was so dense we had to arrange with the dock policeman to hold the men returning from leave until an officer could meet them and lead them onboard. It was impossible to find one's way from the dock gate to the gangway, and we had to crawl on our hands and knees and stretch a life line (rope) from one place to the other so we could follow it.

A group of dockyard workmen walked right over the edge of the dry dock and were killed. Over twenty people lost their lives that night by walking into docks or into the river. We rescued two men who fell into the next dock. In all my experience, I never saw anything like it. It was worse than any London fog I had been in. You could not see your hand held up in front of you, and that is the actual truth. City traffic was held up for hours. The list of killed and injured, as it appeared in the papers next morning, read like the report of a battle.

The big thrill came just before Christmas. I had been ashore to Birkenhead to dine with friends of Lieutenant Davidson. We were returning aboard the ship just about midnight. The ship was berthed at the C.P.R. sheds. I thought I could smell smoke and both of us investigated. We located the fire in the back part of the store-room on the wharf. The store-room was locked and it was full of inflammable material. We could see several barrels of oil in the vicinity of the fire. We gave the alarm, ordered the

Virginian's crew to fire stations, and 'phoned the City Fire Department. We were told to fight the blaze as best we could and, if possible, hold it under control, as every piece of city fire-fighting equipment was in use fighting fires which had broken out simultaneously all over the city. This epidemic of incendiarism was attributed to Sinn Feiners.

The officers and men on the *Virginian* fought like heroes. They smashed open the doors of the burning store-rooms and officers went into the burning shed with two hoses playing on them to protect them from the flames. They trundled out the burning oil barrels and prevented them from exploding. If this had happened, the whole water front might have gone up in flames. The valuable freight, which was in the sheds at the time they were set on fire, was trucked away to the far end by hundreds of willing workers. The fire was kept under control until the arrival of the City Fire Brigade.

We were thanked by the officials of the C.P.R. the next morning. They wanted to replace the uniforms and greatcoats of some of us, which had literally been burned off our backs while fighting the blaze, but when the Captain of the ship took the question up with the Admiralty, they wouldn't allow the C.P.R. to recompense us. The joke of the whole thing is that the Admiralty informed us they could do nothing in the matter, either. We had to stand the cost of the loss of our uniforms. It's a great old war when you are an officer.

There is a restless spirit aboard this ship. All the officers are volunteering for special duty of one kind or another. I have volunteered for service in submarines. Several times lately word has been received that a few navigating officers are required. I do not think it makes much difference where you serve or what you serve in. A person does not die until his time comes, and when it does, it is little use kicking. I have not told anybody about this except Captain Wilding, my commanding officer, who recommended me, and his secretary, Mr. Armour.

"JACK'S GONE ALOFT"

To my cousin E. Thomas, who died in sail

A HUSH is o'er the half-deck,
  Young Jack has gone at last,
He made but little bother,
  As across the line he passed.
It all happened rather sudden,
  In the middle watch last night;
We were up there on the royal,
  With the seas an ugly sight.

He was with me out to starboard,
  Where we'd gone to take in sail,
When by some mischance he stumbled,
  Slipped, and fell to the weather rail.
It weren't his limbs, though badly broken,
  But his innards that were wrong.
Busted legs ain't no bad token,
  If your constitution's strong.

But it ain't much use a-crying
Over men that's done their dying,
  So we stitched him up in canvas good and strong.
And with fire-bars from the fiddly,
  We weighted his young feet,
So that when we put him over
  He'd be anchored good and deep.

Then we took him up on deck,
  And laid him by the rail,
And spread the ensign o'er him,
  While the crew were furling sail.
And when the weigh was off her
  We mustered in the lee;
The "Old Man" read the Psalms
  Ere we dumped him in the sea.

Now it's quiet there in the half-deck,
   Without his happy laugh,
But when you take to sailing
   You've got to stand the gaff.
It ain't much use complaining
   When the things of life go wrong;
At the same time it grows lonesome,
   For you miss his boyish song.

But if I keep a-rambling,
   You'll think I'm growing soft,
For it's taken me a long time
   Just to say " Jack's gone aloft."

CHAPTER XV

March 27th, 1917.

All kinds of things have happened these last couple of months. Life is beginning to move at a dizzy pace. I went home on three days' leave in February. My brother caught measles. I was placed in quarantine and did not mind it a bit. As the result, I missed my ship, she sailed without me—more joy. When the period of quarantine was over I was ordered to report to Admiral Stileman in Liverpool. Lieutenant Commander V——, who was King's Messenger, had taken ill. I was detailed to fill his place. While doing so, I was instrumental in capturing a spy. V—— is better; the spy is in jail; I am in submarines.

Let me record these events as they happened. First of all comes the spy.

When I relieved V——, I found my duties consisted of taking dispatches from the Admiral in charge of the port of Liverpool to Wigan. In Wigan I met the Naval leave trains. These trains ran from the North of Scotland to London and from London back North again. Both of them passed through Wigan within an hour of each other and between the hours of midnight and four in the morning.

The practice was to meet the first train (which was bound South), and give the King's messenger on the train the dispatches Admiral Stileman was sending to the Admiralty. I received from the King's messenger on the train the dispatches the C.-in-C., Grand Fleet, was sending to the S.N.O., Liverpool.

It is necessary to explain that the word " dispatches " covers everything from a few letters to sacks of lead-covered confidential code books and other secret documents. The " dispatches " I sometimes received from the Admiralty often weighed several hundred pounds.

Just to show how we muddle through this jolly old war I might also mention that absolutely no provision is made for the protection of these secret documents during transit from the station to the hotel, or while they remain in the King's Messenger's room in the hotel while he is absent meeting the train from London. It is obviously impossible to carry them with you because they weigh too much and are far too bulky.

Even more extraordinary is the fact that I was not even provided with a revolver.

The King's Messenger's room was in the Victoria Hotel. It was an ordinary room with a very ordinary lock. The distance from the hotel to the station is quite considerable, or seems so when you are struggling along under a load of lead-covered books tied up in heavy duck canvas sacks.

Many thoughts assailed me as I staggered along the dark streets from the station to the hotel that first night. I had one sack on my shoulders and dragged two more along the pavement with my right hand. Even if I had carried my own revolver, and had been attacked, I would have been unable to defend myself until I dropped the dispatches and drew my gun.

The whole situation seemed so extraordinary that I mentioned the facts to the Admiral's Secretary. I am not sure if he said anything to the Admiral at that time.

While having dinner in the hotel the next night, I sat thinking how very easy it would be for an enemy agent to steal the dispatches or, even worse still, enter the room during the absence of the King's Messenger, and after opening the dispatch bags, obtain what information he required and put the documents back again. I couldn't for the life of me see that it would be difficult for an organization like the enemy secret service to find means to duplicate the seals and fasteners which secured the mouth of the bags.

While my mind was thus occupied, I noticed a man at another table watching me. He turned his eyes away quickly as I looked up. He was a middle-aged man, with a heavy Hindenburg type of face and a square head, if ever I saw one.

Without attracting undue attention, I pretended to start a little innocent flirtation with the waitress and when opportunity offered, I asked her who the man was. She told me he was an American who had been living at the hotel several months. His name was H——.

I took a distinct dislike to the man. The first thing I did was to ask the manageress to change my room and put a special lock on the door. I had considerable trouble having this request granted, and had to finally produce my letter of special authority.

There was nothing else I could do that night, so I turned in early, determined that I would check up on the American next day and see if he was registered as an alien. The Defence of the Realm Act, or DORA, as it became known, could be very useful in a case of this kind.

I had hardly moved my things into my new room and put the catch on the Yale lock when I heard a knock at the door. It was the chambermaid. She was young and very pretty. She excused herself, saying she had come to make sure I had clean towels and that the bed was properly made. Having seen to these things, she sat on the edge of the washstand and engaged me in conversation. She mentioned the fact that I was a new messenger, asked why the other officer was away, and wanted to know if I would be taking over his duties permanently.

I replied that I had no information on these matters, and hinted that I was tired and anxious to go to bed. She took the hint, smiled very charmingly as she left the room, and quite familiarly wished me " pleasant dreams."

I had only just got into my pyjamas when there was another knock on the door. She was back again. This time it was to bring me some soap. " Surely you don't intend to go to bed so early ? " she asked, as she stood at the foot of my bed.

" That is my intention," I retorted.

" Are you sure there is *nothing* I can do for you ? I don't think you are tired—you are lonely." There was no mistaking her meaning. Her whole manner and the tone of her voice was an invitation.

I assured her that there was nothing I wanted and to let her know definitely that I was not so dumb that I didn't know her meaning, I informed her that I was married.

She threw back her pretty head, and gave a low musical laugh. " Ah ! I understand. Your marriage must have been quite recent. You are still very much in love with your wife. If you should happen to change your mind and *do* want anything, ring the bell."

I put out the light and lay awake thinking. I tried to convince myself that I was a suspicious fool. If I reported the matter, or mentioned my suspicions again, I would become the laughing-stock of everybody who heard the story. If I mentioned the incident of the pretty chambermaid, they would give me the horse-laugh and put me down for a silly, conceited ass. I didn't know what to do. At the same time, deep down inside of me I was convinced that my suspicions were right. I began to reason the thing out.

If H—— were a spy, if he had designs on the documents I carried, and I was in his place and he in mine, what would I do?

The first thing to do would be to obtain an impression of the key which unlocked the new fastener. If an extra (Yale) lock had not been placed on the door, the chambermaid would have had a pass-key with which to open it.

If I had foolishly allowed her to remain in my room, she would have been able to unlock the door from the inside during my absence at the trains. Was this the purpose of her visit? Was she in league with him, a spy, or was she just one of the numerous butterflies which flutter around the flame of life until they finally singe their pretty little wings or get badly burnt?

Two little demons seemed to be having a tug-of-war inside my brain. One tried to convince me that my theories were ridiculous and nonsensical; the other pulled just as strongly, and told me it was the unexpected that most often happened, and said I was right.

I decided on three things. I would keep all dispatches under my personal observation that night. Next day (it happened to be the one day of the week I didn't have to be on duty) I determined I would look further into the matter. I also made up my mind to send my wife a telegram and ask her to join me in the Victoria Hotel in Wigan. She was staying with my family in Preston at the time. I decided on this later move because I thought if the chambermaid was in league with H—— and it was their intention to arrange means by which they could obtain access to my room, this move would upset their plans and might possibly make them show their hands. It did.

I had an exciting day. I found out H—— was supposed to be the representative of a well-known American concern which manufactures a cheap and very popular watch. I found out he spent most of his days travelling around the country and only made the hotel in Wigan his headquarters. He was a " good fellow," a " free spender " of his money, and was " a ladies' man."

A little further investigation and a talk with the booking clerk at the station showed that his trips out of town took him to such places as Birmingham, Manchester, Leicester, and nearly all the industrial and mining centres of England. More important still, I found out that while he was an alien and subject to the restrictions with regard to travel imposed on aliens by the Defence of the Realm Act, he had never taken the trouble to register nor did he report to the police. This was enough to have him arrested, but I thought there would be no harm in giving him a little more rope with which to hang himself.

That evening I dined with my wife in the hotel diningroom. After dinner, I registered her as my wife and went up to my room where I told her all that had happened and explained my suspicions. I had not finished my story when a knock came on the door and the manageress asked to speak to me alone. She was terribly upset.

One of the guests—one of her most respectable guests—had informed her that I had a woman in my room who was not my wife. She pointed out what a serious offence it was to register falsely, and informed me that her guest had threatened to inform the police if the woman was not out of the hotel by the time he returned from the theatre.

" And who might this guest be ? " I asked the lady, who was so excited she could not stand still, or keep her hands quiet for a single moment.

She informed me that it was a Mr. H——. " He had stayed at the hotel for months." She sang his praises skyhigh. " He was such a nice man," " such a good man," she didn't want to lose him as a guest and she didn't want trouble with the police.

I thought quickly. H—— was at the theatre. I saw

the opportunity I had been looking for. I assured the good manageress that I would have the lady, who was in my room, out of the house before her model boarder returned, and wished her good-bye.

She was no sooner out of sight than I took a skeleton key I had obtained from a hardware store and opened Mr. H——'s door. In his room were two trunks, massive affairs and securely locked. I rummaged through his drawers and felt as guilty as any thief. All I could find were some books. I glanced through the pages. At first I thought what dull reading the man must enjoy. Then light dawned. The books which were lying about were volumes which contained all the vital statistics of the mining and industrial life of Great Britain. I hurriedly glanced through the pages, lists of mines, production, number of men employed, details of labour troubles, strikes, etc. Queer stuff for a man selling watches to be interested in.

I decided to take the bull by the horns. I went to the local police station and asked to see the Chief of Police. He was absent from the city. I asked to see the Chief Inspector. He was off duty. Finally, I did make enough bother to bring the Inspector down to see what it was all about.

I told him my story. He received it as all police officers receive the efforts of individuals who appoint themselves amateur detectives. It was plain to see that he thought I had been bitten badly by the bug which inoculates people with "Spyitis" or whatever you call it.

He tried to discount all my arguments. Mr. H—— had been in the city for months. He was well known to the Inspector. He was a fine man. There was nothing wrong with him. He hadn't registered, but it was simply an oversight. He would call him up and have him come in and register in the morning. Thus the Inspector argued.

By this time I was furious. "This man is guilty of an offence against the Defence of the Realm Act. Under that same Act I have power, as an officer holding the King's Commission, to arrest him. If you don't arrest him, I will." I meant what I said and he knew it.

I have often wondered why they pick a policeman for the size of his feet and the height and weight of his body. If those making the choice would only pay some little attention to what he has in his brain, it wouldn't be so bad. The man I was speaking to excused himself. He went into another room. He picked up the 'phone and gave a number. To my horror, this is what I heard.

"Hello! Is that Mrs.——, Victoria Hotel?"

"Is Mr. H—— in?"

"Tell him there's a naval officer been kicking up a fuss down here about him not being registered. Tell him not to leave the hotel. I'll be down right away to see him."

"No, there's no need to worry. Everything will be fixed up all right."

I was at his elbow by this time, simply furious. I demanded to know why he had 'phoned to warn the man. He told me that there was no harm in 'phoning him—that he was quite sure he wouldn't try to run away. I saw there was no use trying to argue with the Inspector, so we started off together for " our interview."

I expected the man H—— would escape. He would undoubtedly have done so had it not been for the fact that he had more important business to attend to than even trying to escape. We were not more than fifteen minutes from the time the Inspector 'phoned until we knocked on his door for admittance. When we did knock, we were calmly informed that the gentleman inside was just dressing and would be ready in a minute or two.

I turned on the police official and insisted that we tarry no longer, but if necessary break down the door. The Inspector thought I had gone mad. We were delayed fully another two or three minutes, and when we did finally obtain admittance, it was to find the fire grate full of burnt and still smouldering papers.

This man had spent the twenty minutes he had at his disposal burning evidence rather than attempting to escape. The wisdom of his choice was proved at the trial. He was given ten years' imprisonment instead of being condemned to face a firing squad. He might have escaped scot-free through the bungling of the local police if it had not been that certain letters were found in his pocket from a woman who signed herself " Olga." They were written as if she was his wife and signed, " Your loving wife, Olga." This was strange, because he informed us, when questioned, that he was single. The letters contained phrases which were undoubtedly code, but which were of so intimate a nature that the person using them would have to sign herself " wife " or create suspicion should any third party read them.

Even then, I couldn't convince the local officials that this man was a spy. They resented my attitude; they resented my interference; they resented very much being forced to obey the orders of a naval officer. H—— was taken to the police station and put in a cell. While there, he asked permission to send his wife a telegram. This was granted by the Inspector. It was a plain, simple document.

" I have been arrested in Wigan. Will need your help."

An innocent message from a husband to a wife, but a most potent one from one spy to another. It was nearing train time. The Inspector called a constable and told him to send the telegram. I said good night and left. Outside I told the constable I would save him the trouble of sending the wire and explained that I was on my way to the station to meet the naval leave train. The wire with the woman's address in London was sent down to certain officials in the Naval Intelligence Service by the King's Messenger on that train. Their investigations led to the second arrest, further evidence was obtained, and the woman was sentenced to five years in prison.

I was next given the task of changing the arrangements as they affected the receiving and delivering of dispatches. The meeting-place was shifted from Wigan to Preston. The King's Messenger had a room at the Park Hotel which was on the railway property and much better adapted and more private than the Victoria Hotel at Wigan.

H—— was transferred from Wigan to the Preston Jail to await trial. I did receive a communication asking me if I wished to attend the trial and give evidence, but as I had no further interest in the matter, I declined. I would not have known the outcome if I had not read the report of the trial in a newspaper.

I was sent to Glasgow with dispatches upon my return and Lieutenant-Commander V—— resumed his duties as King's Messenger from the port of Liverpool. I suppose the information learned from the arrest of this man will be kept a secret like so many other things that have happened during this war.

Just before I left Glasgow, I met some officers off the *Andes*, another of the 10th C.S. They have been in action with a German raider which they sank. This is supposed to have happened some time ago, but the information has been hushed up. I wonder if we are afraid or ashamed to publish our victories? After what happened at Jutland, I don't think it unfair to record the fact that some people seem to like giving full publicity to any successes the enemy may achieve, and, in the case of Jutland, loading the scales in their favour when announcing the results of a naval engagement.

My trip to Glasgow afforded me a very pleasant surprise. I was able to run down to Dumfries and visit my old school again, St. Joseph's College.

Many of the masters, who had taught me during the years I had studied there, were still carrying on their good work. I wanted to see them.

I was invited to stay to dinner at the college, and all the Brothers of my own time were asked to attend. I don't know of any banquet or dinner that I ever attended which gave me so much genuine pleasure as that little private affair in St. Joseph's.

I rejoined my ship at Busta Voe. I went to sea and was put onboard another ship and brought her into port.

I didn't know it at the time, but on this ship, which was neutral, were the survivors from one of the Manchester liners which had been torpedoed and sunk by an enemy U-boat. My cousin Ernest Beggs happens to be Commodore Captain of the Manchester liners. He heard the story from the Master in question and told it to my mother after he arrived back home. I cannot even now see why they should have made such a fuss over such a simple thing. What happened was this.

I had information that U-boats were exceptionally active in and around the Fair Island Channel. I was ordered to approach the channel after dark and slip through before daylight. In other words, the policy was to dodge them, if possible. U-boats, like whales, have to breathe. For reasons of safety, they usually do their breathing while on the surface, charging their batteries at night. If you happen to meet up with a U-boat during the hours of darkness, even when on the bridge of a neutral ship, you can ram it and sink it, and you don't need to prove that it wasn't an accident.

During this particular voyage we had fog from the time we left the *Virginian*. We had to slow down as we approached the land, for reasons of ordinary safety. The fog didn't lift until nearly noon. When it did, the sun came out and shone bright and clear. Land was in sight and I realized that we were south of Fair Island Channel and almost off the entrance to Stronsay Firth.

It is a very easy thing to make up one's mind when you are only twenty-one, with no certificates to worry about in case your judgment is wrong. If you did pull a bad bloomer and got kicked out of the Navy, there is always an Army ready to take you—they want plenty of men.

When I saw where I was, I thought matters over. It was broad daylight. If we went north and through the channel, it would take us nearly a whole day to make Kirkwall and we would have to run the gauntlet of the enemy submarines. If I went through the Stronsay Firth, we would be in Kirkwall before nightfall. The Stronsay Firth is a narrow, tortuous channel, through which the tides and currents rush like a mill-race. It is seldom used by ocean-going vessels.

There were two points to consider.

Safe navigation and the dangers of submarines in Fair Island Channel and another night at sea, or dangerous navigation but safety from submarines in the Stronsay Firth and a night amongst congenial company in the Kirkwall Hotel. I decided on the latter course and informed the ship's Master accordingly.

He literally threw his hand in. He wasn't going to take any ship he commanded through the Stronsay Firth. He'd never been through it in his life, and he wasn't going through without a pilot. If I insisted on being a dog-goned fool, then he wasn't having anything to do with the navigation of the ship and I could take her through myself, but first of all I would have to sign a document saying I had taken over command and relieved him of all responsibility.

I told him to draw up the paper and promised to sign it.

I was always puzzled to know why some captains in the Merchant Service hate being close to land. I had become an extravagant admirer of naval navigators who disdained to use a pilot and take their ships in and out of port themselves.

I altered course for the Firth, obtained a large scale chart, read the sailing directions, and then took up my position on the bridge near the helmsman. I'll admit I felt quite a man. The tide and current were with us.

The Captain came up on the bridge with his precious document. I signed it. We entered the Firth. I had never been through it before. I received quite a thrill as we raced through the tortuous channel at a speed of about fifteen knots. There are a couple of places where the rocks appear to hem one in until you reach the point where the channel takes a sudden turn. We raced on and through in safety and dropped anchor in Kirkwall harbour. I was in time to land and have dinner in the hotel.

To me it was all part of a day's work. To the old " Shell Back " who commanded the ship, it was an extraordinary piece of war-time foolhardiness. They don't seem to realize that due to the exigencies of war, men who are still boys in years have learned to accept responsibilities which they would not have been asked to assume until they were well on into middle age in peace time.

This was my last trip in charge of an armed guard. When I rejoined the *Virginian* I received a telegram ordering me to report to H.M.S. *Maidstone* for navigating duties in submarines.

CHAPTER XVI

April 1st, 1917. At Harwich aboard H.M.S. Maidstone.

Well, here I am at last. I have wanted to join submarines ever since I saw Commander Max Horton, D.S.O., etc., in Devonport, October 1914. Even then he was wearing a string of medal ribbons which looked like a rainbow. He had been several times into the Bight of Heligoland and had sunk two enemy ships. Nearly every Allied Power had decorated him for his bravery.

To the midshipmen who were in Barracks at that time he represented the "Spirit of Adventure," the Nelson type of British naval officer. I know many R.N.R. midshipmen rushed off and volunteered for service in submarines, only to be told there were no vacancies for Royal Naval Reserve officers except those qualified as navigators.

To be qualified as a navigator, it is necessary to hold your Board of Trade Certificate as Mate or Master and to have experience as watch-keeping officer on one of His Majesty's ships. Strange as it may seem, I have no Board of Trade Certificate. I have never had the opportunity to sit for an examination since the war started. I did, however, pass a naval examination and was awarded a "test certificate." I have persistently volunteered for duty in submarines, and I think Captain Wilding must have forwarded a strong recommendation following my experiences while in charge of armed guards.

Personally, I am not the least bit nervous of undertaking the responsibility. I feel "tickled to death" to have received the appointment. I understand that I am the youngest navigating officer in the submarine service and the only R.N.R. Sub-lieutenant to receive such an appointment.

H.M.S. *Maidstone* is the submarine depot ship. She is moored alongside the Parkstone Quay at Harwich. Next to her is the old *Pandora*, also acting as a home for submarine crews when they are in port.

HELL'S ANGELS OF THE DEEP 207

The whole atmosphere of this naval base is different from Scapa Flow and Cromarty. It is difficult to describe. The difference is comparable to that which exists between men in the front-line trenches ashore and those who are stationed in Boulogne. Everyone I have met is quiet yet cheerful; youthful yet matured by responsibility; happy-go-lucky yet cool and unexcitable; alert yet supremely calm and confident. I think the most noticeable difference is in the relationship between senior and junior officers and all officers and the men. In the " Big Navy," if any little thing goes wrong, the Captain "strafes" the Commander, the Commander " raises Cain " with the Officer of the Watch, the Officer of the Watch turns on the Midshipman of the Watch and gives him hell, while the Midshipman speaks his mind to the Quartermaster of the Watch and blames him. But it doesn't even stop there. The Quartermaster turns on the poor unfortunate Sideboy and tells him more about himself and his past ancestors than the poor kid ever thought possible. He takes the blame because there is no one else to pass it on to. By the time the " strafe " is over, everyone has forgotten what it is all about anyway, and the Commander will be walking up and down with the Captain talking quite friendly. If the watch has ended, the Midshipman may be having a glass of sherry with his Lieutenant, while the Quartermaster and the Call Boy will be down in their mess playing rummy or writing a letter home, " telling the folk they don't need to worry as long as there is a Navy."

I don't want to be a cynic, but these conditions seem conspicuous by their absence here. Nobody seems to be eagle-eyed, hunting about for some minor breach of discipline. One receives the impression that the officers and men have met bigger things, passed through greater dangers, known more bitter disappointments, and enjoyed to the limit the sweet nectar of achievement and victory.

I, who have only been here a few hours, have breathed that atmosphere and feel different already. And why not ? In the " Big Navy " men live and thrive on the traditions of centuries ago. They are sticking the long, weary, nerve-racking, soul-destroying years of deadly monotony and inactivity with admirable patience. Their heroes are Grenville, Drake, and Nelson. These men attached to the

Harwich Base here are imbued with the glorious example set them by their own officers who are with them of the same flesh and blood.

As I stood on deck before dinner last night, the Officer of the Watch pointed out to me the lines of destroyers. The famous Harwich Striking Force. The light cruisers and 1st and 3rd destroyer flotillas. Ships which have been in every naval engagement which has taken place in the North Sea since the outbreak of war. True the "Saucy" *Arethusa* has gone—blown up by a mine February 13th last year—but her Commander, Commodore Sir Reginald Tyrwhitt, still survives to lead these sleek, powerful, swift engines of war. Mines may have wrecked the ship, but they can never efface the memory and inspiration of the glorious deeds performed by the men of the "Saucy" *Arethusa*.

And if we turn from the destroyers and light cruisers, we find leavening the personnel of the submarine service officers and men who, young in actual years, are veterans of the underseas branch of the service ; men who by crashing their way through the mine-infested, net-obstructed, narrow channels which lead into the Sea of Marmora and the Baltic established a new service and a new tradition.

As I stood and drank in this wonderful scene, I thought of the days back at college when I had read with feverish interest the stories of the deeds of gallant "Sea Dogs" and the Spanish Main. Here, right before me, was a modern edition of these stories in the reality of drab greys and modern life. The same spirit prevails, the same names run through the stories, only the scene is changed and given a modern setting. The whole thing seems like a dream. I can't believe it is real and that I am one of the actors in this new drama.

Harwich is called the "Graveyard of the Fleet." More ships have left this base never to return than any other base in naval history. The submarine service is called the "Suicide Club." I am not going to let those things worry me. I am growing to be quite fatalistic. If you are not going to be killed, why worry ? If you are going to be killed, worrying won't prevent it happening, anyway.

I heard the original optimist the other day while on my way down here. He was a "Tommy" returning to the

Front after his leave. The train was crowded, as usual. He climbed into our first-class apartment, and shedding his equipment, apologized for the intrusion, but explained he couldn't find any other place on the train. He was a ruddy-cheeked, happy-looking individual with the sparkle of humour in his eyes.

An old lady spoke to him. She elicited the information that he was on his way back to the trenches. His happy-go-lucky, devil-may-care attitude caused her next inquiry.

"Do you never feel worried or nervous?" she asked.

"Lor' lummy, Missus! Hit's like I told me bruver what hasn't joined up yet. There's no sense in worrying. Only about two out of every three men what enlists ever leave England. Hif you don't leave England, why worry? H'out of every 'undred men what goes to France only about fifty get 'it. If you're not one of the fifty, you don't need to worry. Now, hif you do get 'it, only about fifty per cent get 'it seriously, and hif you only get a 'Blighty' you'd be crazy to worry—you're lucky. Now, h'out of the other fifty per cent only about five are killed or die from their wounds, and if you're not one of them what turns up his toes, you don't have to worry, and if you do turn up your toes, you *can't* worry anyway."

The first thing I did when I arrived onboard the *Maidstone* was to report to the Captain. He is in charge of all submarines in the flotilla. He gave me a brief talk about how honoured I should feel to have been accepted for this particular branch of the service. He tried to impress on me the importance of my duties and the seriousness of the situation. From what he said, I believe there will be quick promotion either in this world or *to* the next.

I was having a cocktail in the smoke-room with some other officers when I was ordered to report to the Paymaster's office. It didn't take me long to reach there. I thought my transfer must have come through, and I expected to be able to obtain an advance from the Paymaster. When I stepped into his cabin, he offered me a seat and placed a form before me. It was headed " LAST WILL AND TESTAMENT OF——."

I asked him what the idea was.

" We ask all officers joining submarines to make their

will. It saves a lot of trouble in case of—accidents," he replied, quite casually.

He seemed rather bored with the whole proceedings, and glanced significantly at his watch.

It didn't take me long to make my will. I had nothing to leave. As I didn't want the P.M. to know that I was as poor as a church mouse, I wrote:

"I hereby leave all my real and personal estate to my wife, her heirs and assigns forever, with the exception of my private diary, which I leave to my friend, Sub-Lieutenant M. D——."

I was next ordered to report to the Medical Officer in the Sick Bay. For the third time since volunteering for services in submarines, I was ordered to strip and do physical jerks prior to being examined, from head to foot. I can't figure out why they are so infernally particular on insisting that men, apparently labelled for the "bone yard," should be 100 per cent physically fit, unless it is they don't wish to contaminate the poor fishes in the North Sea.

According to what I hear, the chances, while attached to this depot, are about even odds when you patrol inside the "Bight," and about four to one in your favour if you are allocated to patrols off the Danish coast and the entrance to the Baltic. Not bad odds when backing horses, but they seem damned short when you're gambling your life against the winning of a tin medal.

April 2nd, at Harwich.

The submarines (or boats as we call them) attached to these flotillas, do the Bight of Heligoland patrols and those off the Danish and Dutch coasts. They are having a rotten run of luck. It is the exception rather than the rule when all the boats which leave for patrol, return safely.

They leave in batches. The flotilla is so organized that some submarines are on patrol in the "Bight" while others are ready for coastal defence work. Those which have just returned from patrol are overhauled and when they are ready and refuelled, they take their place on the coastal defence list, while those longest off patrol go out to relieve the others.

As a general rule, the boats do about ten days on patrol in

enemy waters, a week out of action, and two weeks coastal patrol duty. The other week is taken up going out and returning from patrol.

Most of the destroyer flotillas and light cruisers are based here. They are the "striking force." They protect the channel ports, and have been in more fights than an Airedale in a dog-catcher's wagon.

Patrolling the North Sea down our way is no sinecure. From all accounts, mines in these waters are as thick as peas in a pea-soup, but the officers attached to the *Maidstone* are a very fine bunch of fellows.

Right here attached to this flotilla are such outstanding submarine officers as Commander Holbrook, V.C., Lieut.-Commander D'Oyly Hughes, D.S.O., and a dozen others who distinguished themselves in the Dardanelles campaign. D'Oyly Hughes and I have mutual friends so we enjoyed a chat together.

The submarine depot ship is a lively place, as it is the congregating place for many officers from the destroyer flotillas and other small craft operating from this base.

I am down here awaiting disposal, but have been instructed to go out in E 29 to-morrow to do torpedo trials. The navigator of this boat took me through the submarine and explained what my duties would be as navigating officer.

Last night, after dinner, a rather amusing incident occurred which gave everyone but the victim a real good laugh.

One of the submarines had just returned, and the crew were feeling pretty pleased because they had had the good fortune to bag a "Fritz."

After the King had been honoured, the president of the mess mentioned the fact. He said he had been asked by the other members to make a presentation to Lieutenant-Commander C—— and tender to him their very heartiest congratulations on making such an excellent shot.

The officer in question was, to say the least, dumbfounded. Nothing like it had ever occurred before in the history of the depot. Other officers had gone forth and done battle with the enemy and had far greater successes. No presentations had ever been made to them.

At the president's request, however, he stepped forward

to receive the " gift." It was wrapped in brown paper, and from the outside appearance looked for all the world like a large sized pair of binoculars. As he reached forward to take the present, the officer who had made the speech said : " Would you mind signing this receipt ? Some of the officers who have subscribed have already left for patrol. I wish to attach your receipt to the account of my stewardship."

Lieutenant-Commander C——, still very much embarrassed, signed on the dotted line, wondering what it was all about. Then he unwrapped the present. Layer after layer of paper he removed. As he did so, the general outline of a pair of binoculars became more and more evident. As he was getting down to the last sheets of tissue paper, he said : " Really, you know, this was most unexpected. I don't know why I should have been singled out for such an honour."

" Because you are so popular, my dear fellow," replied the speech-maker, while the rest of those present howled with laughter. The removal of the last wrapper disclosed two empty beer bottles tied together to resemble a pair of binoculars.

When the laughter had subsided, the president of the mess rapped for order and announced :

" Gentlemen, you will be pleased to know that the receipt our friend signed was an order on the wine steward to fill all our glasses. We can drink his very good health and wish him and his crew further successes."

The glasses were filled and his health drunk at his own expense. I think the perpetrator of that joke must be a Scotsman.

April 3rd, at Harwich.

They say it takes all sorts to make a war. Well, there are all sorts here. One submarine Commander is an atheist. For some reason, best known to himself, he hates religion and all things pertaining to it. It is rather tragic that he is like that, because in other respects he is one of the best fellows you could wish to meet.

Religion to him is like a red rag to a bull. I heard that, not very long ago, as he was returning to the depot ship, he passed a Salvation Army band which was holding a service at the street corner. According to an eye-witness, just as Commander S—— arrived abreast of the meeting, the Army Captain was crying in a loud voice :

" Just elevenpence ha'penny more to make the shilling . . . just elevenpence ha'penny more to make the shilling . . . every shilling saves a soul. Just elevenpence ha'penny more and another soul is saved. . . . Ha ! some kind brother has thrown a shilling on the drum. God bless you, brother . . . just elevenpence ha'penny more to make the shilling . . . "

" Hey, there ! Hold on a minute," Commander S—— called, and when he got attention he asked :

" How does a shilling save a soul ? "

" Them's the statistics, Mister. For every shilling the Army collects, we save a soul."

" So a shilling buys a ticket to Heaven ? "

" That's right, Mister . . . that's a good thought. Every shilling buys a ticket for Heaven," said the enthusiastic saver of souls.

" Here's two shillings, give me a return ticket," demanded Commander S——. " If I don't like it in Heaven, I'll be able to come back."

The Salvation Army Captain looked hurt and astonished.

" Give me that return ticket," demanded Commander S——, pointing to the two-shilling piece he had dropped on the drum.

He waited a moment. There was general silence.

" You can't give me a ticket for Heaven any more than I can buy a ticket for Hell. You're a fake . . . all religion is a fakery." Saying this, he put his foot clean through the big drum.

There was the devil to pay shortly afterwards. Certain " Brass Hats " at the Admiralty wanted to have him dismissed from the service. They demanded a court-martial. I don't know exactly what happened, but Commander S—— was not court-martialled. I understand that a certain senior officer informed those who were after his hide that, irrespective of what his idiosyncrasies might be, he was a first-rate submarine officer, and that was the main thing to consider when there is a war on.

Commander S—— is reported to have agreed to purchase a new drum to replace the one he put his foot through. It is reported that he sent a covering letter with the donation which was couched in this style:

"DEAR SIR,
    Please find enclosed my cheque for the purchase of a new drum to replace the one that came in contact with my toe.

Money will purchase a new drum, but I'm hanged if it will buy tickets for Heaven or save souls.

Yours, until long after Hell freezes,

———."

April 4th, at Harwich.

Three submarines sailed this morning. I got up to see them off. It is a rotten experience to see those boats push off in the cold grey of the early dawn. The lines were slipped and the motors of the submarines purred as they worked their way from alongside the depot ship.

Once clear of the other boats they turned into line ahead and proceeded out of harbour. Before they reached the "gates" (anti-submarine defence protecting the harbour entrance) the mist closed down and hid the ghostly procession from view, as they slipped silently out towards the unknown.

There is something sinister about the appearance of a submarine, whether it be friend or foe. I shuddered involuntarily as I turned to go below again. The cold dank mist, as it lowered and hid them from sight, was too much like a funeral pall being spread over three drab steel coffins.

I don't know what is making me write like this. I think I must be sickening for an attack of the hebe-gebies.

April 7th, 1917. Blyth.

Strange how the unexpected happens. I thought I would be appointed to an E-boat operating from Harwich, instead of which I was sent North to Blyth and ordered to relieve Lieutenant Howell-Price, D.S.C., who was navigator of submarine G 6. He has been recommended for a course as first lieutenant of submarines. I hear that several R.N.R. officers who joined the submarine service early in the war have been promoted to first lieutenant and two of them have actually been given command.

The Captain of my boat is Lieutenant Coltart, and the

HELL'S ANGELS OF THE DEEP 215

second in command Lieutenant Redfers Holland-Pryor. The depot ship is the *Titania*, and attached to her are twelve submarines, six G's and six J's. They are numbered G 1 to G 6 and J 1 to J 6. I should mention that we have two C class submarines operating between here and the Tyne doing coastal defence and anti-submarine duties.

Attached to this depot are many of the officers who distinguished themselves in the Baltic Sea and the Sea of Marmora. Commander C. Boyle, V.C., is in J 5, Max Horton, D.S.O., etc. etc., is in J 6, Commander Turner, J 1, while Commander Ramsay, cousin to the officer who married Princess Patricia, is in one of the other boats at present on patrol. Sir Edward Carson's son commands one of the C-boats, and he has a yacht here which is open house for all the officers of the flotilla. Captain Willis is the depot Commander.

We leave for patrol in three days' time. Yesterday we went out for torpedo practice. This is an interesting game but not without its dangers. The attacks are carried out under conditions as nearly approaching those of actual warfare as possible.

The Captain of my boat is a prince of a fellow. He is so damned calm and self-possessed I don't think he'd perspire in the tropics . . . or in Hell.

The torpedo practice was carried out near St. Mary's light. We received information that three destroyers had been sighted in that position and were ordered to attack them. We headed for sea. As soon as we were clear of the harbour we dived and steered for the position indicated. In a submarine nobody sees a darned thing but the Captain. He may allow the first lieutenant or the navigator to use the unifocal periscope and assist him in locating the enemy, and when on patrol the other two officers, of course, take turns keeping the periscope watch when the boat is submerged. During an attack, however, the Captain of the boat is the only one who sees anything.

The " practice " was something like this. C.O. to me, " Weather's fine. Just enough chop to make the feather of our periscope hard to see."

The periscope was " housed " and the boat running blind towards a position five miles north of the lighthouse.

The Captain, glancing at his wrist-watch, gave the order: "Raise periscope slowly."

As the instrument came out of the "well," he stooped and placing his eye against the rubber shock absorber, raised himself with the instrument. The moment the top lens broke surface he shouted: "Stop periscope." He took a quick, cautious look around and seeing nothing, ordered: "Raise periscope slowly."

He swept around and around trying to locate the "enemy." Finally he sighted them away to the North and steaming towards us. "Down periscope" was his next command. Then he turned again to me.

"Nothing to this attack if they don't see our periscope or alter course. They are heading straight for us, and I'll get 'em as they go past."

He raised the periscope several times and left it up just for split seconds at a time. He gave me the necessary particulars and I checked off the deflection for the shot and gave it to him. Then he took another quick look, and the warning: "Stand by to fire."

The torpedoes used in practice are fitted with special heads which collapse like a concertina when they hit. In this way no damage is done to the delicate mechanism of the "tin-fish" or the hull of the target.

Twice more he poked the tip of his periscope above the surface to make sure the "enemy" were not altering course, and then came the order, "Full speed on both motors."

The "enemy" had altered course right at the last minute and were headed straight for us. We had to dive and come up 500 yards away from them.

As we slowed down and rose the next time, I had a queer sensation around the nape of my neck. What if his calculations were out, or what if the destroyers had altered course again? This was all part of the game, but I must admit that I felt as I am sure men must feel at the front when they raise their heads above the comparative safety of the trench.

We had turned like a greyhound doubles on a hare, then up went the periscope again. Hardly had it broken surface when the order came to "Fire!" It did not seem possible for a hit to materialize out of such a snap shot, but as we

LIEUT.-COMMANDER BOYLE, V.C.

broke surface the destroyer signalled that we had secured a hit right under the bridge and added that she had seen neither periscope nor torpedo until she had been hit.

The next attacks were much the same. Once we had to drive hard to head off the "enemy," but we got her just the same. I heard after we returned to port that we had accomplished well-nigh the impossible. We secured three hits out of three attacks and all unseen by the target ship.

This torpedo practice is a most realistic game. I have heard of two cases in which serious accidents occurred. In one, the attacking submarine was rammed and sunk; in the other, the submarine which was acting as target was holed and sunk by the attacking submarine which overran her distance and came up under the bow of the target and ripped her bottom out.

Last night I was speaking to another navigator whose boat had bagged a "Fritz."

"We were on the surface at night, charging our batteries, when I spotted the 'Fritz,'" he informed me. "We weren't more than a couple of hundred yards away. For a moment I didn't know what to do. I don't know what made me do it, but I felt it would be surer to ram her than fire a torpedo. I don't know much about 'tin-fish' anyway, so I called for 'Full Speed' and the Captain at the same time. We were almost on top of her when he climbed up on the conning-tower, and having come out of the light he was as blind as a bat.

"The 'Fritz' saw us coming at her like a ram at a gate. She went into a crash dive, but she wasn't quick enough. We tore through her deck plating as she dipped under and hit her with enough force to drive her downwards, so she hit the bottom with a bump and bounced clean to the surface again. It was quite shallow where we had the scrap, not more than six or eight fathoms deep.

"By the time she bobbed up again, the Captain had the torpedoes ready and his eyes were accustomed to the darkness. He fired one fish. When it hit, there was no question about 'Fritz's' fate."

We went on to talk about navigation. "Say, you'll find out that you're lucky if you see the sun once in ten days," he said. "You are equally lucky if you are able to 'shoot' a star at dusk or dawn once in the same period. When 'Fritz' is not around keeping you under, the horizon is no good or the sky is cloudy. You might as well try to steal the Crown Jewels out of the Tower of London as shoot the sun when you're inside the 'Bight.'"

April 9th. At Blyth.

This is the last time I will write in this diary before I go to sea.

I spent an hour with the depot navigator going over the secret and confidential charts. The chart of the southern portion of the North Sea looks more like a board on which you played " Snakes and Ladders " when a child than anything else I can think of.

On it is marked all the wrecks of ships torpedoed and sunk during the war, in addition to those lost due to errors of navigation before the war. The mine-fields laid by the British are marked in one colour; suspected mine-fields laid by the enemy in their own waters are marked in another; nets and obstructions and dangerous areas which are known, are also marked. A known danger is no danger at all. All areas into which our submarines have been sent to patrol and from which they failed to return, are given special notice and a wide berth.

It is generally conceded that when a boat goes out and fails to return, and nothing more is heard of her, that she has struck a mine.

The enemy U-C class of submarines are mine-layers, and they lay a nest of " eggs " off the coast every tide. We do the same thing inside the Bight, so honours are even, except that their mines seem to be a damned sight more effective than ours.

My first patrol is likely to be in the vicinity of Horn's Reef. Two other submarines are leaving with us.

The boat I have been appointed to is 181 feet long with 22 feet 7 inches beam. She displaces 780 tons and is fitted with two bow torpedo tubes, two beam tubes, and one in the stern. She can make about fifteen knots on the surface and eight or nine submerged. She carries a crew of three officers and twenty-eight men. With the exception of a few veterans who still survive from the days when the

A-boats were in their experimental stage, all the personnel are young men. Quite a number of first lieutenants of boats attached to this flotilla are under twenty-three years of age. Many of the Captains are not a day over twenty-five, and some of these are veterans of the submarine service with three to six years' service to their credit.

Every man is a volunteer. The standard set is so high that only about 40 per cent of those who volunteer are ever chosen for actual overseas patrol.

Discipline here is vastly different from what it is in the " big ship " Navy. You could sum it up in a very few words. " Do your job. Do it well." That is about all that is asked. EFFICIENCY in capital letters is all that is required. The officer or man who does not do his job well, or who is proved to be inefficient, is rooted out just as ruthlessly as a surgeon removes a cancer from the human body during its incipient stage.

The men are highly trained, full of self-confidence, and have confidence in their officers and their boat. They are the type who realize their responsibilities. If, as rarely happens, a man does do something wrong, he is simply told he will be transferred back to general service. That is about the worst punishment with which he can be threatened. I think most of them would rather be sent to Devil's Island than back to general service.

When they volunteered in the first place, they threw out their chests a couple of inches; when they were accepted, they swelled them a bit more. Once they had been overseas they puffed up their chests with righteous pride to the girth of greatest expansion. They feel as much superior to the ordinary " big ship " mattaloe as a high-caste Hindu does to his low-caste brother. To be sent back to general service reacts on them like a nail on a pneumatic tyre.

If a man begins to lose his nerve, or develops " cold feet," he usually cuts up rough, breaks the rules of the service and his leave, and in that manner works his " ticket." Nobody ever tries to stop him. He is just eased out.

Some men can't stand life in submarines. I saw an extraordinary instance of this when I first joined the depot. A boat returning from patrol landed a man they had taken overseas with them as spare hand. He had passed through all the various stages, from volunteering until he was given his final test—that of a trip in a boat under actual war conditions.

Before the man had been at sea a day he was all in. He had plenty of courage in the ordinary sense of the word, but his stomach and nerves revolted against the conditions experienced in a submarine. When he landed at the end of fourteen days, he was a shadow of his former self, a gibbering, nervous wreck. He had put in two weeks of constant nausea, insomnia, and nervous reaction. Some men simply can't stand the thought of being hermetically sealed up in a glorified sardine tin. He actually lost a stone in weight in two weeks.

I have been told that the surest way to find out if a man is submarine minded or not, is to watch him when he is suddenly awakened from sleep by the ringing of the alarm gongs, or klaxon horns, to give them their proper name. If he is the type who will make a good submariner, he will automatically go to his diving station on hearing the alarm. If he is not he will instinctively start towards one of the exits. Once a man shows the latter tendency, he is gently but surely eased out of the submarine service.

I heard of another extraordinary case. An officer with eight years' service in submarines and considered a good all round and efficient commander, suddenly went stark raving mad. News was received that another officer, a great friend of his, had accomplished quite a stunt and torpedoed something worth while. When the officer in question heard the news he was sitting at the dinner-table in the depot ship's ward-room. He got to his feet without saying a word, climbed on top of the table, and began to crow like a cock. His mind had given away completely.

There is little or no comfort for the crews of G-boats. The interiors are cramped for space and crowded with machinery. In the foremost compartment are the twin 18-inch torpedo tubes. They carry Whitehead torpedoes which can be adjusted to run about 3,500 yards at 45 knots, or 10,000 yards at 25 knots. The tubes are built right into the bows of the boat. The torpedoes are fired out of them by compressed air. They can be fired either when the boat is on the surface or submerged. Spare torpedoes are carried

HELL'S ANGELS OF THE DEEP 221

which can be loaded into the tubes while the boat is submerged.

The exits of the tubes are fitted with "bow caps," which can be opened or closed from the inside of the boat. The torpedoes lie ready in the tubes with the bow caps closed when the boat is on patrol. When the enemy or a suspicious vessel is sighted, the order is given, "Flood bow tubes." The bow caps are then opened and the tubes fill with water. When the order is given to fire, a charge of compressed air, with a pressure of about 350 pounds to the square inch, is released into the tubes at the rear of the torpedoes, which are forced out of the tubes. As they are driven out, the starting lever, which is situated in the top of the torpedo, is forced back by a little catch, and the compressed air in the air chamber of the torpedo itself is, in this manner, allowed to enter the heating chamber. After it has been expanded, it passes on into the air engine, which in turn drives the propellers of the torpedo. The compressed air chamber in the torpedo is tested to about 3000 pounds to the square inch.

The depth at which a torpedo travels is regulated by a hydrostatic valve situated underneath the balance chamber. If the rudders are set for twelve feet, the increased pressure on the valve, should she go below that depth, causes a weight or balance to operate the horizontal rudders and bring her back to her proper depth. If the "fish," as we always call the torpedo, runs too shallow, the opposite action takes place, and the rudders operate so they cause the torpedo to dive. A gyroscope acts in exactly the same way on the vertical rudders and steers the "fish" straight. The gyro revolves at many thousand revolutions a minute and takes up its position at right angles to the fore and aft line of the torpedo when it is fired. If the "fish" starts to run off its course the vertical rudders, which are attached to the gyro, are pulled over to the right or left, as the case may be, in exactly the same way as a man driving a horse would guide it with the reins.

The explosive charge, consisting of T.N.T., is in the head of the "fish." In the nose of the torpedo is inserted the pistol; a miniature propeller extends out beyond the nose like whiskers. When the torpedo is fired, the propellers revolve and cause the pistol to be screwed back onto the fulminate of mercury detonator, which is next to a black powder blasting charge in the head. When the pistol is screwed back into this position, the slightest blow the whiskers receive will set it off. As explosives of this type have the property of seeking the line of most resistance, the force of the explosion strikes inwards causing a gaping hole in the side of the ship it hits. Torpedoes cost about £1200 each. They can be set to either float or sink after they finish their run.

April 7th, 1917.

I'm all dressed in white woollies like a patient waiting to go into the operating theatre. They call this outfit our " running gear." It is wonderful stuff, and should keep one warm if anything can.

It is just breaking dawn. I've been in the boat to make sure the Sperry is running O.K. I started it before I turned in last night. I didn't sleep much. I guess I'll feel better once we get started. Even a murderer's troubles cease after the trap is sprung.

I feel like a chap about to jump into the water, who fears it is going to be cold.

CHAPTER XVII

As I thumb over the pages of my notes, I find difficulty in picking out the remaining chapters for this book. I have already told the most interesting adventures experienced by the officers and men of the submarine service in my book *By Guess and by God*.

The only thing left to tell are some of those more intimate and personal events which occurred while I was serving in submarines G 6, K 12, and R 12, which have not already been recorded.

The first incident which stands out most clearly in my mind was the "stunt" we were rushed down to Harwich to take part in.

These stunts, as we used to call them, were of frequent occurrence. Summed up in a nutshell, they were carefully thought-out operations in which the whole British Navy stationed in home waters took part.

The Battle of the Bight in August 1914 was the result of one of these stunts. We were able to coax the enemy to sea, lead them into a trap, and sink five of their ships before they really got wise to what was happening. But the enemy, like a fox which has once been caught in a trap, became very cautious as time went on, and they, in turn, tried to trap our ships in a manner which would have given them the advantage and caused us serious losses. The war at sea, as far as they were concerned, became one of attrition.

In the midsummer of 1917, the general atmosphere became "windy" indeed. There was much talk of invasion by the enemy. In fact, troops were rushed to the East coast and guns were mounted, and for some weeks we men in submarines lived the life of firemen. We were always at short notice, always on the alert, ready to rush to sea and attack the approaching enemy ships and transports.

Both officers and men serving in submarines were not only allowed, but were encouraged, to have their families live near the depot ships. It was felt that home life was the greatest antidote to the terrible strain experienced while away on overseas patrols.

When in port, married men were allowed to sleep at home, the only stipulation being that they could be down to the depot and aboard their ship in less than twenty minutes after the alarm had been received and the order " All boats to sea ! " given.

I was at home this particular night. I had retired early and was in a sound sleep. In the same house, occupying the front bedroom, was an Army officer and his wife. Onboard the depot ship in charge of the officer of the watch was a complete list of the married officers and men, with the street and house number where they were staying. As soon as word was received, orderlies would jump on their bicycles and each man would race away to warn a given number of officers and men.

It was about midnight when I heard the Army officer pounding on my door. " Some chap outside threw a handful of gravel at my window and told me all boats were ordered to sea. I think it must be you he wants."

Dashing the sleep from my eyes, I mumbled my thanks, climbed into my greatcoat, pulled my socks over the legs of my pyjamas, and tied on my boots without taking time even to lace them. I kissed my wife a hurried good-bye and in less than one minute was racing down towards the docks where the boats were moored.

All submarines were at sea in less than half an hour, and we took up our position ten miles off the coast and about two miles apart. All through the remaining hours of darkness we stayed on the surface, trimmed down, ready to deliver a torpedo attack against the enemy ships and then dive for safety.

Dawn came and nothing had happened. We were ordered to return to harbour. We refuelled and went to one hour's notice. That meant that the danger still threatened and nobody was allowed to leave the depot ship.

Next night we went to even shorter notice, which meant " stand-by for sea." Most of us were playing bridge or poker, when one of the submarines, returning from patrol, sent a wireless message and reported she had sighted a squadron of ships, without lights, steaming east. As no British ships were supposed to be in that vicinity, we went to sea again, and when we returned at dawn the following day the coast line from Blyth to St. Mary's Lighthouse looked like the coast of Belgium. Troops had been rushed to the threatened zone. They had dug themselves in like moles, and the ugly snouts of field guns and howitzers poked hungrily from behind sand-bagged emplacements all along the shore line. I say "hungrily" with due deliberation. One was so hungry for trouble it took a crack at us as we hove into sight returning to harbour. That was night Number Two. Night Number Three, we were still on standby. We spent the evening onboard Lieutenant Carson's yacht and had a very pleasant time indeed until about 2:00 A.M. We had just decided to call it a night and return to our cabins onboard the depot ships, when an orderly rushed onboard with the same old message. As we climbed on to the wharf, we could hear the Bos'on's mates going along the mess-decks in the depot ship piping, "Away submarine crews; man your boats!"

This was going beyond a joke. I began to wish I had left my wife in Preston. I determined to try and send her word to go home again, because I realized how nerve-racking it must have been for the womenfolk who saw all the activity yet knew not the why or wherefore.

The approaches to the wharf had been sand-bagged, and barb-wire entanglements stretched all along the shore. Sentries, Army sentries, were stationed guarding the approaches to the depot, and the troops were actually standing by in the trenches.

After we got to sea, Coltart, Pryor, and I matched coins to see who would stand the first watch. I was odd man, so settled down to do four hours on the conning tower while they had a sleep. Just as day was breaking, we received the recall signal again.

My boat, G 6, was one of three next on turn for overseas patrol. As we crept alongside the depot ship and moored, I reminded Coltart of this fact and told him I had had no opportunity to buy in the provisions for the two weeks' trip. The navigating officers usually acted as caterer of the officers' mess.

P

Coltart told me to slip home (it was then about 5:30 in the morning), have some sleep, and purchase the needed provisions on my way down to the depot ship in the morning. He told me that I did not need to hurry down as it wasn't likely there would be any further activity during the day. If there did happen to be another "panic," he promised he would let me know.

So that I could make faster time in case I was called, I borrowed a bicycle from one of the other officers. I had no trouble passing the sentries, for I had the pass-word. In five minutes I was home and in bed.

I did not seem to have closed my eyes properly when I heard my wife say, "Wake up, dear. A seaman is downstairs and wishes to speak to you." I hopped out of bed, threw my greatcoat over my pyjamas, and went to see what it was all about.

"Excuse me, Sir, but your boat is ordered to sea. Mr. Coltart told me to tell you to come like Hell."

It is one thing dashing half-dressed through the streets in the middle of the night when plenty of others are doing likewise. It is a totally different matter doing the same thing alone in broad daylight.

There was nothing else to do. The message was urgent. I pulled on my trousers, socks, and boots over my pyjamas, yelled out a "Good-bye, dearie, see you later" sort of adieu to my wife, and still wearing my greatcoat, rode hell-bent-for-election through the streets towards the depot on that hot summer's day.

I had been tired out when I arrived home, and my wife had allowed me to sleep on.

I forgot everything but reaching that infernal submarine before she put to sea. I forgot about trenches and sentries, for they were something new in Blyth. I was pedalling like a blue streak and going full speed ahead as I turned from the road down the approach to the depot entrance. I can just recollect seeing a figure jump out in front of me. I saw the flash of a bayonet. I heard the command, "Halt!" I swerved to the right to avoid running the man down or receiving the bayonet in the guts, my wheels locked in the deep golden sand which had drifted to the side of the road, and I sailed high in the air and landed "ker-plunk" right on top of some very astonished soldiers in the trench.

My greatcoat was up over my ears. My pyjama coat was in full view and the pink and white trousers were sticking out of the top of my uniform pants. I felt a perfect sight, and it did not improve my feelings any when I heard a voice say, " Too bad, Sir, but you should lay ofen married women. Yuh never can tell when their hubby's 'll come 'ome."

I felt so confoundedly angry I could have hung, drawn, and quartered that infernal sentry without the least compunction. He and nobody else was the immediate cause of my downfall. The silly ass might have known I wasn't an enemy trying to capture a whole line of trenches, twelve submarines, two destroyers, and an armed liner, alone.

After a moment the truly humorous side of the situation dawned on me. It was no use being angry; it was no use trying to explain the why and wherefore of the sleeping suit. I sat and laughed with the men. I explained to a second lieutenant who happened along that I was a submarine officer, extremely anxious to rejoin my boat, and informed him that if the sentry with the pig-sticker had no objections, I'd be getting along.

I was just in time. The submarines were actually pushing off when I rushed aboard. Lieutenant McKenzie, an officer who was serving with us as a " spare," had seen the depot navigator and obtained the confidential notices and sailing orders. A few minutes later we were at sea.

When I opened the sailing orders I found we were all ordered to Harwich. This was something new. Big events were about to happen or the powers that be would not have disorganized the whole system of submarine patrols to concentrate every available boat on Harwich.

We were all elated as we steamed south. We felt there was going to be " Something doing " at last.

We arrived in Harwich. We moored alongside the depot ship and waited. The Captains of all submarines were sent for and they were closeted with the Captain S—— in secret session for nearly an hour.

From Diary.

Last night the Huns raided the South-east coast with

Zeppelins and 'planes. It was one of the worst raids so far. I don't know how the women and children stand them as well as they do. You feel so helpless. There is nothing you can do. It is impossible to stay out in the open once your own guns begin to fire, for what goes up has got to come down, and that applied to anti-aircraft shells as well as other things.

Harwich is still having hard luck with her submarines. The flotillas based here lose the regular quota of one or two and sometimes three each month.

I saw an incident yesterday that will live in my mind for ever. I wouldn't have the Sky Pilot's job in this depot for all the money in the Mint. It is his job to break the news when a boat's overdue.

It's Hell doing the patrols. It must be worse than Hell for the women who wait for their husband's boat to return. God! I never gave much thought to the horror of war till I saw several women standing out there on the end of the wharf watching, dry-eyed and weary, for the boat on which their husbands had sailed . . . the boat which was overdue.

They stood there a pathetic little group. Officers' wives, wives of petty officers, and wives of seamen and stokers. They stood there bunched together. Common sorrow the great equalizer. Many of the women who were married to the lower-deck ratings carried babies in their arms. Mere girls most of them . . . pretty girls . . . widowed before they really knew what marriage was. They face the future alone . . . mateless . . . with a pension of one pound a week.

And their courage? Could anything be finer? The wives of the officers, dressed in the height of fashion, reach out and take into their own arms the grubby little youngsters which are just about breaking their own mothers' backs. And the kiddies themselves? Too young to realize the grim truth, made matters worse by continually jabbering, with chuckles of delight, to every man who passes in uniform: "Da da! Da da!"

And they stood and talked for hours watching towards the East for the boat which will never return. They buoy up each other's courage. "Remember, dear, how Mr.

HELL'S ANGELS OF THE DEEP

Johnston's boat got back . . . it was three days overdue . . . the boat which had to come back stern first because it had its bow blown off with a mine ? " I heard one say to the others.

Oh ! the cruelty of it all. Each and every one of them knew in their hearts they were widows. Each one knew that by the time they got back to their lodgings or their apartment in the hotel, there would be a telegram waiting for them couched in these words :

" The Admiralty regret to announce that the submarine on which your husband served is now overdue and must be considered as lost. Their Majesties tender their sincere sympathy to you in your hour of sorrow." And then would come a visit from the Depot Chaplain. A few days later you would see the same pathetic little group boarding the train with their belongings, bound for various parts of the country. They are saying good-bye to Harwich . . . good-bye to the " Grave-yard of the Fleet " . . . good-bye to the place where they had lived through months of anxious waiting . . . through nights of repeated air-raids so that they could give to their men-folk, when they came back from patrol, cold, tired, and weary, with nerves on edge, the relaxation . . . the sympathy and comfort of married life. Now they themselves were deprived of that happiness for ever.

What can be worse than for a young healthy woman to be widowed when she has just matured into the full bloom of motherhood ? The doors behind which lurked the secrets of nature during her years of childhood have been opened. She has learned the happiness which accompanies love and companionship, and most women are satisfied with the love of one man. How black must be the despair of the woman who is robbed of the man she truly loves ! How terrible must be her loneliness and how utterly barren and hopeless the future must appear ! A year of what we go through in submarines could not be compared to one sleepless night of any woman who remains at this depot when her husband is at sea.

If his boat hits a mine or is destroyed, his troubles are over—hers have just begun. If she values his memory and her own reputation, she must for ever be a slave to the conventions of society. The most powerful fires have been set aglow; the most potent influences turned loose; the most intense feelings stirred to life, and then, a woman, because she is the victim of bereavement, is expected to gather up the most powerful forces of nature and smother them, just when they have been fanned into the fiercest blaze by motherhood. She must weep resignedly over the smouldering ashes of her love. That is what is expected of a woman. There is at least something to say for the Indians who burned the widow on the funeral pyre together with her husband.

God! but such thoughts make me feel morbid. I'm going to quit writing now and join the others in the wardroom. I guess they have a "Binge" well under way . . . they always do when a boat is lost. Nobody ever refers to the loss deliberately. Some fellow who has been on leave or just come in from patrol may enter the mess, glance around, and ask: "Where's Watson . . . why the Hell isn't he at the piano?" And somebody else will answer: "He's not got back . . . yet." They never forget to add that word . . . YET . . . even if they were overdue a week. They like to think of them as just away on a longer trip than usual.

We went to sea and we had our stunt, but it turned out to be a proper washout. As far as I can gather, and that is not very much, the idea was to send out a flotilla of destroyers to a certain rendezvous in the "Bight." These destroyers were to act as a support to a number of minelayers; the latter were to lay a mine barrage across that particular section of the "Bight" which appeared to be regularly used by the enemy submarines when going out and returning from their commerce-raiding cruises.

It wasn't thought the enemy would sit quiet while our small surface craft steamed insolently around in what might be termed the enemy's own backyard. The British submarines were sent out to secrete themselves in certain strategical positions and attack the enemy. It was the old game. We tempted the enemy with a mouse, they were expected to send out a cat to gobble up the mouse. A terrier, in the form of our battle-cruisers, was intended to tackle the cat. The cat would naturally be "up a tree" and would have to stay there until the High Seas Fleet came to drive off the terrier. When that happened, the big British bulldog, represented by the Grand Fleet, was intended to be turned loose and clean up all comers.

That is what was undoubtedly intended. What happened was a very different thing. The enemy let us lay our mines. Next night they sent sweepers to clean them up. These little vessels were set upon by our destroyers which had been left to guard the mine-field and two of the enemy vessels were sunk.

Nothing further happened. We remained at sea until recalled. We waited, watching every hour, every minute, every weary second for the enemy to heave into view and give us a crack at them. It was hard enough waiting during the day; patrolling on the surface at night, never knowing what second the enemy would dash into view out of the darkness, was worse than some nightmares I experienced when a child.

While we were busy laying mines, so were the enemy. We were ordered back to port. Just as darkness settled over a war-weary world, we steamed into Yarmouth Roads. As we did so, two ships blew up on mines. We did the sensible thing and dropped the anchor right where we were and remained there until the mines were reported as swept up.

The following day was one of those glorious summer days such as we long to enjoy down by the seashore. The sun shone out of an almost cloudless sky. What clouds there were looked like puff-balls floating across an azure sky.

The sea was a sheet of shimmering blue streaked with the tiniest wavelets sporting little white caps. The golden sands threw back the warmth of the harvest sun and blended perfectly into the background of sandhills clothed in star-grass.

Hundreds of people came down for their early morning dip. Some used the conventional bathing vans; others were content with little bell tents open to the sea. One of the seamen who was keeping the anchor watch on the conning-tower with me swept the beach with his glasses and remarked:

"Them people ashore hevidently don't know 'ow close a pair of binoculars can bring things to the 'uman heye, Sir."

"Remember," I admonished him, jocularly, "he who

casts covetous eyes at his neighbour's wife already commits adultery. You better put those glasses away."

"Blimy, Sir, if looking at thim skirts what have nothing on over ashore is sinning, then I guess I'm going to keep the Recordin' H'angel busy to-day. Gor Blimy hit's better than going to a leg show at the theatre, strike me 'ansome if it ain't."

He sinned and so did many others also, for the story of the fox and the grapes had nothing on those men who were cooped up in the belly of a submarine while the world played before their eyes.

As the day wore on, dinner was eaten, and during the afternoon we three officers turned in to read or rest while the coxswain kept the anchor watch on deck. One man was at the high power periscope and the rest of the crew listened to his broadcast of events which were happening ashore.

I was reading in my bunk when I heard the seaman, who was looking through the periscope, say:

"Gor blimy! Say, 'Dusty,' what a bleedin' beauty. Strike me 'andsome if she ain't got a figure like Venus de Milo, or whatever the 'ell her name is. Just imagine being cooped up here while there's a skirt running abart ashore just longin' for 'e men like you and me, Dusty."

"What yuh see?" demanded Dusty.

"See? I can see the prettiest piece of skirt wifout anything on I ever saw in me life. She's sittin' there insider her tent wipin' the bloomin' sand off'n 'er feet and the flap of the tent's wide open. Tell 'Pincher' Martin to come and take a look. I don't think Pincher ever saw a girl à la natural in his life yet. 'E's that shy hit's simply bloody awful."

Pincher arrived.

"Say, Pincher, take a look on bearing red ninety. There's a target yuh ought to try and torpedo."

Most of the crew were gathered in the control room by this time enjoying the fun.

"What yuh mean, Dusty? What yuh want me to see? Is it them donkeys runnin' up and down wif kids on their backs?" replied the innocent one.

"Gawd blimy. Can yuh beat it?" the other demanded of the assembled crowd.

HELL'S ANGELS OF THE DEEP 233

In turn the crew looked through the periscope as the pretty young maiden completed her toilet all unconscious of the interest she had aroused aboard one of His Majesty's submarines. I think her ears must have burned, at least.

Suddenly there was a renewed burst of excitement. The signal rating had eyes like a lynx. He spotted a Marine and his girl sitting in the sand-hills which skirted the shore line. Sailors and Marines never did hit it off very well together.

"Can youse beat hit? A damned old 'leather-neck'[1] havin' luck like that!" he demanded of all and sundry. "And ain't she a beauty? Say, fellers, she's a peach. And 'e ain't half tellin' 'er the tale. Strike me 'ansome if 'e ain't. Damn the luck, says I."

"What they a-doin' of, Dusty?" asked one of the crew.

"They ain't a-doing nothin' yet . . . nothin' much, but 'e's a-lovin' 'er and huggin' and kissin' of 'er as if he wanted to eat 'er up," replied Dusty.

"Let's 'ave a look," demanded one of the men.

"G'an. Nothin' doin'. You're too young. Go and get the tea ready. You're cook of the mess to-day."

"Get on wif the news, Dusty. Don't mind Pincher."

"What they doin' of now?" demanded another.

"'E's just a-lovin' of 'er. She don't seem to take it none too kindly. Don't blame 'er a bit. If I wus a girl I'd never trust a Marine, strike me pink if I would."

"Girls are funny that way, Dusty. Most of 'em acts as if they were sore at yuh, but they get mad-as-hell if you quit lovin' 'em. When they say 'No!' they mostly mean 'Yes,'" the Chief L.T.O. opined.

"Hi treats 'em wif indifference. Let 'em think ye want sumfing and see if ye gets it. Make 'em believe yuh don't give a damn and they'll pester yer worse than a West African mosquito." Thus argued one man, with the conviction which only comes with long experience.

"Now take that Marine. 'E don't know nothin'. 'E's trying to stroke her leg and gettin' all excited. She's tryin' to make 'im behave 'imself. Instead of treatin' her calm and indifferent and approaching the subject slowly like, he's wrestlin' wif 'er as if 'e was trying to throw Ackensmith. 'E's in a 'ell of a 'urry. 'Is leave must be up to-night."

[1] Marine.

Then followed a detailed account of the amorous scene being enacted ashore. The broadcast terminated with these words:

"Gawd blimy! What a swipe. The bloke got too fresh. She fetched 'im one right to the point of the bleedin' jaw. What a wallop. I guess *that* 'ud kill 'is ambition. Come on . . . let's eat."

Next morning at daybreak the mine-sweepers reported all clear and we proceeded on our way to Blyth. As the sun rose up over the Eastern horizon and melted away the shadows of night, the mists rose from a sea so calm that it looked like a huge container of molten metal with a scum formed here and there. I found it hard to realize that only short hours before the very spot we were passing over had been the scene of sudden death and swift destruction.

I always think that it was this fact that affected one more than any other. The sea is ever the same in times of peace and times of war, whether it be stirred to anger by mighty tempests or is glossy calm under azure skies; it is the same old ocean sailors were born to and had learned to love in all its various moods. When sudden and hidden death sprang at you from the very bosom you had been reared upon, it all seemed so unnatural . . . so unreal. Human passions, human intelligence, had made it possible, even against the fundamental laws of nature, for mother ocean to kill with deadly hidden engines of destruction those born of her. To lose your ship, and perhaps your life, instantly, as the result of a deadly torpedo or a treacherous mine seemed strangely at variance to fighting a losing battle against the elements. To die when your vessel foundered under you because she could no longer battle against mountainous seas and the raging winds of Heaven is one thing. You went down awed and inspired by the majesty of the elements which had encompassed your doom but you could feel no anger against them. It is different to being struck a mortal blow unwarned and often in the dark. To be mined or torpedoed seems like falling victim to an assassin's knife stuck treacherously in your back.

We are back at Blyth. A lot has happened since I last wrote in this diary.

The weather was wonderful this last trip. Never had a

bad day. Little bit hot and stuffy in the boat towards the end of the day after a long dive . . . batteries gas a good deal in the hot weather . . . but on the whole, not so bad.

I thought I was developing nerves this last trip over. Got the jumps . . . or the jimmi-jambs, or whatever you like to call them. Thought I had begun to imagine things . . . see things . . . and all the rest of it. . . . All the time I was that way (and it lasted for over an hour), I kept saying to myself . . . What's the matter with you ? . . . You haven't been drinking . . . pull yourself together.

What happened was this. I relieved the Captain on the conning-tower at midnight. I was to keep the twelve to two watch. The sea was almost calm . . . there was a sort of lazy swell, the kind that would remind you of a well-gorged tiger wagging its tail.

It was dark . . . dark and still. . . . There was no wind except the little we made ourselves as we plodded along at a ten-knot clip. There was to me a peculiar oppressiveness about the atmosphere that night. . . . There was something uncanny about it . . . the silence . . . the extraordinary darkness . . . the lack of wind . . . almost a lack of air to breathe . . . the close sultriness . . . all seemed to accentuate the sound made by the surge of the bow as it cut into the dark water . . . and to give a more mournful tune to the sob of the water as it switched along the sides.

The sea itself looked like nothing so much as a huge bowl of ink. It was so dark that the phosphorescent glow of the myriads of marine organisms was increased a hundredfold. I couldn't help it. I felt uneasy. I felt something was about to happen. I felt as if some evil thing was about to befall me or the boat. I felt just like I did before we were wrecked in the typhoon out in China.

I felt as I imagine the criminal must feel who for ever is expecting the hand of the law to descend upon him.

I tried to put the feelings away from me . . . tried to master my nerves . . . for I honestly thought I was suffering my first real attack of nerves.

I swept the arc of the horizon with my night glasses . . . what there was of it. . . . It was one of those nights when the sea and sky melt into each other. There was no clear-cut dividing line. You seemed to be in a gigantic oven.

There were stars . . . but they gave no light. There was no moon. Suddenly my hair seemed to stand right up on end. A prickly sensation ran like icy fingers up and down the entire length of my spine. I gripped the rail and held my breath. Then I recovered myself and yelled down the voice-pipe to the helmsman to put his helm hard a-starboard.

Coming straight for me through the water were two parallel streaks of light. I had seen the tell-tale streak of a torpedo too often to mistake it . . . but I made a mistake that night. Just as I was resigned to the sensation of being blown to blazes . . . just when the two streaks were within ten yards of the bow . . . and coming straight as a die for them . . . they turned in perfect unison . . . and jumped out of the water.

Two porpoises were responsible for the scare, but on a night like that nobody can tell the difference between the streak of a porpoise cutting through the water and that of a " tin-fish." I cursed myself for a fool and steadied the boat back on her course, and asked Clark, one of the seamen, to bring me up a cup of strong black coffee.

But it was no use. Neither the presence of Clark nor the coffee could dispel the terrible feeling which had settled down on me like a blanket that night. The middle watch is not called the " Graveyard Watch " for nothing.

About one o'clock Clark went below again. I was for ever turning my head and looking over my right shoulder . . . some unseen force seemed to be drawing my attention to that direction. I took the night glasses and gazed long and earnestly into the darkness on our starboard quarter. The powerful lens showed me nothing.

Another fifteen minutes went by. I was getting really angry with myself. I was as jumpy as a jack-in-the-box. I had to take a grip on myself with both hands to prevent putting over the helm every time another porpoise played the same trick as the pair had done earlier in the watch. A pair of magnets might have been attached to the back of my head so powerful was the attraction which pulled my eyes from the darkness ahead . . . to the darkness on our starboard quarter.

Finally, to satisfy my instinct, perhaps to calm my nerves,

I surrendered myself to the subconscious urge. I called down the voice-pipe to Clark and told him to come up on the conning-tower. When he arrived, I told him to keep a sharp look-out ahead. I hung my arms over the beam which bridges the gap between the for'ard and after periscope and concentrated my gaze in the direction that unexplainable but irresistible force demanded.

And I hadn't been doing so long when I thought I saw something. I could not define what it was . . . but a sailor's eyes become like a cat's. I sensed there was something strange out there in the darkness. I was so sure that I asked Clark to look and see if he could make anything out. He couldn't. Nothing more was said and the watch continued. I still felt as if I was sitting upon a mine which was timed to go off any minute.

Again I saw something. It appeared only for a moment, but this time I was sure. It appeared white and as if it was illuminated with a dull phosphorescent glow. It looked ghostly as it showed for a moment against the absolute velvet blackness of the night.

After that it gradually began to appear more often, more regularly. It began to look like an enormous bird, its white wings hovering low over the water on our starboard quarter. As it took more distinct shape it looked as if the body of the bird was black and the outspread wings white . . . and frosted . . . like the frosting one sees on Christmas tree decorations. But by this time I knew what it was. It was the bow-wave of some low-lying craft . . . the dark body was the vessel's bow outlined by the phosphorescent glow of the water.

I pulled Clark by the sleeve and pointed in the direction. He lifted his glasses. " Hit's a blinkin' submarine, Sir. . . . Hit's headed just abart the same as we are, Sir. What do you think ? Can it be one of our own ? "

" No, it must be an enemy vessel," I whispered. . . . " None of our boats should be in this vicinity. You better slip down and call the Captain."

There were three things could be done. It was evident the enemy had not seen us. She had been gradually overtaking us. Steering exactly the same course as we were . . . travelling perhaps half a knot faster. We could turn and fire our torpedoes at her. . . . We could try and hit her with a shell out of the after gun . . . or we could try and ram her.

I ordered the for'ard tubes flooded . . . the gun crews to their stations. . . . I spoke down the voice-pipe and instructed the helmsman who had been steering from down below to connect with the upper steering position and hand over the helm to me.

By this time the Captain had come up on deck . . . but he was blind as a bat. . . . He couldn't see a thing, having just come hurriedly up out of the light into the darkness.

In a few terse words I explained the situation and asked his advice. . . . " Damned if I know. . . . Do whatever you think best. . . . I can't see a thing."

I told Clark to report if the gun-layer could see the enemy through his sights. He reported he couldn't see a thing. That settled it. I had to act and act quick, or the Fritz would be so near they would see us, and then it would put us in a bad position. We would be just ahead of her . . . and at her mercy. . . . I gave the order to stand by the for'ard tubes. To have turned towards her would have put us right on top of her, so I called down for full speed and gradually edged away . . . praying all the time she wouldn't see us until too late. . . . I told the Captain my intentions and he agreed.

When I had considerably increased the distance between us I put the helm hard over and turned towards the unsuspecting enemy submarine. . . . As our bow was just about to swing past her, I yelled down the voice-pipe to the crew to fire both torpedoes.

The " fish " streaked their way towards her. We went after them. If they had hit, I believe they would have destroyed both of us, we were so close to her. But the one thought uppermost in my mind was to sink that Fritz . . . never mind how . . . but sink her.

Both torpedoes ran deep. They passed right under her . . . but we were on top of her a moment afterwards.

We slid right over her stern and then put the helm hard over to bring her ahead again. We knew we had damaged her to some extent . . . but we didn't know how much. During the manœuvres following our attempt to ram her, she had drawn ahead several hundred yards.

Our engine-room crew responded to our appeal, and soon we were tearing through the water after her at a speed never before attained by a boat of our class . . . we logged over fifteen knots.

But the enemy must have been able to make a fraction of a knot more. She was evidently in no condition to dive . . . she stayed on the surface. We opened fire on her with our for'ard gun . . . our shooting was bad . . . it was almost impossible to see the enemy through the sights . . . and impossible to see the fall of the shells. . . She didn't reply.

After a time we gave up shooting at her and settled down to doing everything in our power to overtake her.

Daybreak came at last . . . the enemy submarine was one of the big cruiser type. She had a closed-in, dome-shaped conning-tower . . . she was about 8000 yards ahead of us when it came light enough for us to see properly through our gun-sights. . . . No matter how hard our engine-room staff worked the Fritz seemed to be just able to gain a little on us.

We opened fire at a range of 8000 yards. Our shooting was good, but the stern view of a submarine's conning-tower is not a very big target at 8000 yards, especially when your gun-platform is within four feet of the water itself and anything but stationary.

The damage we did to him was certainly not to his engine-room. He decided he had had enough and went off like a streak over the rim of the horizon. I don't know why she didn't shell us in return.

"THE SUBMARINE PATROL"

To the widows of the Submarine Service

DARK sinister forms, the product of man's ingenuity,
   Sallying forth into danger wrapped in obscurity,
Out from the harbour of that East Coast Town
   Slyly they steal as the sun goes down.

Through darkness and fog, through tempest and rain,
   They just " carry on," for it's part of the game,
Though death may lurk near, and conditions are vile,
   You'll ne'er hear them grumble, they're trained just to smile.

They are all volunteers, and the pick of our men,
    Determined to keep the foe locked in his den ;
They lay off his harbours and shut him in tight,
    Not daring to send his fleet out to fight.

But the dangers are real, and there's always a doubt
    That ere the trip's over and they turn about
To run through the mine-fields that lay in the way,
    They never may reach that East Coast Bay.

For there're planes in the air, and destroyers at sea,
    That search night and day. They are never left free ;
They hunt them with mines, and depth-charge, and net,
    And they've no means to tell where these dangers are set.

There are women who wait, faces anxious and drawn,
    Who scan the horizon from break of the dawn,
But day follows day—their boat's overdue :
    They have paid with their lives for devotion so true.

And hot briny tears have streaked many a face,
    As they choked back their sorrow and relied on God's grace
To give them the courage to start life anew,
    And raise the proud offsprings of the submarine crews.

WILLIAM GUY CARR.

CHAPTER XVIII

THE first week in January 1918 was cold and stormy. On the night of January 8th, the wind blew with hurricane force and a blizzard of sleet and hail accompanied it.

We had returned from our trip around the British Isles and were attached to the depot ship *Lucia* moored in the river Tees. On the night in question the flotilla officers had just finished dinner and were sitting comfortably engaged in a game of cards in the smoke-room of the depot ship. They had nothing to worry about, for they had taken the precaution to put out extra mooring wires from their boats while daylight lasted. They were satisfied that everything was safe and secure, and that the officer of the watch and the sentries on the boats would be more than ever alert in the face of the bad weather.

Lieutenant Chapman, D.S.C., who had been home for a few days' leave, blew into the smoke-room, stamping the ice off his clothes.

" Why didn't you get a taxi ? " someone asked.

" Taxi ? " snorted Chapman. " I never saw such a night. The taxicabs and motor-cars are all frozen where they last stopped. The street-car tracks are filled with ice."

The card game was just about well under way when a seaman entered the smoke-room and announced : " The officer of the watch ordered me to report that a coal hulk has broken adrift in the river and is endangering your boats, Sirs." The man was hastily questioned by some of the senior officers and we all realized that real danger was imminent. Everyone rushed to don oilskins.

What a sight met our gaze when we reached the sea-wall to which the flotilla was moored. Two boats were berthed next to the sea-wall and the other four were moored outside of them, making two tiers of three boats each. The icy wind was blowing with hurricane force, and the atmosphere was full of driving sleet.

At the moment we arrived a huge coaling hulk had drifted down on to the first three boats. They were all mixed in a tangle, and the coal hulk, which at one time had been a wooden sailing ship, was lifting up and down with the surge of the angry seas, threatening to pound herself and the submarines to pieces.

A big barge loomed up out of the storm and wedged itself between the hulk and the sea-wall. The seas lifted the two wooden vessels on their crests and crashed them down on the sterns of the three submarines.

There was only one thing to do and that was to get a hawser off to the coal hulk, make it fast, and let the seamen ashore haul the hulk clear with the aid of the steam capstans.

I got safely on to the barge, which was tossing about like a mad thing, and hanging on one moment as a wave broke over me, I scrambled across the heaving decks the next. The sides of the coal hulk towered high above the deck of the barge. She lifted high in the air on each succeeding wave-top and came hurtling down with a sickening crash on the stern of the submarines.

The task of getting aboard her seemed almost impossible. However, I noticed the end of the cable, by which she had been moored when she broke adrift, was dangling over the bow. I knew that would enable me to get aboard if only I could reach it.

Both the hulk and the barge were adrift, free from any kind of control and at the mercy of the wind and waves. They were alongside each other one moment and thirty feet apart the next.

I scrambled along to the bow of the barge, hoping they would drift close enough together to enable me to catch hold of the end of the parted cable.

After several attempts I managed to catch hold of it and started to climb aboard, but the cold had begun to get in its work. My hands were growing numb; my water-soaked clothes and the drag of the heaving line were added burden. It took every ounce of my will power and energy to climb each extra foot up the cable that swung back and forth with the pitch and roll of the old hulk.

I could feel every jar as she pounded down on the partly

submerged sterns of the submarines. I realized that it would only be a question of time before she would either break them adrift or sink them, so I renewed my efforts to climb aboard.

Finally I got within reach of the deck and pulled myself aboard. I beat my arms across my chest to get the cramps out of them and start the circulation again, then I signalled ashore that I was ready to haul off the heavier hawser. They bent it on to their end of the heaving line and I hauled it off and made it fast. I saw the men ashore take the hawser to a steam capstan, but the thing wouldn't work. It was like everything else that night, frozen stiff.

Few people can realize what wet cold really is like. You can have zero weather on a nice dry day without the slightest discomfort, but the damp cold seems to penetrate into the very marrow of your bones. Your fingers and toes seem to swell to bursting-point. The pain becomes excruciating.

As I stood there in agony, my clothes froze stiff as a board. However, I saw through the blinding storm dozens of men, yes, hundreds, collecting ashore. At first I didn't realize what it meant, but soon I saw them lay hold of the six-inch manilla line and start to haul the hulk clear by sheer brute strength. The officers laid hold with the men and lent their weight, while I could see Lieutenants Chapman and Bradshaw urging them on to superhuman efforts like coaches do a tug-of-war team. Slowly but surely their efforts were rewarded. I no longer felt the sickening bumps as the hulk crashed down on the submarine.

I had grown numb. The pain in my bones had mercifully grown less and less. A kind of tired, drowsy, comfortable feeling took the place of the excruciating torture I had at first experienced. Then I sensed something was wrong. I thought I heard tiny voices calling as from a great distance. I made a superhuman effort to arouse myself. I tried to beat my arms again, but they were simply made of lead. My legs were little better, but I could just move them. Forcing my eyes open, I dimly saw the figures ashore excitedly waving to me. They were apparently yelling at the top of their voices, but they were shouting into the teeth of the gale. My senses seemed to register the fact that they were trying to warn me about something. I made another effort to collect my senses and force my intellect to function, this time with success. The coal hulk was sinking under me. She had pounded a hole in her bottom.

It is extraordinary what the sense of self-preservation will enable a man to do. The shock of the discovery seemed to give me renewed energy. I realized I had to act to save myself, so I dragged myself over to the rail which was almost level with the water. The coal hulk was at this time about forty feet from the dock wall and about the same distance from the submarines.

The top of the dock wall was at least twenty feet above the water, and I realized that it was useless to swim to it, so determined to try and reach the barge, which was low in the water.

Frantically I tried to beat some feeling back into my limbs. The old coal hulk, which had in her day been a fine sailing ship, settled lower and lower. As she sank, the water actually felt warm. It revived me.

I don't think I would have made the barge if Chapman and Bradshaw hadn't come to my assistance, because the next thing I remember clearly was being with them in the barge, which was full of water to the gunwales. The waves were washing right over her, and the barge was still pounding herself on the sterns of the submarines.

The men ashore threw down a line, and Bradshaw and Chapman made it fast to the thwart of the barge. Then the men ashore hauled the barge clear, but she also was in a sinking condition, so the three of us entered the water again and swam to the submarines.

This was the most dangerous part of the experience. The sterns of the boats projected quite a distance just beneath the surface. The after hydroplanes and propeller guards also formed ugly obstructions to avoid. The seas were running quite high and broke in a smother of foam against the sloping decks of the submarines.

I was nearly exhausted by this time, and the waves threw me up on the slippery decks of the submarines, only to suck me back again before I could catch hold of anything.

Bradshaw and Chapman managed to get on to the deck of a submarine, and then they pulled me out also.

One of the mooring lines had parted, and when we

recovered sufficiently we proceeded to get the submarines securely moored again. Under the existing weather conditions, this was no easy task. It was the wee sma' hours before we got back on the wharf and staggered to the depot ship, where we were given medical attention.

Following my experiences that night I took a severe cold, but one simply hated to report sick when the flotilla was having a run of bad luck. Several of the G-boats had failed to return from their last patrol. When these things happen you feel that to report sick might be taken by others to indicate that you had developed an attack of cold feet. Too many officers and men remained on duty in the submarine service during the war when they should by rights have gone to hospital.

.   .   .   .   .   .

The exposure and cold, followed by an attack of the measles and the worry of passing my examinations for Master Mariner, proved too much for my physical condition. Weakened by almost eighteen months' service in G 6, I grew weaker and weaker. I developed a bad cough and lost forty pounds in weight. May 2nd found me onboard a hospital train bound for Haslar Hospital labelled " Observation Case—T.B."

I was discharged from the submarine service and my training certificate book marked " Unfit for Further Service."

From Haslar I was sent up to Peebles, where the Admiralty had taken over the huge hydro as a convalescent hospital for officers of the Royal Navy and Royal Naval Flying Corps. It was a wonderful place, situated on the banks of the river Tweed, among the Lowlands of Scotland, amid scenery which had inspired the masterpieces of such men as Scott and Robert Burns. It was here that men who had been broken by the war were nursed back to health and strength.

My wife came up to join me, and the following morning, which happened to be Sunday, we went to church. Just as the preacher was about to start his sermon somebody came in late. It was a naval officer and a lady. They tiptoed to vacant pews just behind where my wife and I were sitting. The officer stumbled as he entered the pew and fell, making a most awful racket. I automatically turned my head, as did most of the other members of the congregation. My eyes met those of the other naval officer as he picked himself up. It was Jock P——. The same old Jock I referred to earlier on. We had served on the same ship together at the outbreak of the war. He is one of the best linguists in the British Navy, and when volunteers were called for he had offered his services to the Intelligence Department of the Admiralty. After he left the D—— Jock disappeared completely. None of us knew where he had gone. Rumour had it that he had gone into the enemy's own country as a secret service agent. That turned out to be the truth.

Commander P——, as he now is, was always a rather excitable sort of fellow under ordinary circumstances, but cool as a cucumber when circumstances warranted it. As we looked at each other in mutual recognition, we both forgot we were in church. Jock held out his hand and said in a voice audible throughout the church, " Good God ! who expected to see you here ? "

The titter which went up from the congregation brought us both to our senses. Our wives flushed to the colour of ripe tomatoes, and Jock and I buried our heads in our arms in an attitude of devout prayer.

After the service was over . . . and I never attended a sermon which seemed to last so long, we all went to the hotel and had dinner. What a time we had. Jock had just escaped from Northern Russia, where he had been engaged in counter-revolutionary work, and when he escaped he took with him the lady who was now his wife. She, too, had had a price upon her head. She was a daughter of one of the best Russian families. While Jock was working in Russia, a romance started which ripened into love, and when he escaped he took his fiancée with him.

.   .   .   .   .   .

Followed weeks of complete happiness. Weeks of wonderful fishing, good food, fresh air, and hospitality as only the Scotch (much maligned) are capable of. There were two other submarine officers in the hospital (or supposed to be, because we were seldom ever in the place except for morning inspection, and we avoided that if it were possible to manage it). But there is a war on. I can't explain why, but I noticed that all those who were not out-and-out malingerers wanted to get back into the service again. They had started out to do a job of work and they wanted to finish it. Early in July I applied for and was granted leave. Previous to getting it, I had asked to be discharged from hospital and sent back to submarines, but the Medical Officers simply laughed at me.

When I was granted my leave I went down to London. I called in to see Admiral S. S. Hall, who commanded the British Submarine Service. "Why, I thought you had been knocked out for good," he greeted me. "I thought from what the Medical Officer said in his report that it was a wooden jacket for you. . . . I'm more than pleased to see you looking so well." Admiral Hall was one of the best liked officers in the Service. He had that great gift of being able to remember every officer who served under him by name.

I told him I was feeling fit again and would like to get back into submarines. "You do? Well now, if you feel equal to it, you are just the man I'm looking for," he replied, and added: "The Navigating Officer of K 12 has been taken suddenly and seriously ill. I don't know just how to replace him. If you feel equal to going up to Rosyth and taking over his duties, I'll relieve you as soon as I can get somebody to take your place. I'll give you a shore-berth for a time and give you a chance to get really fit again," he told me. A couple of days later I reported to Lieutenant-Commander Bowers, the Captain of submarine K 12.

What gigantic vessels these K-boats are. They are, roughly, 400 feet long, 2000 tons displacement, and carry a crew of fifty-seven officers and men. They are simply submersible destroyers. They carry an armament of ten 21-inch torpedoes and three 4·1-inch Q.F. guns. They are capable of steaming 25 knots when on the surface and 10 knots submerged. That was a distinct departure from any other type of submarine then built. They are driven by steam engines when on the surface and are so constructed that the engines and boiler room can be shut off and the boat dived in from four to five minutes after the alarm has been given. Their purpose is to operate with the battle fleet. Should the fleet succeed in making contact with the enemy, the plan is to have these huge submarines so that they can dive and attack the enemy ships.[1]

In the early part of 1918, they were ordered to sea ahead of the battle cruiser squadron which was also based on Rosyth. The enemy had been reported as having put to sea. They rushed out, keen to test their skill. Just as they reached the entrance to the Firth of Forth, one of the rear boats developed engine trouble. It was a pitch dark night. The crippled boat signalled her predicament to the Senior Officer, who was in the leading submarine. He replied that she was to return to base. The signal was taken by the officers of the other boats to be intended as a general signal. They proceeded to make a sixteen point turn. The battle cruisers, which were tearing along in their wake, crashed into them. In the terrible darkness indescribable confusion ensued until signal lamps flashed their warning into the night.

When it was all over, two K-boats lay at the bottom of the Firth of Forth. They were K 4 and K 17. Others were badly damaged but they had been saved from sinking by the heroic conduct of their crews. Lieutenant Antrim, the Navigator of one of the boats which was lost, had served with me in the Blyth Flotilla. I can well remember the day he came into my cabin and told me that the Captain of the boat he was then serving in had been appointed to take command of the new K-boat.

"He wants me to go with him," Antrim told me. "I'd like to and yes somehow I don't like leaving this flotilla." (Antrim was married. His wife was expecting a baby.) I knew what a terrible time of worry and anxiety a woman went through during that trying period. My wife had told me how the days had dragged and the nights been hours of slow torture while she waited for the message which told her that G 6 had safely returned from patrol. K-boats did not do those patrols in enemy waters. Their great task would only mature if the enemy came out to fight. This possibility seemed unlikely.

---

[1] They were never given the opportunity of showing what they were capable of in a general fleet action, but, as a flotilla, they suffered one of the greatest tragedies of the war.

Then again there was the period during which he would be standing by while the new boat was completing construction, the period when the trials were being done. I pointed out to him these things. I told him if I were in his place I would most certainly accept the offer and go to the bigger and more comfortable boat. He went. The boat he left continued patrolling into enemy waters and survived the war. Antrim's K-boat sank with nearly all her crew as the result of the accident. K 1 was also sunk as the result of an accident. If I remember rightly it was in the latter part of 1917, and K 13 sank during her trials in the Garlock. She was raised to the surface again and most of her crew saved. Some forty men, many of them dockyard men, who were just aboard for the trials, lost their lives. Such was the luck of the K-class.

Admiral Hall kept his promise and in August I received a letter telling me that another officer was on his way to relieve me and that I was to report to the Admiralty for instructions. What a surprise I got. I was informed that I had been appointed as navigating officer of submarine R 12, which was then under construction in the yards of Cammell-Lairds in Birkenhead, Liverpool. She would not be ready until the end of October.

My home was in Preston, just near Liverpool, and for the next two months I had little to do except visit the boat and learn all about her. She was another experiment. She had been especially designed and constructed to operate against enemy submarines. She could only make about seven knots on the surface, but her surface speed had been sacrificed for battery space and motors which would drive her when submerged at a speed of nearly 15 knots.

Experience had taught us that very often an enemy submarine on the surface escaped when sighted by a British submarine which was patrolling submerged, simply because the British submarine had not sufficient speed and battery power to head her off and get within range. Often when on patrol in enemy waters, we sighted U-boats proceeding on the surface at approximately 12 to 14 knots and we didn't sight them until they were almost abeam and just at the extreme range of our periscope horizon. That meant we had to chase off after them to close the range and often be satisfied with an acute angle shot, which promised little hope of making a hit. It was hoped that the R-class submarines, with their great submerged speed and the fact that they carried six torpedo tubes built into the bows, would not miss many submarines they were fortunate enough to sight through their periscopes. It was possible to fire all six bow tubes at once. From our point of view, it made all the difference in the world. Up till now we had been like a man trying to shoot rabbits on the run with a rifle. Now we were being handed a scatter gun.

The yards at Cammell-Lairds were busy night and day. R 11 was just about completing. Several L and H class submarines were on the slips under construction. The weeks flew by. R 11 did her trials and made a submerged speed of nearly 12 knots. Lieutenant Barry, D.S.O., who was my new commanding officer, conceived the idea that streamline could be applied to submarine constructions as well as to aeroplanes. After considerable trouble and many trips to London, he got permission to have certain alterations made in the shape of the superstructure and conning-tower of R 12. When we did our trials we made a submerged speed of 14·75 knots.

Lieutenant Barry, my new Captain, is only a young man. He had previously sunk the German submarine U B 72. For this he had been decorated with the D.S.O. and appointed to command the new R-boat. Lieutenant Lowther, R.N.R., has been appointed first lieutenant of R 12. He is a reserve officer who volunteered for navigating duties in submarines at the outbreak of the war. He has had a great deal of experience and had served in E, H, D, and K-class submarines before coming to R 12. He was navigator of the H-boat which torpedoed the Italian submarine when on patrol in the Adriatic. The two boats had gone out on patrol together and were supposed to patrol miles and miles apart. Due to poor navigation, the Italian vessel wandered off her patrol and drifted into the area Lowther's boat was in.

The British submarine sighted her just as it broke daylight. As no other friendly submarines were supposed to be working in their vicinity, they attacked and torpedoed her.

HELL'S ANGELS OF THE DEEP 251

They didn't know their mistake until they were fishing a couple of survivors aboard.

Lowther was also on one of the K-boats which was rammed by the battle cruiser squadron in the entrance to the Firth of Forth. His calmness and courage in remaining below to shut the water-tight doors after the boat had been rammed and severely damaged was responsible for saving the boat herself and many lives. He is a very capable officer, highly efficient, and with a length of service in submarines equalled only by one or two other officers of the Royal Naval Reserve, yet he has not received a decoration.

Early in October H 33 was launched and Admiral and Lady Hall arrived down for the occasion. Lady Hall had been asked to christen the new H-boat. An invitation was extended by Sir George Carter, the General Manager of the shipbuilding yards, to all officers and their wives then in Birkenhead, to attend the luncheon which the firm was giving in connection with the launching ceremony. There were a number of American officers present as well as Army and Air Force officers stationed at the various camps in the vicinity.

After the tapes had been cut and the champagne broken over the bow, luncheon was served, and what a wonderful meal that was. Food was pretty scarce at that time in England, but there was an abundance of good things on the table that day. Lady Hall, replying to a toast, stated that she had never aspired to be a public speaker, and asked if she might pass the responsibility on to her husband. Admiral Hall rose and made one of the finest speeches it was ever my pleasure to listen to. He had the whole company in roars of laughter at the start, and the tribute he paid to the men who served under him left many in tears at the end.

" I don't know why my wife should be embarrassed when asked to make a speech on an occasion like this," he remarked, when he rose to speak. " This is not the first launching ceremony she has attended and been the principal. Neither is she backward at speaking her mind at home. She has been the principal at five launching ceremonies. She launched five children of mine onto the sea of life. . . . I sincerely hope and trust they will grow up to be men who will be of equal service to their country as those I have the honour to command to-day."

He then went on to outline the work of the submarine service for the benefit of those who were strangers to it, and finished with such a glowing tribute to the officers and men who served under him that those of us who happened to be of the service didn't know what to do to hide our blushes. He ended by paying a wonderful tribute to those who had made the supreme sacrifice.

He asked those present to drink a silent toast to the 33 per cent of the officers and men of the submarine service who lie in their steel coffins on the bed of the ocean in various parts of the world. That was probably the first occasion on which the actual losses amongst the personnel of the submarine service were made public.

"THE SINKING OF UB 72"

A tribute to Lieut. Claude Barry, D.S.O., one of my submarine Commanders

SHE was built by Cammell-Laird's,
O'er there in Birkenhead,
They laid her keel, and wrought the steel,
Into shapes that nations dread,
She was neat and trim, but of sinister shape,
And more deadly than ships of yore,
As she left the stocks, and broke the tape,
To start on her life of war.

She was fitted out 'mid the noise and shout,
Of the ever boisterous throng,
Then they tested her out in the Mersey's mouth
To make sure that nothing was wrong,
And when she returned from her first speed trials,
And dive and other stunt,
She was handed new to the special crew,
Who would take her out to hunt.

HELL'S ANGELS OF THE DEEP

They sailed her out of the Mersey's mouth,
And passed by Holyhead,
Then south by west in the rolling swell.
The sky looking heavy as lead.
Blowing half a gale, she was like a whale,
As she made the Lizard Light.
Then she straightened away, at break of day,
And steered for the Isle of Wight.

In a submarine it is easily seen,
It is best to keep out of sight,
For none are your friends, and all ready to send,
The shell that will end your life.
So in the cold grey dawn of the early morn,
She dived and her watch did keep,
Through her powerful eye, sweeping sea and sky,
While she lurked in the waters deep.

It was just four bells, and the heavy swells,
Rolled in from Biscay's Bay,
When the eagle eye of the watchful Lieut. (Lute)
Saw something his breath did stay.
Yes! certain now, on the starboard bow,
Was an object that roused his hate,
So with warning shout, he brought her about,
And called to the coxswain's mate.

" Port-a-bit " . . . " Steady " . . . " As you go "
A Fritz by the living God.
And away to the right a smug of smoke,
Just like a wisp of fog.
She is nearer now scarce a thousand yards
As she rides the heaving swell,
But the " fish " in the tubes are soon released,
To point out the road to hell.

They braced themselves to withstand the shock,
As the four " Fish " end their race.
And when the explosion had done its work,
Of the Fritz there was scarcely a trace.
So they blew their tanks, and offered up thanks,
For a day's work nobly done,
And went o'er the surface thick with oil.
To rescue a half-drowned Hun.

The sole survivor of all that crew,
Which numbered just thirty-two.
He was fished aboard, rubbed down and thawed,
With a mug of steaming brew,
The smug of smoke was thickening fast,
And the hulls of the ships appeared,
So they filled their tanks and quickly sank,
As the ships of the convoy neared.

They passed them by on that morning tide,
Six transports filled with men,
And they laughed and sang, and little knew,
The difference *now* from *then*.
They were headed for homeward shores,
For leave and joy supreme.
But they'll never know, what they really owe,
To that British Submarine.

CHAPTER XIX

ALL was bustle and hurry in the shipbuilding yards, and the day fast approaching when R 12 would be ready to take her initial dip below the surface. She was only a small submarine as far as length went, not 200 feet over all, yet she was absolutely the last thing in submarine construction. Her control system was something we were all proud of. The control was in very fact the brain of the boat, and all her diving machinery and armament could be handled right from under the eye of the officer on duty in the control room. As an added safety measure, most of her machinery could be operated by electricity, hydraulic power, by compressed air, and by hand. Hundreds of tons of batteries and equipment were lowered into the boat, and it was subject for amazement to those unfamiliar with a submarine to know where it could possibly be stowed.

But everything had its own particular place even to the last little wrench. The mass of machinery and equipment which covered the greater part of a huge freight shed gradually disappeared into the bowels of the tiny craft, and the day arrived when the inside of her hull looked like the interior of a watch. The dry-dock in which the finishing touches had been completed was flooded and R 12 turned her motors for the first time. Gradually she slid astern, passed through the dock gates and turned into the trial basin.

Up to this moment, she was only a boat. The next hour would prove whether or not she was a submarine. Everyone went ashore except her crew, who had arrived from the depot ship *Platypus*, and a few technical and other experts attached to the submarine branch of the Admiralty and the naval dockyards. Calculations had been made to ascertain her centre of buoyancy, her metercentre height, her centre of gravity. The capacity of her tanks was known, the weight of every ounce in her hull was known. The weight of her crew and the extra men she carried was figured out, and then a simple calculation was made to find out the number of gallons of water which would have to be admitted to her ballast tanks to overcome her surface buoyancy and cause her to sink to the bottom of the harbour.

Barry was busy with the experts in the control room. Lowther and I had the men who were now our crew stationed throughout the boat ready to report any leaks or weaknesses they could discover in the hull. We heard the order given to flood the tanks. All hatches had been closed; all eyes fastened themselves on the depth-gauge. Just as the right quantity of water had been admitted into the tanks, the needle of the gauge began to flicker. There was a sigh of relief. No need for another check-up of weights. Nothing had been overlooked. The calculations had been correct to the last final pound. That great silent engine of destruction was ready to respond to the will of her human masters. A valve was *cracked* and the depth-gauge needle swung round slowly and steadily to stop at 50 feet. We were resting on the bottom of the trial basin. Officers, men, and experts crawled throughout the length and breadth of the submarine. Each carried a piece of chalk, a note-book, and a flash-light. Every seam and rivet was examined. Every place where the slightest sign of dampness showed was encircled with a white chalk mark and the position jotted down in a note-book. If a seam or rivet leaked ever so slightly at 50 feet, what might happen at two or even three hundred feet was something nobody intended to take chances on.

When everyone was satisfied that all weak places had been detected, air was put in the tanks and the water ballast gently forced out of them. R 12 rose to the surface, and a cheer went up from the hundred men who were lined up on the wharf watching the spot where she had disappeared an hour earlier.

Back onboard came the workmen. Rivet-guns hammered tightening up all seams and loose rivets. Defective rivets were removed and replaced by new ones.

Next morning the big and real test was made. Just as the sun raised itself over the top of the Liver Building across the river, we eased our way out into the river and headed

SUBMARINE R 12 COMING UP AFTER HER FIRST DIVE IN THE TRAIL BASIN

This photograph, presented to the Author by Sir George Carter, is extraordinary in as much as it shows H.M.S. *Donegal*, H.M. Submarine K 12, and H.M. Submarine R 12, on all of which the Author had served during some period of the War.

down the Mersey. New Brighton, with its miles of promenade and acres of amusement places, slipped by on our port beam as we drove the surface engines at full speed and covered the measured mile. We only made seven knots, but the engines ran like a seventeen-jewelled watch. There was not a knock or a sign of heating. The pistons thrashed up and down, music to the ears of the engine-room ratings who calmly and carefully wended their way among them, feeling here, bending their ears to listen there, stroking them with their hands full of oily waste like a mother would pat her new-born child with a powder puff.

I had my own work to attend to. Checking the compasses, keeping her on her course, checking her speed, examining her surface and diving steering gear, both hand and electric. I checked the gyro-compass with the magnetic and the magnetic with the range marks ashore. In a few minutes we would crash under and hurl ourselves along under the surface with every ounce of power our motors were capable of. The first trial would be at periscope depth, the second at 100 feet. I needed to be sure of my compasses. We didn't want to dive into a sand bank 100 feet below the surface when travelling at nearly twenty land miles an hour.

Barry was on the conning-tower with me. Lowther down below watching his precious machinery and getting his motors ready for their cruel grind.

"Let me know when you are ready, Pilot. We'll drive her one mile out at eighteen to twenty-two feet and then turn and dive to one hundred feet and come back over the same course."

A quick bearing of the Formby and Crosby Lightships and the lighthouse at New Brighton gave me a definite position. I laid off a course which gave us good clear running.

"Let her go. . . . I'm all set."

C-L-A-N-G! C-L-A-N-G!

The klaxon horns were sounding throughout the boat for the first time. Barry slid down into the control-room. I followed him through the hatch and pulled it down on top of me and adjusted the clamps.

"Steady her at twenty feet." Barry gave the order. The crew were handling the boat now.

A few more orders were given as he juggled with the ballast tanks and adjusted the fore and aft trim of the boat by means of the trimming tanks situated in the bow and stern. Lowther was busy preparing his torpedo tubes for *Dummy-shots*. I had steadied her on her course and checked it once again with bearings through the periscope.

" Everyone all set ? " The reports came back from the for'ard compartment, the motor-room, that everything was ready.

" Two hundred on each . . . four hundred on each . . . six hundred on each. . . ." At intervals of two or three minutes Barry increased the power of the motors until they were going at their top speed. I had set the Forbes log and saw the indicator was ticking away merrily. We gave her sufficient time to gather her full measure of speed, then timed the log for a mile. Her speed worked out at just a fraction under fifteen knots, the fastest any submarine in the world had ever travelled under the surface.

We turned and dived to 100 feet. No leaks or undue strain had been reported by the men stationed at their various posts throughout the boat up till now. How would she stand the strain of being driven through the water at fourteen knots with an additional pressure of forty-five pounds to the square inch on the hull ? That is what we were there to find out. Down . . . down we sank, slowing down as we made the turn of sixteen points, then speeded up again.

Barry is a great fellow for the submarine game. He loves a thrill. Excitement is the spice of his life. " You take her, Pilot, I'm going along to that motor-room. If there's anything to bust or blow up, we might as well do it right here and now, rather than when we are hot on the trail of some Fritz."

The men who belonged to his crew sat at their stations and grinned. Those who belonged to the dockyard looked at each other but said nothing. These dockyard men were paid highly for being onboard a submarine during her trials. It was easy to see by the expression on their faces that submarine men are born, not made. You have got to be submarine-minded to enjoy the life, just the same as one must be air-minded if you wish to make a success of flying.

Hollow but cheerful, Barry's voice filtered through the voice-pipe from the cramped motor-compartment right aft.

"We are going to give her all she's got tucked away, Pilot. I'll pass you the word when to start and clock her ... we are out to knock fifteen knots out of her or bust!"

"Crazy as a loon," I heard one of the dockyard men mutter to his pal standing close alongside of him. "Must be, or they wouldn't sail in these God-damned contraptions.... If the bloody motors blow up, we'll be a nice kettle of fish."

"Exactly!" This from one of our crew. "You'd be a nice kettle of fish alright alright ... same as that bunch which went down in K 13 ... but they wuz boiled fish ... gor blimy if they wusn't." (Those who died had been imprisoned in the boiler-room of the K-boat.)

The man's attitude of calm disgust towards the uneasy land-lubbers, and his reference to those dockyard men who had been scalded to death in the engine-room of K 13 when she sank during her trials, caused the rest of the men standing crowded in the control-room to laugh at the two who had evidently got the fidgets badly.

R 12 began to shake and vibrate like a man with the palsy. You could literally feel her tearing her way through the depths. You could sense each added ounce of power. She seemed almost like a human being trying to snatch victory from defeat in the last few yards of a flat race.

"All ready, Pilot ... time her!"

"Aye-aye, Sir!"

For four long minutes she trembled and shook as she was forced through the water at 100 feet with every ounce of power her motors were capable of. Barry watched the motors, Lowther the hull and the hatches, while I remained in the control-room. Slowly the tenths ticked off until the finger which registered on the mileage dial flicked off one more mile. I pressed the lever of the stop watch. Four minutes and four seconds to cover one mile—14·75 knots. We had established a world's record and beaten the speed R 11 had made by nearly three knots. Barry had proved his contentions about streamline and justified his insistence that the alterations to the superstructure and shape of the conning-tower should be made. I reported the speed to him as I heard a " Whoop ! " come through the voice-pipe which would have done credit to a North American Indian on the warpath.

R 12 was tight. She had fulfilled all our expectations and those of her builders. We came cautiously to periscope depth, took a look around, fired our dummy-shots, rose to the surface and returned to port. The formality of officially receiving her from the builders on behalf of the Admiralty was gone through and she was ours.

November 7th found us heading out of the Mersey bucking a heavy north-westerly gale. We were going on our first patrol. Our instructions were to proceed around by the North of Ireland and report to the base which had been established at Killibegs on the north-west coast of Ireland. Hydrophones on trawlers, the deadly depth charges, mined nets and minefields had made operating in the water around the British Isles a very unenviable occupation for the German submarines. News had reached us that the German authorities were finding great difficulty in getting crews to man their underseas boats. We heard that several of the crews had absolutely refused to sail after returning from their last voyage. We had also learned that the life of an average U-boat during the last six months of the war was figured at about three months.

We had our own troubles, but they certainly were having theirs. The few boats which were operating were doing so off the coast of Ireland and in the Bay of Biscay. We had information that a group of six or eight U-boats had passed through the Straits of Gibraltar and were returning to Germany from the Mediterranean. We were to lie in wait for them as they made their way past the north-west point of Ireland.

Rumours that the war was coming to a close reached our ears. If the truth must be admitted, we didn't want it to finish just then. We all felt that we had had our noses rubbed pretty deep in the mud and dirt for four long weary years, and we were far from anxious to hear the whistle blow to stop the game just as things began to go our way. None of us wanted an armistice. We wanted nothing but a complete victory and surrender by the enemy.

Just as darkness took the place of day, when grey skies

and black clouds made it impossible to distinguish where the sea finished and the sky commenced, we were fired on by an armed trawler. That was nothing unusual, but it is always annoying. We gave the necessary signals and passed on. We wondered if it were the same craft which had given R 11 such a shelling as she left the Mersey only a few weeks ahead of us. As we worked our way across the Irish Sea, making about five knots, we rolled and pitched until we all began to marvel how in the name of fortune she stopped before she went right over. I had sailed in every kind of craft that ploughs the ocean, from Chinese junks to the lordly trans-Atlantic liners; from humble fishing boat to the picturesque full-rigged sailing ship; from crazy destroyers to mammoth battleships; but I never experienced anything like the way R 12 rolled that night. She was built without rolling-chocks, and she jerked through the arc of her roll something like a prize-fighter swings an upper-cut.

The roll indicator showed that she rolled through an arc of about 74 degrees and she did it in about one second flat. She seemed to snuggle her nose into one sea and roll herself over the top of the next in a jerky corkscrew motion; she would stand on her tail as if to look at what next was ahead of her, and having seen it she would fall into the trough of the next wave just in time to miss the creaming crest and dive under it. As one man said to me, holding his false teeth firmly in his hand to keep from losing them overboard, " It's not sailors they want in this bloody tub, Sir . . . it's broncho-busters . . . strike me 'andsome if it ain't . . . ouch . . . gurr-r-r ouch . . . and me payin' tuppence hap'ny a pint for that 'alf-and-'alf just before we sails, Sir . . . beggin' your pardon . . . but I can't keep it down . . . much as I'd like to, Sir . . . this is sure awful . . . strike me pink if it ain't."

Barry relieved me on the conning-tower. He was as white about the gills as a cod-fish which has laid on a fishmonger's slab for a week. It was November and cold, but the sweat was running off his forehead in rivulets. I grinned at him. So far I was feeling O.K., except that my legs and ribs were sore from gripping the periscope standard and from the chafing of the rope which we called a soul-and-body lashing. We lashed ourselves to the periscope standard with this rope and it kept us from being washed overboard as she dived through the seas.

We R.N.R. officers always tried to make believe that we were tough and seasoned sailors (as we should be, having followed the sea all our lives). I was feeling proud of the fact that I had not parted company with my last meal. Barry was too ill to speak, but he tried to look cheerful. I gave him the course and speed and promised to be back on the conning-tower before very long. I wanted to get down below, check my position, and lay my course for our passage through the North Channel. We were supposed to have an escorting destroyer, but we had lost her in that smother of flying foam hours ago.

Lowther was lying in his bunk trying to read when I entered the officers' quarters, just off the control-room. His legs were drawn up so that his knees wedged him back solidly against the other side of the narrow bunk.

"I can stay in the saddle as long as she is satisfied to roll, damn her, but when she starts to sun-fish and sideslip like a broncho or a blasted aeroplane, I can't do a thing," he remarked, as I pulled my way along to the chart drawer, never daring to leave hold of some fixture for even a single second.

It was impossible to use a rule or dividers on the chart. A man has only two hands, and he needed both of them to keep from being shot around the room like a squirrel in a cage. We had shut off the gyro-compass. With the way R 12 rolled that night, the floating ballistic was swinging like the pendulum of a clock, only ten times faster. Then the sweat began to form on my forehead. That cold, clammy sweat. My insides began to feel as if someone was trying to use my diaphragm for a concertina. Figures and markings seemed to fade from off the chart at which I gazed. A haze formed before my eyes. My stomach seemed to gasp just like a fish which has been taken from the water. I reeled towards the toilet. I was no better a sailor than any other man in the boat.

I crawled back to the control-room. If you are afraid of death and are a poor sailor, just arrange for your last illness to take place at sea, preferably aboard a trawler or a submarine. When old man Death says "Come!" you'll welcome him with a smile.

I climbed up the conning-tower ladder, feeling weak as a day-old kitten. I felt that my face was a sickly green like a limburger cheese. "It's no use, Barry, I don't know where we are exactly and I'm too damned ill to find out. I couldn't make the North Channel to-night if I was offered a million pounds. I can't even see to read the chart."

"What shall we do?"

"I would suggest we head over under the lee of the coast of Ireland and wait for daylight." I told him we were making hardly any headway and were drifting sideways, like a crab. We had lost our escorting destroyer during the night, so I headed for Belfast Lough to shelter from the terrible weather.

Daylight found us safely anchored. If anyone wants to really know what we all felt like, let him ride the figure eight for twelve consecutive hours without a break.

. . . . . .

But sailors mostly take their troubles as lightly as their loves. By noon we had put off in our small boat to rustle some fresh grub for the rest of the crew. We all knew that there was no shortage of food in Ireland, and we thought it would be a good time to stock up with those commodities which would keep. We had signalled the S.N.O. (Senior Naval Officer) of the port, who had ordered us to remain where we were until he received a reply back from Admiral Stileman at Liverpool. The destroyer escort was evidently somewhere searching around the Irish Sea, wondering where in Heaven's name we had got to.

While ashore, I met the officer in charge of the Submarine Defence Boom. He had a sweet job. Lived at the local hotel and was newly married. He thought everyone should be as deeply interested in his better half as he was himself. Notwithstanding the fact that I looked more like a pirate than a naval officer, and that my brand-new white woollen running-gear was filthy from coming in contact with oil and grease, he insisted that I go into the hotel and have a cocktail and meet his bride of a few weeks.

As I never needed a cocktail so much in all my life as I did at that moment, I accepted his invitation. His wife was as nice as the cocktails he ordered. She was a most charming girl, and so deeply interested in submarines that she begged to be allowed to go aboard and see R 12. I extended the invitation to her husband, they arranged to visit us during the afternoon and promised to stay and have dinner with us that evening.

"Have dinner onboard a submarine. . . . Oh how lovely," she thrilled, and so it was settled. Then before I had left the beach, news arrived that the Armistice had been signed. After what we had been through the night before, it would be hard to describe just how we felt. It was, as we all know now, the news of the false Armistice, but we accepted it as gospel truth. I repaired on board R 12 with the news of the Armistice, a case of champagne, and several cases of stout. We always thought of the men in submarines.

Everyone knows how men, women, and children celebrated the false Armistice. We did that night. The boom defence officer arrived aboard with his wife, and the signal rating and I rustled the food along. I had bought two roasted chickens while ashore, and with champagne, cheese and crackers, and other extras, we served a very nice dinner to our guests.

We had a portable gramophone and that supplied the music, and I don't remember having so happy and informal a party for a long time. Barry and Lowther were both single and good fun. The lady guest was equal to them on all occasions. Stories, jokes, and laughter rang throughout the hollow steel hull. Why shouldn't it ? The war was over. The Armistice had been signed. The men were served with an extra ration of rum. They were also given stout with their evening meal. The hours slipped by just as quickly as they had seemed to drag the night before.

We were safely anchored and the coxswain was keeping the anchor watch from eight to twelve. The wind was still blowing a gale, but we were sheltered from the force of it by the land. About nine o'clock the wind changed. We were sheltered no longer. It blew with hurricane force right into the harbour. A signal was received from the boom trawlers to say that one of the boats had broken adrift. Five minutes later a motor-boat was alongside R 12 and the officer who had been our guest was heading off into the teeth of the blinding storm to try and rescue his derelict trawler. His wife stayed aboard R 12. He said he would come back for her as soon as he had the boom fixed. He promised to get her oilskins to keep her dry during her passage to the shore.

Midnight came and the officer had not returned for his better half. The wind blew " big guns." The rain descended in torrents. R 12 swung about at the end of her cables like a huge fish on the end of a line. She pitched, she rolled, and she tried to dive. She became absolutely unmanageable and I noticed she was dragging her anchors. There was nothing for us to do but dive. The water was deep and there was a good bottom. We told our guest what our intentions were, and she behaved like a real heroine. Many girls would have gone off the deep end if they had been in her shoes. There she was aboard a submarine which was rolling and pitching to beat the devil, alone amongst a crew of men, and we were taking her down with us to the bottom of the sea to prevent being wrecked on the rocks or driven ashore.

I've often laughed since about that night we spent at the bottom of Belfast Lough. The three of us, Barry, Lowther, and myself held a consultation in the control-room. As my bunk was by itself on the port side of the officers' quarters I offered to give it up for our guest. We had curtains we could draw to give her some privacy.

It was arranged that one of us would keep two hours' watch and then turn into the bunk his relief had just vacated. Both Barry and Lowther had their bunks on the starboard side.

As I mentioned before, the unfortunate girl had been aboard since about four in the afternoon. It was after midnight when we settled to the bottom. We had enjoyed a good dinner and consumed considerable liquid refreshment. This fact caused me to go along to the officers' toilet. When I came back I mentioned the fact to Barry and pointed out that I had heard of people being made seriously ill owing to the fact that they had been forced to restrain nature. This caused Barry to worry.

The toilet aboard a submarine is a very complicated affair. When the submarine is submerged you must first shut off the inside valve, and then after opening the outside valve you blow the water out of the outside tank and shut the outside valve. You have made an empty tank inside the boat shut off from the outside pressure of the water. To flush the toilet, the inside valve must be opened, and after the toilet has been flushed it must be closed again before the outside valve is opened prior to flushing the outside tank with compressed air. This is all a rather complicated operation and to forget to close the right valves immediately turns the toilet into a very fine water fountain. That is what caused Barry to worry. Our problem would have been a comparatively simple one if we had only to show the lady where the " wash-place " was. The trouble was that once inside there it was almost possible for anything to happen if she tried to pull the plug or flush the toilet.

" What the devil are we going to do about it ? " demanded Barry anxiously.

" What you mean ? What are *we* going to do about it ? Less of the *we* stuff. You're the Captain of this boat," Lowther chided him unmercifully.

" You're responsible for the safety of the boat, Barry. It's up to you to explain how the thing works. Besides she's really your guest," I pointed out, rather enjoying his predicament.

" You're a married man, Carr. You take her along." He grasped at the excuse, but I wasn't having any. I pointed out once again that he was the Captain of the boat and she was his guest.

I often wonder now what the unfortunate girl must have been going through while we were arguing in the control-room. But the resourcefulness of the British Navy has always been one of its strong points, otherwise they would never have got the naval guns ashore and taken them to the relief of Ladysmith. Barry's face brightened. He obtained a nice new garbage bucket. This he took along with him and after switching out the lights in the compartment where our guest was, he placed the bucket inside the curtained cubicle and rattled the handle, then he withdrew and switched on the " Police " or emergency lights. Thus he saved what might have been a serious situation.

Next morning the weather moderated. We came to the

surface much to the relief of a very distracted husband, and he took his wife ashore. We were sent to sea to continue our patrol. None of us was feeling very enthusiastic.

We came to the surface about 10.30 A.M., November 11th, and kept a surface patrol. The weather was cool but fine, and the sea comparatively calm. About half an hour later Barry came rushing up the conning-tower ladder.

" The war's over. The Armistice is signed ! " he gasped, more excited than I had ever seen him before.

" What are you trying to do ? Pull my leg ? " I demanded, thinking of the previous message.

" I don't blame you being sceptical. I can hardly believe the news myself. Here, read this," saying which he handed me a signal. I read :

" Cease hostilities unless attacked. Armistice signed 11:00 A.M."

This is a very small world. It is perhaps not so very extraordinary that sailors should meet friends in all kinds of strange places, but the experience I had the other day was the strangest coincidence imaginable. Going down Water Street, Liverpool, I bumped into no other person than Captain B. V. Smith. He knew me at once and remarked on how I had grown, and asked all about my doings since I had seen him last. He paid me the compliment of inviting me to serve as Second Mate with him on a new ship he had just been appointed to. I declined his offer with thanks, and informed him that now I was married two-year voyages on the Eastern Trade had no very great appeal for me. He laughed and made some remark that I would soon change my mind. He said it was very nice to come home for a holiday once in a while, but he always felt that while aboard his ship he was Master and when home only Chief Mate. You have to know Mrs. Smith to appreciate that joke. She is as small as " Big Ben " is large. She is as kindly and gentle as he is masterful and domineering.

Meeting Captain Smith again was an unexpected pleasure, but just after I left him I ran into none other than Mickey Robinson, and while we stood talking, who should clap me on the shoulder than Bellamy, who was Third Mate of the *Dacre Castle* when we were serving our time.

We all walked into the " Oriel " to celebrate the occasion, and no sooner entered the bar than we spotted Charlie Bonner, who was one time Second Mate of the *Muncaster Castle*, and who is now a V.C. and national hero. He served under Captain Gordon Campbell, V.C., in " mystery " boats.

We all sat and had lunch together, we all adjourned to a table in the marble bar and told our different stories over liqueurs.

Robinson had served in various kinds of warships and he had been decorated for saving the lives of several men whom he rescued after their boat had capsized. I heard afterwards that when the boat turned turtle he helped the non-swimmers and made them secure a good hold on the boat, and after seeing they were as comfortable as possible he swam ashore with them one by one until he had landed them all safely. Mickey had also been " hitched up," as sailors put it. It turned out his wife was a relative of mine. She had nursed him while he was in hospital recovering from his experience when he rescued the seven men from drowning. From all accounts he was absolutely all in by the time he had made the journey between the upturned boat and the shore about twelve times. Charlie Bonner hadn't changed a bit. True, the ribbon of the Victoria Cross decorated his rather shabby uniform jacket. He had won it half a dozen times over while serving aboard Q-ships with Captain Gordon Campbell, V.C. Bonner had also married and his first-born was named Gordon Campbell Bonner.

Asked for what particular act of valour he had been decorated, Bonner replied, true to form : " Oh, I just sat under the lee of a deck-house telling smutty stories to my gun's crew and trying to keep them amused until the ' Fritz ' would come near enough to give us a crack at her with our gun."

That was literally true. He did sit telling stories and keeping his men amused waiting for a chance at the " Fritz," and he had continued telling stories and keeping his men amused and their minds occupied while hell broke loose all around them, while the ship was torpedoed three times, while the inside of her became a raging furnace, while the magazines threatened to blow up. When the magazine finally exploded Bonner was blown forty feet in the air. He only missed being killed owing to the fact that he landed on the bridge awning. Bonner received his V.C. because after all this had happened he crawled back dazed and half dead and gathered the remnants of his crew together again and told them another story or two until the "Fritz," believing nothing human could remain alive aboard that ship, came to the surface to question the "Panic Party" which had previously taken to the boats. Then it was that Charlie Bonner stopped telling stories and went to work seriously on the German U-boat.

Such was the type of men that were turned out by tough ships and hard-boiled skippers like Captain Smith. I wish he had been there to sit and listen to the stories of the younger generation of seamen. I could picture what a self-satisfied smile he would wear on his weather-beaten face; he the "Daddy" of us all. Old Ben had been carrying on, just carrying on, like thousands of others. He had carried on at the age of seventy-five just because "No damned German U-boat had been built that could make B. V. Smith quit until he was damn well good and ready to retire."

I had to tell my story, and as I came to the end of it I suddenly remembered that I had promised my wife to be home early that particular afternoon. I had missed the train.

There was no use crying over spilled milk so I joined the others, and we ended up by having dinner together, and I missed the next train and the LAST one also.

By the time I had missed the last train we were all of the same opinion. It would have been too bad to break up the party then.

It came closing time. No more drinks could be served. Everybody had left the bar except our little party. All the help but one had rushed away to meet their boy friends. We tried to coax the girl who remained to sell us a bottle of whiskey. She said it was utterly impossible, and informed us that she thought we had had enough. Perhaps she was right. But this was a very special occasion.

We held a council of war. I went and ordered a taxi. Bonner persuaded the barmaid to cut us some sandwiches. While she was gone he swiped the big glass container filled with whiskey off the bar-counter and left a five pound note to settle the damage. We finished up the reunion party at my home in Preston, driving there from Liverpool in the taxi-cab.

We talked and we laughed and told each other about old times until the ladies got bored and retired to bed. The time must have simply flown. Re-telling the story of the feed I cooked for the officers after the *Dacre Castle* had been wrecked reminded us that we were hungry. I appointed myself emergency cook. I rustled some hash, and might have been busily engaged frying those eggs over the gas-range until this day if it hadn't been that my wife came downstairs and pointed out to me that I had forgotten to light the gas jets. She informed us that it was time for breakfast. We went upstairs for a wash and left the cooking to her.

" CHRISTIANS ? "

He's a Christian who kneels in the church and prays,
And raises his voice in heavenly praise
    On Sundays.
He's a Christian in the eyes of the world,
Though he keeps his banner tightly furled
    On Mondays.

Men argue o'er doctrine, define fable from fact,
And damn all who differ (an unchristian act);
They start new religions every day,
And all of them wrong but theirs they say.
    These Christians.

They forget that Christ said, " If ye would be saved
There are two things to learn ere you reach the grave,
To love your God, and earn heavenly wealth,
And love each man as you love yourself,"
    As Christians.

If only each man who has heard the word
Would humble himself and learn to serve,
And direct his life, not for selfish gain,
But to acts of love and relief of pain
    Like Christians,

We'd soon forget self and the greed of gain,
Spreading joy, not sorrow, sunshine, not rain,
And the hearts of men would grow mellow and kind,
And peace and contentment easy to find,
      For Christians.

No Christian can harbour an unkind thought,
For one whose freedom Christ dearly bought,
As He hung on the Cross and shed His Blood,
That we'd all unite in one Brotherhood
      Of Christians.

There could be no war, there could be no strife,
If we'd follow the " Golden Rule " through life,
And remember the command to " Sheath thy sword,"
Then rely on His teachings when making awards,
      As Christians.

It isn't our God who willed each war
That robbed us of loved ones and heartstrings tore.
We Christians, so quick in our pagan hate,
Ignore His teachings and decide our fate :
      Blind Christians.

Has God, who has planned and made all life,
To look down on other hideous sights,
And see all the heathen races fight
Against us ere we will yet unite
      As Christians ?

If we of the West all war would ban,
And settle our quarrels as Christians can,
Our very example would teach them grace,
And convert to God every pagan race :
      All Christians.

Though our Faith in strength like the tempest be
And our Hope like the boundless sea,
All this and much more is of no avail,
If no beacon of Charity light our trail,
      As Christians.

A Charity meek as the meekest lamb,
A love that will hatreds always ban,
A compassion that sees in the darkest heart,
Some virtue which will if given a start
      Make Christians.

But perhaps as long as this world does spin
Men will lay aside God earthly gains to win,
And will foolishly think that all is well,
Till they struggle engulfed in the flames of Hell,
    False Christians.

Does it matter at just which shrine we kneel,
To profess our faith and the love we feel
    On Sundays?
If we go forth into the world *and do*
And practise CHARITY the *whole week through*
    On Mondays?

WILLIAM GUY CARR.

CHAPTER XX

CONCLUSION

February 1932. Toronto, Canada.

I finally reached a position in life which gave me access to the seats with the Mighty. It was my pleasure and my privilege while checking data contained in my first book, *By Guess and By God*, to meet once again Admiral S. S. Hall, C.B., and his very charming wife. The Naval Conference was in session in London and the question of abolition of submarines very much to the fore.

In the seclusion of their country home, "The Shelters," Hamble, near Southampton, I dined with them and talked over the old war days and the present situation as it affects the maritime interests of Great Britain. Few people have heard much about Admiral S. S. Hall. He wears no lengthy string of decorations, he has received no great distinctions or honours from the Government, yet in my opinion he did as much if not more towards winning the war for the Allies than any other British Admiral at sea or afloat during the Great War. He is undoubtedly the greatest living authority on submarines and submarine warfare. He served in underwater craft from the days they were in the experimental stage. He was soon given command of the British submarine service; he organized it for war, and held that position for the entire period of the war. He was responsible for all the rapid developments in submarine design which the war produced, and is proudest of the fact that the organization, which he had effected six years before in peace, worked unchanged and without a hitch during the whole war. The British Submarine Service claims to be the only branch of the Navy which can show a Credit Balance Sheet; by this I mean that they inflicted greater losses on the enemy than they themselves sustained.

It is difficult to get Admirals to talk of their own services, even when they are retired, but during my visit to Admiral

Hall's country home near Southampton, I elicited the following little simile from him, in reply to a question I had put to him about abolition of submarines, which I will give because it seems to me to strike at the root of the matter:

"If I quarrel," he said, "with my neighbour to the extent of fighting him, and he has a dog which without necessarily biting me compels me to keep on running on a zig-zag course, I shall soon be winded and my capacity for fighting will be reduced to vanishing point.

"Here you get in a nutshell one of the great truths about Submarine Warfare. The torpedo is not a weapon of precision. The chief and foremost value of submarines is a moral one, when you are considering their military value apart from their qualities as commerce destroyers," he contended.

"The mere possession of a submarine fleet 'in being,' which need not necessarily be at sea, compels your enemy to proceed always at high speed on a zig-zag course. Further, all valuable ships and cargoes require the escort of destroyers or similar nimble ships. The endurance of the latter is very limited, since they must proceed at even higher speed or have this at immediate call. The result of all this being, that the endurance of your surface fleet is automatically cut down by more than half of what it would be if submarines were abolished, and submarines produce a universally restrictive effect upon all sea operations which gives them a military value which no other naval weapon can approach."

This is one part of the truth. In the light of it, how futile and, may I say, how undignified to ask for their abolition. Futile, because this portion of the truth about submarines was common knowledge to Naval experts at any rate. Undignified, because our delegates should have realized that it was almost a naval platitude, and that they were merely giving the impression that they were squealing about submarines because they had hurt in the last war. The pretext of humanitarianism was not likely to deceive anyone.

What were the other reasons that caused Great Britain to pursue this ostrich-like policy with regard to submarines? Part of the reason I have already shown, but there was more than this in it, and this is concerned partly with the last war and partly with post-war development. At the termination of the war, the public was led to believe, in fact it still is, that submarines had been completely outclassed by the anti-submarine methods employed by Great Britain and her Allies.

It is necessary here to state at once and most emphatically, that this was not the case.

That the sinkings of British and Allied merchant ships were reduced to a bearable number is true, but the cause of this does not lie in the discovery of any appliance or sovereign remedy evolved by the anti-submarine fleet, not even that of numbers when it grew to upwards of five thousand vessels. Nor has any such been produced since the war.

It must not be forgotten that it always has been, and to this day remains, a settled British policy to decry submarines and exaggerate any success obtained against them.

When the United States came into the war, the situation was such that Admiral Sims repeatedly cabled, emphasizing the necessity of America contributing without delay every ship and man that could be used for anti-submarine work. When the war ended Britain had had the shock of her life. German U-boats had almost brought her to defeat. *If the campaign of unrestricted submarine warfare had continued uninterruptedly from the commencement and, more important still, had been conducted in an original manner with the right types of submarines, there is little doubt but that German submarines would have won.*

Once again let me say it was not our anti-submarine fleet that caused them to fail, there were many reasons besides this. First as to the type of submarine used. There is no doubt that Germany had not seriously considered or made any plans for a submarine war on commerce before the war. It was indeed fortunate for us that she had not. It was an omission that was to have a far-reaching effect upon results. German submarines were designed as torpedo vessels for attacking men-of-war by submerging and firing torpedoes at them, and it is necessary to realize that such a vessel is poorly equipped for attacks upon merchant ships.

As it turned out, the war on commerce was soon forced

upon them, as it was bound to be, and it found them quite unprepared with a suitable type of submarine for the job. It may have been lack of originality, of sea sense, or of time to try out a new design, or all of these, which caused her to carry on with the type she already had. Probably she thought that they could be adapted for the work. In order to adapt these torpedo vessels, they were equipped with a gun or even two, and a supply of bombs, but the guns were necessarily small and close to the water, and the whole outfit made them even more cramped and complicated than they were before.

It had this further result which was of such immense value to Britain and her Allies, a result which helped as much as anything else to restrain the activities of German submarines, in that it enabled the Allies to employ all and every class of vessel that could mount a small gun in their anti-submarine fleet.

Yachts, paddle steamers, trawlers, torpedo-boats, destroyers and even sailing ships, all were pressed into the service. Anything that floated was good enough to make these vulnerable and feebly armed submarines dive and keep under water.

Over five thousand of them were used, and owing to the wonderful geographical conditions of the war they could all be sent out on patrol without any support.

Here is another of the causes that brought failure. The atlas may be searched in vain to reproduce such a splendid geographical position as that held by Britain and her Allies during the last war. Japan holds exactly the same advantage in the Far East at the present time.

This should never be lost sight of, in reading the lessons of the war, particularly in the case of getting at the truth of the submarine campaign.

All German submarines proceeding to the trade routes had to pass through the Straits of Dover, or else cover the extra thousand miles or so by going round North of Scotland. In both cases they had to run the gauntlet of this huge anti-submarine fleet which was working only at short distances from its own bases along the shores of the United Kingdom, without any fear of molestation from the enemy's cruisers.

That the proper type of submarine cruiser would appear on the trade routes was a constant nightmare to those who knew the weak spots in the Allied armour.

We can all recall the exploits of the *Emden*, the German light cruiser, which caused such havoc in the last war. It was a submersible *Emden* that was indicated and expected. As month after month went by, it seemed almost incredible that we were to have such luck. But so it was. Quite late in the war something of the kind did appear; whether it was that the rot in her personnel had by this time set in, or the design of vessel was unsatisfactory, they did not accomplish much. Some convoys were badly mauled by them, including, in one case, the escorting cruiser, but the attacks were half-hearted and poorly executed.

It will be realized what the effect on the naval situation would have been if Germany had equipped only half a dozen submarines for dealing with these anti-submarine patrols which were restricting her submarine activities so much. Armed with 6-inch guns and adequate protection, all the outlying patrols would have been mopped up in detail, and those not destroyed would have had to be withdrawn, or support provided for them: the latter being quite impossible for there was already a shortage for the convoys. THIS BRINGS US TO THE CONVOY QUESTION.

It has become quite general to assume that resort to the system of convoying merchant ships in large numbers under the protection of one or more cruisers, is one of the sovereign remedies for attacks on commerce by submarines.

There is no doubt that under the circumstances of the last war, the Allies, by putting their vessels under convoy, did considerably reduce their losses. Alas! propaganda again! Truth demands a deeper inquiry into these circumstances to see whether they are likely to be repeated.

When convoy was put into force, the war had been going on for some three years and the exhaustion of German submarine personnel had been considerable, particularly of the type of commanding officer that they wanted. It is no ordinary man that is required as captain of a submarine. The vessel is cramped and noisy, meals are indifferent, and the Captain is never sure of any proper rest except that brought on by extreme physical fatigue. Once submerged he only has the use of one eye and that very close to the surface of the sea. Above all, no one can help him. Everything depends upon whether he is of the calibre to rise superior to all the complicated mechanism of his vessel; to all the privations and physical discomforts of the voyage, and be able to make his opportunities and take advantage of them, or, at the least, seize them when they come to him.

Admiral Hall told me that although Germany had some four hundred submarine commanders during the war, 60 per cent of the damage done to Allied shipping during the war can be credited to twenty-two of them. In other words, it is not the number of submarines which a nation may possess, but the type of men who command them that matters. The Japanese are typically suited for submarine work temperamentally.

To return to the convoy question again. Was the right type of commanding officer available to attack them? We know now that it was not. The drain on her first-class personnel had been too great, their successors were unequal to the task. It was common knowledge that submarine attacks on convoys were ill-timed and half-hearted.

There is very grave doubt whether the collection of vessels in convoy would have reduced losses against well-officered submarines in the last war. The favourable geographical position to which I have already referred, precluded any attack on the convoys by enemy cruisers. The German submarines were of the wrong type and poorly handled, so that results were unsatisfactory. The situation out East is entirely different. It must be remembered that the mere fact of putting vessels into convoy makes it legal for an enemy cruiser to sink them out of hand without the loss of time caused her by the tedious process of visit and search which the law compels her to follow, when a single merchant ship is intercepted.

This applies also to a submarine attack on a convoy. The torpedoing of ships without warning became fully legitimate the moment they were put into convoy; in fact, it was long before that. *The practice of zig-zagging was quite sufficient to render a merchant ship open to be sunk without warning, for it implied an intention to resist.*

With the termination of hostilities, Great Britain concentrated upon really finding an antidote for submarines, which would make it impossible for a similar situation to arise again ; well knowing, of course, that the much advertised remedies were in reality only quack or partial ones.

She enlisted the aid of the best scientific brains in the country, supplied them with money, and placed at their disposal all the information that the war had made available, together with the necessary submarines and antisubmarine vessels. A committee was formed, called the Anti-Submarine Detection Investigation Committee. The word " Asdic," formed from the initial letters of the five words of the title of this Committee, is the name given to one of the methods they perfected for locating submarines.

A great deal of mystery surrounds this method, which involves the use of highly delicate and sensitive apparatus. What the hydrophone claims to do by sound waves, Asdics achieved by high frequency electrical impulses.

Both were in use during the war, but great improvements were made by the Anti-Submarine Committee, and results were obtained under favourable circumstances, which were considered sufficient to warrant a great deal of rejoicing and some discreet propaganda to the effect that submarines were no longer to be feared. With such a weapon in her hands, if she believed in it, Great Britain had no need to press for the abolition of submarines. Was it because her naval experts shuddered at the thought of exterminating enemy submarine crews who might be reckless enough to put to sea against them ? Certainly not ; the reason was because of the short qualification I made in describing the experiments as successful " in favourable circumstances." The same limitations attach to Asdics as to the hydrophone in all its forms. Both will show off well under academic conditions. Anti-submarine craft equipped with either of these devices can, in moderate weather, locate a submerged submarine and then follow her to her destruction by depth charges. But the dice are loaded, the operation in peace lasts only a short time, listeners and operators of the devices go to sea fresh and knowing that a submarine is there, and approximately its position. The submarine also has to play up to a certain extent. Admiral Hall stated, " Neither Asdics nor hydrophones can be relied upon in rough or roughish water on the high seas, over long periods and distances. There is no sovereign remedy against the far-flung activities of submarines."[1]

During the post-war trouble between Britain and Turkey, when hostilities nearly broke out again, a British fleet was anchored at the entrance to the Dardanelles. They were believed to be safe from submarine attack by the stationing of anti-submarine vessels fitted with hydrophones and Asdics, in the channel above them. The use of these methods, coupled with the assurance and enthusiasm of those who ran them, had convinced everybody, until the arrival of a British ex-submarine officer on the staff of the Commander-in-Chief. This officer did not place full credence in the new inventions, and considered the fleet was being exposed to unnecessary risk from the threatened attack upon them by Soviet submarines from the Black Sea. To settle the difference of opinion, it was decided to pull a stunt and test the anti-submarine vessels without warning, in fact without the "favourable conditions." The British submarine, sent up under cover of darkness, came back the next day, made a tour of the anchorage, and returned to her base without being detected either by Asdics or hydrophone. The shock which the commanding officers of the British ships received can be realized. It explains more fully another of the reasons why Great Britain asked for the abolition of submarines, since this was all the result of ten years' intensive research and experimental effort.

The truth is that the problem of locating with certainty the position of a submerged submarine is not in sight of solution. Academic results can be obtained, but in doing so the mechanisms become so complicated and delicate, that when they get up against the hard practical difficulties of the open sea, they break down.

Post-war developments of submarines have, in fact, more than kept pace with any antidote. Several of the disabilities under which they laboured in the last war have already been removed. Some may be given here in connection with the torpedo attack. German submarines were provided with, at the most, two discharges for torpedoes in the bow.

---

[1] The failure to locate the wreck of submarine M2 in time to save her crew proves this statement.

Post-war submarines have at least four and usually six of these. This means that six torpedoes can be fired simultaneously and the chances of hitting a difficult target are multiplied by three, since the torpedoes can be spread out in the form of a fan, and in the case of a certain shot, six torpedoes can be exploded against a valuable ship known to be provided with under-water protection against explosion.

The torpedoes themselves have been made faster and carry a heavier charge, and their discharge rendered invisible. During the war, when German submarines attacked a convoy or any vessel with any kind of escort, they had the unpleasant knowledge that the moment they fired their torpedoes, a large milky patch would appear on the surface, which would serve the dual purpose of helping the ship fired at, to avoid the torpedo, and of fixing the position of the submarine to which the nearest escort dashed at full speed to drop depth charges. This, in its turn, caused the German submarines to fire at greater ranges, when they were more liable to miss, and after firing to dive to greater depths, thus missing an opportunity of any further attack on the convoy.

When a torpedo is running towards its target, the exhaust air from its engines, unless suitably dealt with, will leave a white milky line behind it; another tremendous asset to us in the last war, as it so frequently enabled the torpedo to be avoided, unless the range was very close. This disability has also been removed.

It will already be realized, I hope, that post-war developments of the submarine have shown up the disabilities under which these vessels laboured in the last war and the difficult conditions with which the German submarines had to contend. Some of the latter were due to her geographical position, some to the fact that her submarine fleet had to be built, manned, and trained during the war, when she had so many other calls on her personnel and material. These, it may be said, were beyond her control; indeed, taking everything into account, she overcame them remarkably well. But there was another factor as great as any other, in producing failure, which was within her control; I allude to the incessant chattering that emanated from German submarine aerials. I have heard it said many times that if German submarines had preserved wireless silence when they went to sea, they would have won the war. They seemed incapable of believing that their messages could be picked up and decoded or of realizing that every time they made a signal their position was fixed by British directional stations, enabling ships and convoys to be diverted from their neighbourhood. The number of vessels saved for the Allies by this means was enormous. I have gone at considerable length into the causes of the failure of the German U-boat campaign, in order to explain the truth of the matter. In doing so I have tried to show that the principal of these causes are preventable, that many of them have already been remedied, and that few, if any, of them are likely to happen again. The picture painted is not a pleasant one for those who fear submarines and have been baulked of their abolition, but it explains accurately why these nations pressed for abolition and why the smaller powers stood firm for retention.

The European situation is full of difficulty and there is no lack of inflammable material in the Far East. I do not wish to leave the impression that in the event of another conflagration the submarine is necessarily going to carry all before it, but Admiral Hall definitely states: " Given the perfect submarine, even up to to-day's standard, and the perfect skipper, the position at sea will be entirely dominated by them. The first is possible for any nation, but what about the more vital second ? What about the Captains ? "

Admiral Hall, notwithstanding his trying experiences and the heavy responsibilities which rested on his shoulders during the war, is still an optimist. " In my opinion," he said, " submarines will always dominate the naval situation, vessels that can only move in one plane cannot, in the end, compete with those that can move in two, especially when their movements in the second plane are invisible. Thank God," he continued, " it is not every nation that can produce the type of men to put up an insurmountable submarine menace. I don't mind confessing to you, that though there were many difficulties with material, they could always be circumvented ; the only real difficulty was to find a sufficiency of commanding officers of the right type to command the submarines as we produced them and to replace our losses. During the war I had to send submarines to bolster up those in the Baltic and Adriatic : our experiences with the French submarines were also unfortunate."

Unfortunately for us the Japanese naval officer seems typically suited for submarine service both temperamentally and physically. They are cool, courageous, and patient, and above all fatalistic in their beliefs. I met several of the Japanese officers who were attached to the British Submarine Service during the war for training purposes. They were anxious and keen to accompany us on our overseas patrols into enemy waters, although at the time it was about even money that you didn't return. Very few people realize that Great Britain lost 33 per cent of her submarines. That was little wonder considering the tasks they were asked to perform, but it is to the undying credit of the officers and men of the Submarine Service that they accomplished all tasks they were asked to do and they accounted for no less than 57 enemy warships, in addition to 374 transports and ships engaged in contraband trade. What is even more significant is the fact that they accomplished all this without costing one single non-combatant the loss of his or her life. This last statement being true it can perhaps be realized why the delegates at the last two naval conferences paid so little attention to the request of Great Britain and the United States when they asked for the abolition of submarines for humanitarian reasons.

The submarine is here to stay. The new cruiser type with a cruising radius of 10,000 miles, mounting as they do 6-inch guns, has reduced all naval vessels carrying smaller guns and with less than twenty-five knots speed to the value of scrap-iron. Great Britain and the U.S.A. might well ask for the abolition of battleships. They are valueless. They would be no more use out East than an elderly policeman whose corporation is of greater girth than his chest. Japan knows it.

Admiral Hall certainly threw a great deal of light on what must be a very obscure question to most of the world, but it remained for me to meet, once again, the man who has become one of Britain's greatest characters. I refer to Admiral of the Fleet the Earl Jellicoe. The first time I met this famous sailor will remain for ever in my memory. I was "Snotty" of the duty picket boat of the 7th C.S. attached to the Grand Fleet and based in Scapa Flow, December 1914.

The particular day in question was cold as professional charity. A blustering wind from the Nor'-west whipped the waters of the harbour into waves and then knocked them into spume. It was hardly fit for a picket boat to be in the water. I was hugging the stove down in the gunroom when I heard the Bos'on's Mate piping, "A-w-a-y! picket boat's crew." I struggled into my oilskins and reported to the officer of the watch on the quarter-deck. He told me to report to the flagship to take dispatches from the Admiral in command of our squadron to the C.-in-C. Grand Fleet.

My coxswain was one of the party who had accompanied both Shackleton and Scott on their voyages of Arctic and Antarctic exploration. He was a man of wonderful experience both in steam and sail. He was *a man* in every sense of the word; I was a mere boy, but I was in charge of that picket boat and I was determined that I would steer her over to the flagship and alongside and gangway or take her to the bottom.

We got our orders and shoved off. I had one of the greatest thrills that day I have ever experienced. The small picket boat was pitched and tossed about like a cork by the fury of the storm. We were heaved about and thrown all over the place by the rough seas. I knew the eyes of the Grand Fleet were on my particular duty picket boat.

We sailors of the Merchant Marine prided ourselves that we were second to none as seamen, and I was going to show them I could handle that boat. It says a lot for the discipline of the Royal Navy, but my coxswain never even so much as said, "Would you like me to take the wheel for a while, Sir?" He stood there holding on to prevent from being washed overboard and watched me ease the boat over the wave tops and creep slowly over towards the flagship's stern. The stoker had two jobs. He had to attend to his engine and he had to keep the water below his fire-box door.

I got alongside the flagship and delivered my dispatches,

and then started off for the *Iron Duke*, Admiral Jellicoe's flagship. I looked upon him as the midshipman of 1800 looked upon Nelson. I was thrilled at the thought that I might possibly see this famous man. I wondered if I would take the dispatches into him personally or just hand them over to the Flag-Lieutenant. I was very green in all things pertaining to the Royal Navy. I did meet Jellicoe personally, although it was not quite the way I thought might be possible.

I went aboard the *Iron Duke* and saluted the quarterdeck. I was instructed to go below and take the dispatches to the Admiral's quarters and deliver them to the Flag-Lieutenant. To say that I was disappointed is putting the matter mildly. I started down the iron steps of the companionway. My leather-soled seaboots were slippery. I was about half-way down when my feet shot from under me and I went bumping and crashing down the next half-dozen steps and came up all standing slap-bang into somebody who looked all white collar and gold braid. It was Admiral Jellicoe himself. He let what seemed to be a snort out of his hooked nostrils. Those gimlet eyes of his bored clean through me. I was twice his weight in bone and muscle, but I just seemed to shrink like wool in hot water. I saw the thin lips open and shut. He seemed horribly close to me and yet I seemed leagues away from him. He said something about a young man who was a careless damn fool, and something further about there being no need to kill myself or any other person before the proper time came.

I struggled to my feet. Stuttered and stammered and agreed with everything he said and tendered him the dispatches. He directed me to the proper door and proceeded to where he was going when I tried to knock his pins from under him. That was in 1914. In 1931 I had the pleasure of assisting on the committee of Naval officers and men who were to entertain him during his stay in the Queen City of Canada.

His visit to open the Canadian National Exhibition and attend the convention of the British Empire Service League gave me the opportunity to meet him once again. This second meeting proved to me that Admiral of the Fleet the Earl Jellicoe is one of the most illustrious and yet typical of "Hell's Angels of the Deep." It proved that the man we admired and incidentally feared during the war, second only to the way we feared and loved God, was delightfully human when stripped of the artificial atmosphere which, like his gold-braided uniform, became part and parcel of his character when serving as head of the whole British Navy.

Admiral Jellicoe's visit to Toronto made history, for it was during this visit, and while guest of the ex-naval men, that he made public a statement which cleared up a situation which has been the hub centre of controversy ever since the day following Jutland.

Admiral Jellicoe had accepted the invitation of the ex-naval men to spend one evening with them. He wanted to spend the whole evening with them. When he got up after the banquet to make his speech he told all and sundry that he didn't intend to make any speech but wanted to take the opportunity to talk old ships with the many comrades who had served with him prior to and during the war. Three times he said bluntly, "I did not want to leave you, but others have arranged for me to do something or other to-night and I suppose I'll have to do it, although I really don't want to. I'd much rather spend the evening with you. It is one of the happiest days I have had since I retired. Men, you showed the world to-day that the Navy still knows how to march even if you didn't have a band to march to."

The great sailor then went back to his earliest days at sea, and such is his memory that, although he had only shaken hands with the individual men as they filed past him into the ball-room of the King Edward Hotel, in his talk about "Old Ships" he recalled almost every man present by name, who had served with him during his early days at sea. He ruefully remarked that it was only after he had risen to the rank of commander and captain of big ships that he lost personal contact with his men. When he came to Jutland it was plain to see he was visibly affected. He was far from well. He paused, and then as if to put himself right with the hundreds of men who by their reception had shown him they had remained loyal to him in spite of the many stories and statements which politicians and others had made to belittle the part he had played in naval history, he said :

"Men, I am not going to say much about Jutland except this. If it had not been for that damned fog, and IF I HAD BEEN TOLD THAT THE ENEMY WERE PASSING TO MY REAR THE DAY WOULD HAVE FINISHED IN A VERY DIFFERENT MANNER."

The men went wild. The city of Toronto heard the cheers for city blocks. Jellicoe, the great sailor, the greatest naval strategist of all time, had vindicated himself to his own men. He had kept silent to the world in face of public criticism directed at him by politicians who were not fit to tie his shoe-strings. Jellicoe had not cared what the world might think. His conscience was clear, but he did care what those men sitting with him that night thought. They had shown their loyalty by coming from the North, East, and West of Canada, and some had come North from the United States. They had shown themselves staunch members of the greatest of all crafts, the "Freemasonry of the Sea." They had come to pay their respects and do him homage, and he rewarded their loyalty by making that momentous statement, "IF I HAD ONLY BEEN TOLD THE ENEMY WERE PASSING TO MY REAR THE DAY WOULD HAVE ENDED DIFFERENTLY." A lot of changes will have to be made by accepted authorities who have published naval histories if British naval history is to be passed on correctly to the future generations.

After the cheering came a hush. The tears showed unashamedly in the gallant old sea-dog's eyes. "Men," he said, " I *do* wish I could stay with you for the rest of the evening. I don't know why it is, but I've never felt happier in my life."

The tears rolled down his cheeks as he repeated for the fourth time, " I'm so sorry I have to leave you. I'll see you in the morning, Carr. Come and see me, Davis, before I go . . . any time . . . I . . ."

But the door had closed. There was a roar, the noise of changing gears, and Admiral of the Fleet the Earl Jellicoe had gone.

"THE GLADE"

In Canada

There in the deep, dark shadows of the pool,
   Bright speckled beauties sport in waters cool;
While to the right in that luxurious glade,
   Stand timid deer and wait for day to fade
That they may venture forth to pastures new
   And graze upon the grasses wet with dew.

Slowly shadows deepen o'er this world of ours;
   And timorous wild things leave their hidden bowers.
Night advances, darkness holds its sway,
   But a million glories light the Milky Way.
Humans deeply slumber while ferine creatures play,
   Till the chill dawn heralds forth the coming of the day.

William Guy Carr.

www.ingramcontent.com/pod-product-compliance
Lightning Source LLC
Chambersburg PA
CBHW032101090426
42743CB00007B/199